Board Members and Management Consultants

Redefining the Boundaries of Consulting and Corporate Governance

A volume in
Research in Management Consulting

Series Editor:
Anthony F. Buono, *Bentley University*

Research in Management Consulting

Anthony F. Buono, Series Editor

Board Members and Management Consultants: Redefining the Boundaries of Consulting and Corporate Governance (2009)
edited by Pierre-Yves Gomez and Rickie Moore

Mastering Hidden Costs and Socio-Economic Performance (2008)
by Henri Savall and Véronique Zardet

Socio-Economic Intervention in Organizations: The Intervener-Researcher and the SEAM Approach to Organizational Analysis (2007)
edited by Anthony F. Buono and Henri Savall

Challenges and Issues in Knowledge Management (2005)
edited by Anthony F. Buono and Flemming Poulfelt

Creative Consulting: Innovative Perspectives on Management Consulting (2004)
edited by Anthony F. Buono

Enhancing Inter-Firm Networks & Inter-Organizational Strategies (2003)
edited by Anthony F. Buono

Developing Knowledge and Value in Management Consulting (2002)
edited by Anthony F. Buono

Current Trends in Management Consulting (2001)
edited by Anthony F. Buono

Board Members and Management Consultants

Redefining the Boundaries of Consulting and Corporate Governance

edited by

Pierre-Yves Gomez

and

Rickie Moore
EM Lyon

Information Age Publishing, Inc.
Charlotte, North Carolina • www.infoagepub.com

Library of Congress Cataloging-in-Publication Data

Board members and management consultants : redefining the boundaries of consulting and cor-
porate governance / edited by Pierre-Yves Gomez and Rickie Moore.
     p. cm. -- (Research in management consulting)
  Includes bibliographical references.
  ISBN 978-1-59311-805-1 (pbk.) -- ISBN 978-1-59311-806-8 (hardcover) 1. Boards of direc-
tors. 2. Corporate governance. 3. Business consultants. I. Gomez, Pierre-Yves. II. Moore,
Rickie.
  HD2745.B579 2009
  658.4'22--dc22

                                                                                      2008042373

This volume is jointly sponsored by the Office of Research on Teaching in the Disciplines at the
University of Alabama.

Printed in the United States of America

CONTENTS

PREFACE

Boards of publicly-traded corporations—not limited to those in the United States—are operating under greater scrutiny and transparency than, perhaps, at any point in history. And the corporate governance-related concerns they face are likely to remain a significant point of emphasis in the coming years. Directors will continue to face a myriad of pressures, requiring them to attempt to balance a broad range of growing demands with their more fundamental role of providing strategic guidance to—and oversight of—the firm's management. An underlying challenge is that this type of "balancing" is largely a judgment call, requiring significant insight, informed analysis and independent thought (see Grace, 2005; Stinner, 2007). Indeed, as the standard of what actually constitutes "good" corporate governance practice appears to be a constantly moving target, directors will have to continually show flexibility on such matters, while providing due care in their principal duties of tending to the long-term interests of the corporation and its stakeholders (Cogut, 2007).

These changes are also creating broad new mandates and challenges for the management consulting realm. The intensified emphasis on these governance issues has driven the need for qualified consultants to assist boards and senior-level management teams in dealing with what seem to be an ever growing variety of concerns—a need that is being increasingly encouraged by regulators, institutional investors, and the legal community and other key stakeholders (Grace & Haubert, 2006). Chief executive officers (CEOs) and boards of directors, of course, have drawn on an array of consulting services for decades. The nature of these services, as well as the role played by consultants and the relationship between consultants and such high-level and high-profile clients, however, have undergone significant change, especially in the wake of the recent spate of corporate scandals (Nadler, 2005). This expanding and evolving role of governance consultants—with the underlying goal of improving governance practice —has created significant challenges for the consultants themselves and the boards that use them.

Boards Members and Management Consultants, the eighth volume in the Research in Management Consulting series, explores the growing complexity associated with these changes. Edited by Pierre-Yves Gomez and Rickie Moore, professors at the French business school EM LYON, the book brings together noted international academicians and practitioners— from Australia, Italy, France, Germany, Norway, Spain, Switzerland, and the United Kingdom and United States—to examine the changes that have and are taking place in the governance realm. As a way of better understanding the ramifications for management consulting, particular—and timely—emphasis is placed on the evolution of expectations and needs in relation to boards and their operation.

The chapter authors, as noted above a truly international group of experts, more than succeed in raising the reader's awareness of the consequences that the evolving nature of corporate boards are having on the function of directors, how this function is being redefined by the players themselves—and what all of this change means for consultants and the realm of management consulting. Significant questions are raised and explored throughout the volume, from the extent to which these changes will lead to new social, moral, ethical, and professional challenges and opportunities, to how the relationships between consultants and their traditional clients—managers, administrators and employees—might evolve. As management consultants become more actively involved in governance issues, their role will clearly change, but will such changes enhance or constrain the role they have traditionally played in organizations?

Gomez and Moore are to be commended for bringing together such a talented cast. The contributors explore the link between the role of the consultant and the new roles of directors through their examination of different facets of this relationship. The chapters illustrate how, in general, the evolution of corporate governance, and, more specifically, the new expectations towards directors, both directly and indirectly, impact and transform the roles played by consultants and their relationship with directors and their boards. The goal of this volume—and the Research in Management Consulting series—is to stimulate new ideas, new perspectives, and new opportunities in examining consulting, its changing role, and the interaction and collaboration between consultants and their clients (in this case, directors and CEOs). There is clearly an urgent need to more fully understand the changes taking place in governance, the role and function of directors, and the shifting boundaries between consulting and corporate governance. As Nadler (2005) has argued, consulting in this realm poses unique challenges, serious questions and significant risks —and this volume goes a long way toward providing a fuller understanding of these complex issues and concerns.

Anthony F. Buono
Waltham, Massachusetts

REFERENCES

Cogut, C. (2007). Directors continue to face new pressures from new directions. *International Financial Law Review, 26*(June), 80–118.

Grace, H. S., Jr. (2005). Reflections of a non-executive chair. *Corporate Board, 26*(152), 11–13.

Grace, H. S. Jr., & Haupert, J. E. (2006). The search for qualified governance consultants. *Corporate Board, 27*(158), 15–19.

Nadler, D. A. (2005). Consulting to CEOs and Boards. In L. Greiner & F. Poulfelt (Eds.), *Handbook of management consulting: The contemporary consultant—Insights from world experts* (pp. 151–171). Cincinnati, OH: Southwestern/Thompson.

Stinner, M. (2007). The right stuff. *Directorship, 33*(5), 74.

INTRODUCTION

In Occidental countries over the last 20 years, corporate governance has been evolving rapidly and dramatically. The massive and spectacular growth in the number of shareholders throughout the world—in essence the "massification of shareholding"[1]—estimated at several hundreds of millions of people, has radically changed the relationship between publicly-held companies and the society as a whole (Gomez & Korine, 2005). A firm, especially a large one, no longer belongs to a restricted and exclusive minority of individuals but to millions of people, and their capital is spread throughout society. Their performance and results concern countless citizens who, directly or indirectly through pension funds and mutual funds, have invested their savings in capital. Citizens count on these funds (their savings) to generate revenues for a range of purposes, including investment, consumption and retirement. As such, more and more people are thus concerned with the performance of their investments and the "good" governance of these firms. Massification has, in part, thus led to the demand for more control on the part of shareholders, and is one of the major reasons why the roles and dimensions of corporate governance, with particular emphasis on corporate boards, are undergoing such a fundamental transformation—as we will explore throughout the volume.

Concomitantly, however, globalized firms are less and less regulated by a single national political power as they operate in numerous different international economic regions and countries, each having its own specific rules. As a result, the control of these increasingly global companies and their activities has become particularly complex as was illustrated by the recent subprime crisis. In sum, this profound modification, driven by the globalization of firms and the financial markets and the difficulties of the macroeconomic regulation of such global firms, explains why firms are attempting to find solutions to the problems through changes in their governance. We are witnessing the implementation of new rules and a redesign of corporate governance—its principles, its practices, and its institutions.

THE GROWING POWER OF DIRECTORS AND THE NEW APPROACH TO SHAREHOLDERISM

This major evolution of capitalism has led to the modification of the way in which power in the firm is applied and organized. The era of managers as the main holders of power (more commonly known under the concept of managerialism[2]) is changing (in fact, nearing its end) with the massification of shareholders. Today, other stakeholders—employees, communities, special interest groups, and so forth—are increasingly influencing the governance of firms. Fundamentally, with this massification, shareholders are increasing their demands to be put in a position to influence the corporate strategy of "their" firms and to exert control over the realization of promised objectives. In managerialism, shareholders are supposedly dormant, that is, they completely trust the management which is understood to be acting for the general interest of the firm and the specific interest of the owners. From the 1970s, the situation changed: shareholders were no longer interested in only the firm itself, but were now investors preoccupied with the value of the share. With the massification of shareholders came the "boomification" of investment funds, and the balance of power between shareholders and executives changed fundamentally. Investment funds managers became mediators and "go-betweens" interrelating between the funds' investors and depositories (i.e., citizens/savers who placed/invested their savings in the funds) and the firms themselves, and answerable to the investors and depositories for the funds they have invested. For this reason, fund managers often feel obliged to provide control over the management of the firms to ensure that the forecasted results were, in fact, attained, thereby giving value to the share. This evolution, accelerated by the global financial crisis in 2008 and calls for increased transparency and quality control of firms and investments, will have two consequences: first, it brings about changes concerning the place of control (i.e., the board of directors); and second, it calls into question the matter of executive and managerial expertise. With the burn out of the markets, the role of financial analysts has become even more important. Executives and managers are now routinely challenged by new experts such as financial analysts or fund managers.

Transformation of the Boards

From a legal perspective, the board of directors is where control of management is carried out. Because the results of the firm have accrued in importance for millions of shareholders, the role of the board is increasingly being reassessed as the key instrument of control. Through this control, which is by all accounts brought to bear by shareholders during the general assembly and through daily operational direction, the board is the only intermediary institution that can assure stakeholders that the company's management is performing its functions diligently, coherently and in keeping with its proposed undertakings. Given this responsibility, boards have been put under the spotlight as being the guarantee against the possibility of management straying off course, especially on such matters as compensation, leadership succession, quality of information given to the market, and so forth. This, in turn, has led to a substantial modification of expectations in relations between the board and the management of the firm, and the need for new types of directors, such as the nonexecutive director (NED).

Not only have boards been required to act in line with valid control (e.g., regular board participation, council/committee participation, evaluation of their real impacts), but the very composition of the board itself has also been tackled. Since the beginning of the 1990s, it seemed necessary to introduce the notion of independence of the NED, so as to underline that their role was by no means subordinate to management. This change in the nature and role of the directors radically upset existing opinions because, up until that time, it had been considered that a good director, even a non-executive, was linked to the firm in a *affectio societatis* relationship (i.e., there was a certain personal interest or relationship). With mass shareholding and an obligation to now control the firm, the situation is quite the contrary—independence and certain "distance" with respect to the firm are now considered to be key "required" virtues and a means of assuring that NEDs are not inclined toward collusion or conflicts that could pollute their judgment.

A New Expert is Born

In just a few years and in almost all occidental countries, the new role assigned to the NED has profoundly modified the way in which directors are designated, including who should sit on the board and how should it work to ensure an effective fiduciary duty. This transition has given birth to a new expert—the "outside expert" as the NED. While this change reduces and eliminates potential conflict of interests, it has also given rise to a number of problems. As the expertise required of the board is nonnegligible, performing the function of a real controller of management requires particularly far-reaching expertise and knowledge, not only in strategy and finance but also in the different techniques that the firms use for investment and management. To be aware of the risks, it is necessary to have a certain, even sometimes in-depth, knowledge of ever-more sophisticated technological mechanisms or financial packaging. This requirement is all the more difficult as the members of the board are not supposed to have any links with the company so as to conserve their independence. The result is the "silosification" and "dissectation" of required board expertise into an array of specializations.

As the need for NEDs grows, we find ourselves faced with tough questions about the essence of their knowledge. Can these external individuals sufficiently know the firm? What type of expertise can they bring that is not merely repeating the expertise already present among directors and managers? To what extent is it repetitive with the expertise supplied by those who are contractually linked to the firm (notably independent external consultants)? As soon as problems of "good conduct" have been dealt with, we can see that modifying the role of administrators gives rise to very complex questions concerning the effective skills that are required of the administrators, the articulation of their roles and responsibilities with the board and the management of the firm, and their interrelation with other internal and external (independent) experts. These questions are of particular interest to researchers and practitioners concerned with consulting because it has a twofold impact on the consulting profession: (1) it casts doubt on the limits of "external knowledge" brought by the external (independent) consultant; and (2) it creates a necessary link between the services of the NED and those of the external (independent) consultants.

Setting the Boundaries: NEDs and External (Independent) Consultants

What should be the boundaries between the services of the NED and those of the external (independent) consultant? With the emergence of a new generation of NEDs, the link between "internal" and "external" knowledge is no longer as clear as it has been in the past. External independent consultants are supposed to bring the firm "external" knowledge; but today this knowledge is also a requirement of NEDs, who have higher prestige and legitimacy as they sit at the summit of corporate governance authorities. These different levels of skills have to be set out, notably when a firm solicits the assistance and expertise of generalist management consultants, in particular in strategy. How can we actually appraise the skill and contribution of an external independent strategy consultant relative to that of a NED, given the weight and impact of the NED's opinion on the recommended strategy? To take this further, we can wonder whether it even makes sense for a CEO controlled by NEDs to solicit the services of external (independent) consultants, especially when it is the role of the board to essentially do the same thing. In fact these questions challenge the level and extent of contractual relations between external (independent) consultants and the firm: (1) should the external service providers provide services to just the board (NEDs) that ensures control of the management?; (2) should management that is responsible for the performance of the firm utilize the services of the external service providers?; or (3) should the external service providers provide service to both the firm's management and the board? The potential conflict is obvious, creating a new dilemma for all involved.

A related issue focuses on the question of boundaries between the functions of the NED and the external (independent) consultant. If it is true that the NED is considered as the firm's "super-consultant," not only in terms of competence and independence but also in terms of legal responsibility, one can wonder whether there is much interest in such a profession. External (independent) consultants, in contrast, are not legally responsible, as their interventions are limited to the context of the contract (that links the consultant to the firm) and they are paid for the hours and actions noted in the contract. Also, for external (independent) consultants, there is rarely any contractual obligation in terms of results. The disproportion between the expectations of NEDs and those of the external (independent) consultant is thus very significant. Small- to medium-sized enterprises (SMEs) represent one group of firms that would be particularly affected—the expectations and legal responsibilities for the NEDs would be just as high, for which, in return, their earnings can be low.

These issues and questions underscore the extent to which the modification of corporate governance, in general, and corporate boards, in particular, are affecting the consulting profession, as there are emerging opportunities and a distribution of new players. The main objective of this volume is not to necessarily answer these crucial questions, but to inform the reader about the issues and to help to clarify the challenges that are at stake. We have asked specialists in corporate governance—both academicians and practitioners—to highlight the changes that have taken place and the constraints that they operate under. We have intentionally emphasized the evolution of expectations in relation to boards, in order to better understand the ramifications for management consulting. The contributors, who represent an international group of experts, are from the United States, Europe (United Kingdom, France, Switzerland, Germany, Spain, Italy), Scandinavia (Norway), and Australia. To some extent, this wide representation has given rise to inevitable repetitions, because the perceptions in different countries overlap. Such repetition, however, has also allowed us to avoid the cognitive bias of generalizing from a limited number of cases, or from focusing on an evolution that is strongly marked by a specific cultural context. In their diversity as in their convergence, the contributions show that there is not only a redefinition of powers but also of skills and expertise in firms. The choice of contributors was also influenced by the fact that their experience or their field of research is not limited to large, publicly-listed companies—where we find that corporate governance is often and unjustly restricted—but includes a diversity of firms, including SMEs.

THE NEW EXPERTS:
RISING EXPECTATIONS TOWARDS DIRECTORS

The first part of the volume focuses on the recent shake-up in corporate governance. In the first chapter, David Finegold and Edward Lawler present a comprehensive examination of the evolution of expectations about corporate boards in the United States. Based on a study of board members of publicly-held *Fortune 1000* firms (2003 and 2004), they create a model of new roles and performance expectations. In their findings, Finegold and Lawler show that the shake-up has led to greater board independence and an increase in influence of directors. The boards also perceive themselves to be more effective having come to grips with the issues of compliance and are no able to focus more on aspects of governance. However, one challenge remains—recruiting the appropriate directors who fit with the new criteria.

The next chapter by José Luis Alvarez and Joan Ricart illustrates that this evolution is not restricted to boards in the United States. Corporate governance has evolved considerably in all the countries of the world, which is shown through the Spanish case examined in this chapter. Their analysis shows how this evolution has modified the relationship between shareholders and firms, even in countries that are apparently less familiar with shareholder logic. Noting the rapid proliferation of associations for defending the economic interests of shareholders, they observed that many of the associations were just fronts for legal consulting. These associations promote shareholder activism because annual general meetings (AGMs) are considered to be simply "rubber stamp" meetings and do not play a real role in corporate governance. In positioning themselves as professional service firms, the associations are promoting and defending the interests of their members, and are serving as knowledge intermediaries in articulating the collective action of shareholders and promoting reform in the AGMs.

Continuing this logic, Harry Korine examines, on the basis of his experience in advising capital investment in Switzerland, the paradox of why, when it comes to publicly-traded companies, fewer investor representatives sit on the boards compared to private firms (except if the capital is owned by large blocks of families or restructuring agents). In outlining the various impediments and by showing why these interventions are not more widespread, Korine argues that investors want to be more active. This implies that new experts, different from the manager, have the opportunity to place themselves at the heart of the firm. In analyzing the board-investor paradox, Korine identifies a number of strategic evolutions for firms, boards and especially for consultants, notably in terms of strategy and the blend of skills, in order to add value to boards.

DEFINING THE BOUNDARIES OF THE NEW EXPERTISE

The volume's second section seeks to understand how the operation of NEDs is being defined and regulated. As the demand for administrators is ever-growing, notwithstanding demands in terms of responsibility, it is necessary to understand how these administrators attempt to fix the limits of their function and, as a result, their responsibilities. In the first chapter in this section, Xavier de Sarrau and Thierry Tomasi, two expert lawyers in the field, show how administrators seek to limit their personal responsibility should their judgment be called into question. This judicial counterreaction to the legal reaction of Sarbanes-Oxley (or equivalent laws in other countries) illustrates that the law is at the center of the current redefinition of the boundaries of the administrator function. In outlining and analyzing the various protective measures utilized by directors, they argue that the new rules of governance require a shift in mentalities on the part of board members, as they are now seen as a corporate team and not just a ritualistic gathering.

The next chapter by Australian researchers Gavin Nicholson, Geoffrey Kiel, and Kevin Hendry shows how the growth of expectations in relation to the NED creates conflicts between the different roles that administrators are expected to fulfill. By drawing on social identity theory, they help us to better understand how this function is structured, as administrators learn to fill several roles simultaneously by creating routines and ad hoc procedures. These elements are particularly important to understand, through comparison, in terms of the difference that can be established with the profession of consultant.

David Risser focuses on this difference, drawing on his personal experience as consultant in corporate governance. Risser makes a parallel between the expectations of NEDs (e.g., code of good conduct and texts of reference that describe them), and the expectations he himself perceives in relation to his practice as consultant. This parallel is very revealing to understand how the boundaries can be portrayed between these two functions. For Risser, adding value to the board should be the key criteria in selecting board members and that diversity is one effective mechanism for achieving the goal. He concludes that consultants, beyond observing the changes impacting NEDs, would have to adapt their ways of working in order to help directors add value to their boards and organizations.

"SUPER" MANAGER OR "SUPER" CONSULTANT? THEORIZING THE ROLE OF THE DIRECTOR

The third part of the volume delves deeper into the role of the director, focusing on how this role may continue to change in years to come. In the context of post-Enron fever and the strong demands placed on NEDs, it is necessary to step back and carefully define what is reasonable to expect of these individuals, without overestimating what is humanly possible and economically necessary. Within this context, Morten Huse, Jonas Gabrielsson, and Alessandro Minichilli look at the contribution of the outside director in the corporate value chain. Using a value chain perspective, their analysis examines how NEDs participate and contribute through a review of all the roles that can be expected from the board of a high performing corporation. They demonstrate how outside directors, even though they face numerous dilemmas, challenges and hindrances, can contribute to value creation and not just value distribution, and help create accountability in boards by aligning board role expectations and actual tasks.

The next chapter by Pierre-Yves Gomez and David Russell focuses on the underlying motivation of nonexecutive directors. Agency theory supposes that directors seek to maximize their personal interest, even against the interest of the company, as they have their own interests as well. The chapter posits that we must avoid cornering ourselves into approaches that are too restrictive in terms of motivation and that these approaches can incorporate emotional and moral dimensions, which are just as important as economic factors.

Michael Nippa and Jens Grigoleit conclude this section with an in-depth look at issues of trust and their impact on management consulting, examining the central role that confidence plays both in the nature of corporate activities and the roles and actions of administrators. They analyze the dominant use of agency theory-based approaches and their impact on corporate governance. In arguing for the use of trust-based corporate governance systems as opposed to agency-based ones (monitoring and sanction) they demonstrate why the latter crowds trust and leads to a self-reinforcing cycle of distrust. They conclude by proposing a new direction of research that compares and evaluates the economic consequences (costs and benefits) of trust and distrust on corporate governance systems.

A NEW PROFESSION:
THE CONTRACT, THE RESPONSIBILITIES, AND THE FUTURE

The basic objective of this volume is to raise our awareness about the consequences that the evolving nature of corporate boards will have on both the function of director and the redefinition of this function by the actors themselves—and its ramifications for management consulting and consultants. To what extent will such change open new opportunities and herald new social, moral, ethical, professional, and so forth, roles and responsibilities for consultants and directors? Will the evolution redefine the relationships between consultants and their traditional clients (managers, investors, administrators)? Will these actors become more actively involved in corporate governance, further shaping the role that consultants will play?

Susan Adams draws attention to one of the issues that continues to plague the composition of boards. In addressing the subject of discriminatory board practices and the scarcity of female board members, she looks at the state of female board participation in the United States compared to other countries, and the role and responsibilities of consultants that enable and facilitate the neglect of qualified women to be board members. She concludes by making the case that consultants have the responsibility to play an active role in advancing the cause of diversity in corporate boards.

The volume's final chapter by Rickie Moore examines the unfolding impacts and consequences of the Sarbanes-Oxley Act (SOX) for consultants and their clients (i.e., different stakeholder groups within the firm, including the board, executive management, middle management, investors, employees, and unions), as firms seek to comply with the new legally defined and enforced requirements. Highlighting a number of conflicts and challenges that consultants are made to face as a result of SOX,

Moore depicts the impact of the new corporate governance reform (r)evolution on the practice and profession of consulting. Through his analysis of some of the resulting dilemmas and tensions that consultants will have to address in conducting their engagements, Moore sheds light on the future of the consulting industry.

The volume attempts to build a link between the role of the consultant and the new roles of directors by examining different facets of this relationship. The chapters illustrate how, in general, the evolution of corporate governance, and, more specifically, the new expectations towards directors, both directly and indirectly, impact and transform the roles played by consultants and their relationship with directors and their boards. We hope that the various approaches offered by the book will stimulate new ideas, new perspectives, and new opportunities of collaboration between directors and consultants. Both of these functions are becoming increasingly crucial for the improvement of strategic decision-making processes, the control and supervision of those decisions, and the governance of firms. There is an urgent necessity for a better understanding of the function of directors, hence the need to reexamine its facets and characteristics in light of this important evolution. In exploring the redefinition of the boundaries of consulting and corporate governance, our intention is to better understand the evolving roles and relationships between directors and consultants, and to facilitate the exercise of both functions. We would have achieved the goal of the book if readers improve their understanding of the current situation, the new paradigm and its emerging context, and are better able to deal with the resulting issues and repercussions.

We would like to thank all our colleagues for their motivation to be part of this undertaking and contribution to the volume. We are grateful to them for their generosity and their willingness to share their expertise with the field, and to help constitute a common body of knowledge on a topic that is still emerging and a subject of many debates.

NOTES

1. After mass consumers we now have mass shareholders, and are witnessing an ongoing explosion in the number of shareholders from 30M to 200M worldwide. This phenomenon is comparable to mass consumption dating back to the 1930s. Massification is the evolution towards mass ownership in global economics.
2. Managerialism is characterized by the power of the top executives, the absenteeism of shareholders and the weakness of institutions of corporate governance (Berle & Means, 1932).

REFERENCES

Berle, A. A., & Means, G. C. (1932). *The modern corporation and private property.* New York: Macmillan.
Gomez, P. -Y., & Korine, H. (2005). Democracy and the evolution of corporate governance. *Corporate Governance: An International Review, 13*(6), 739–752.

PART I

**THE NEW EXPERTS:
RISING EXPECTATIONS TOWARDS DIRECTORS**

CHAPTER 1

BEHIND THE
BOARDROOM DOORS

Changes Underway In U.S. Corporate
Governance Post Sarbanes-Oxley

David Finegold and Edward Lawler, III

The United States entered the twenty-first century in a corporate governance crisis. A series of high-profile scandals in major corporations—Enron, Worldcom, Tyco International, the New York Stock Exchange (NYSE) itself—had sharply eroded public and investor faith in how U.S. companies were being run and the corporate boards that were meant to be overseeing them. In response, the Federal Government and regulatory bodies introduced the most significant set of governance reforms in the U.S. for many decades, trying to restore public confidence in the governance of public corporations. The Sarbanes-Oxley Act (SOX) was enacted quickly in 2002, followed by major changes in the rules for publicly-traded companies adopted by the stock exchanges and the Securities and Exchange Commission (SEC).

The purpose of this chapter is to understand how the boards of U.S. public corporations operate today and are changing in light of the new

Board Members and Management Consultants: Redefining the Boundaries of Consulting and Corporate Governance, pp. 3–25
Copyright © 2009 by Information Age Publishing
3

legislation, regulations, and guidelines. We begin by providing an overview of the key elements of recent governance reforms. We then present a framework, derived from the literature on group effectiveness, to analyze the key elements needed for creating a successful board. The main body of the chapter is devoted to analyzing the results of the 2004 version of an annual survey of the directors of U.S. public companies that we have been conducting since 1998 that gathers data on each of the categories in the board effectiveness framework. We conclude by analyzing the likely impact of these reforms on the effectiveness of corporate governance in the United States and the ramifications of these changes for management consultants.

NEW RULES: LEGISLATON, REGULATIONS AND GUIDELINES

SOX established a new public accounting oversight board, imposed new regulations regarding the auditing of public corporations, and instituted a number of new requirements for public company boards. The main changes for individual company boards are: (1) all members of the audit committee must be independent directors; (2) at least one member of the audit committee must be a "financial expert;" (3) loans from the company to any director or executive are prohibited; (4) any transactions relating to the company by directors must be disclosed; and (6) the chief executive officer (CEO) and chief financial officer (CFO) must attest to their company's financial records and are personally liable if their company has been found to be breaking the rules.

In 2003, both the NYSE and the NASDAQ (National Association of the Securities Dealers Automated Quotation) adopted new corporate governance rules that went into effect the following year. The substance of these two sets of reforms is very similar, so we will summarize them together. First, listed companies must have a majority of independent directors. "Independence" now means that individuals have "no material relationship with the company"—that is, that they are not recent employees, family members, nor part of an interlocking directorship. Second, a number of practices related to board committees were mandated. For example, (1) charters for nomination and compensation committees, and annual evaluations of committees; (2) audit committees must establish an audit function, and all of their members be financially literate; (3) only independent directors can serve on nominating and compensation committees; (4) shareholders must be given an opportunity to vote on equity-compensation plans; (5) boards must hold regular executive sessions with nonmanagement directors; (6) the full board must approve compensation packages and director nominations; (7) corporate governance guidelines and a code of business ethics must be adopted; and (8) boards must include training for directors and annual board evaluations.

The common theme in these reforms is an agency-theory perspective that, by increasing the independence of directors, seeks to strengthen the role of the board as the representative of the company's shareholders. Though the reforms' emphasis on the monitoring function of boards aligns with the agency-theory focus of much of the board literature, it stands in contrast to the conclusions of most of the experts on corporate governance (e.g., Conger, Lawler, & Finegold, 2000; Johnston, Daily, & Ellstrand, 1996; Zahra & Pearce, 1989) who stress the multiple roles that boards play.

A comprehensive review of the last 15 years of research on corporate boards and company performance (see Finegold, Hecht, & Benson, 2007) finds that another common element in these reforms is that there is little evidence to suggest that any of the new practices have had a demonstrably positive effect on corporate performance. This is not to say that they will be ineffective, but rather that none of these practices *appear* to have been derived from, nor to have received clear support from, corporate governance research.

A FRAMEWORK FOR BOARD EFFECTIVENESS

To judge the impact these reforms are likely to have, it is important to understand the key elements that shape how boards actually operate. Our work over the last decade has applied insights from research on knowledge work teams to the highest level group in an organization—the corporate board. We identify five features that interact to impact governance effectiveness: roles, composition, structure, processes, and dynamics (see Figure 1.1). These features are derived from research and practice on the core elements of the design of effective organizations and teams (Galbraith, Downey, & Kates, 2002; Mohrman, Galbraith, & Lawler, 1998).

Roles

This variable refers to the role the board plays in key activities, such as providing strategic direction and counsel, monitoring financial performance of the corporation, evaluating and rewarding the CEO, planning for CEO and senior management succession, and preventing and managing crises. One of the key aspects in defining the board's role lies in developing an understanding of the boundary between the board and the management of the organization.

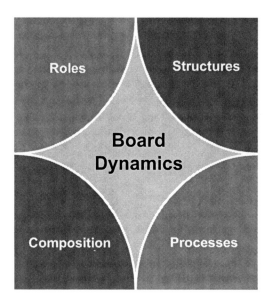

Figure 1.1.   Governance effectiveness.

Composition

The mix of skills and experience among directors will influence the board's ability to work effectively on different problems. It should align closely with the organization's strategy so that board members can deal effectively with the challenges their company is likely to face. A company that experiences growth through acquisition strategy, for example, needs a board whose members have experience with integrating mergers and acquisitions, while a company looking to expand globally may place greater emphasis on director awareness of foreign markets and cross-cultural issues. The extent to which directors share common values and perspectives will significantly influence their interactions. Board composition issues also include director term and age limits, and restrictions to serve on other boards.

Structure

This refers to how the board is organized to carry out its work, including its size, leadership, and committee structure and composition. There are some limitations on board structure imposed by statute, stock exchange regulations, and even by a company's bylaws.

Processes

These involve the mechanisms by which the board does its work and include the meeting structure, agenda management, pre-readings, presentations, and process for making decisions. Board assessment—a key process – is now required by the NYSE for all companies listed on the exchange.

Dynamics

The dynamics of the board members' interactions are represented at the center of Figure 1.1 because they impact the overall effectiveness of the board. Are board discussions open and capturing multiple perspectives or narrow and perfunctory? Do all board members participate in decision making, or does the board tend to polarize into opposing camps? It is vital for boards to identify those patterns of behavior that are critical to their effective performance.

RESEARCH METHODS

In order, to identify how U.S. firms have responded to these governance reforms, we worked with Mercer Delta to survey board practices. A survey was sent to all of the directors on the boards of public *Fortune 1000* in 2003 and again in 2004. Directors who sit on more than one board were asked to fill in the survey for the largest U.S. company on which they served as a director. In 2004, we received responses from 221 directors, from approximately 200 different firms, and included CEOs/board chairs (12%), inside directors (3%), outside directors (72%), CEOs/nonchairs (4%), nonexecutive chairs (3%), lead directors (5%) and "others" (2%). The directors in our survey served on an average of 2.5 boards. Most of the questions were composed of Likert scales (1–5) and to simplify reporting of the results, choices 4 or 5 on these 5-point scales are treated as a "favorable" response.

RESULTS

Board Roles and Effectiveness

In response to the many new governance reforms, boards in the United States appear to be focusing more on monitoring the financial accounting and ethical behavior of their companies, with less time devoted to the many other ways in which boards can add value (e.g., helping to shape long-term strategy, developing potential successors to the CEO). This emphasis reinforces the historical trends within U.S. boardrooms, as directors indicate that monitoring has always been the area where their boards are most effective.

The vast majority (91%) of the directors rated their boards highly on overall effectiveness, but gave much higher scores on monitoring than other board roles (see Table 1.1). Boards were seen as most effective at providing fiduciary oversight (94%), with slightly lower, but still very positive ratings (87%) on monitoring ethical behavior. In contrast, only 63% of the directors responded favorably when asked to rate their boards' effectiveness in shaping long-term strategy. This is an improvement over the 2003 results (55% favorable), but still a low number. The results are similar for identifying threats and opportunities. CEO succession is another area where boards could strengthen their involvement, although there was a significant improvement from 2003 (up from 50% to 69%). In particular, only 26% of the directors responded favorably when asked to rate the extent to which their boards participate in the development of internal candidates for future senior management positions (only slightly better than the 2003 results of 21%).

The good news appears to be that the greater focus on boards monitoring management does not appear to have undermined their ability to work well together. Despite greater focus on board independence, only 8% of respondents felt that it had become much "more difficult for outside directors to work in close partnership with management."

RESPONSIBILITY TO STAKEHOLDERS

One of the major distinctions between European and U.S. models of governance is whose interests boards are serving. Although most U.S. states, like European countries, have laws that indicate boards should take into account the interests of all relevant stakeholders when overseeing the company, in practice, as our survey shows, most U.S. public companies put a much greater emphasis on the interests of the owners than other stakeholders (see Table 1.2). Interestingly, directors draw a sharp distinction between long-term shareholders, who they feel they owe the "most duty to" (62%) and institutional investors (24% "owe most duty to"). One quarter (25%) of the directors surveyed feel they owe the most duty to employees and less than one quarter to other stakeholders.

Table 1.1. Board Roles and Effectiveness

Rate the Effectiveness of the Board on the Following areas:	Very Ineffective	Ineffective	Somewhat Effective	Effective	Very Effective	% Favorable (% of Directors who Responded Effective/Very Effective)
Overall, how effective do you consider the board to be?	1%	0%	8%	60%	31%	91%
Monitoring the firm's financial performance	1%	1%	4%	41%	53%	94%
Representing the interest of shareholders	1%	0%	5%	45%	49%	94%
Advising during major decisions such as mergers or acquisitions	1%	1%	10%	41%	46%	87%
Ensuring ethical behavior within the company	0%	1%	11%	51%	36%	87%
Shaping long-term strategy	1%	6%	29%	47%	16%	63%
Identifying possible threats or opportunities critical to the future of the company	0%	4%	31%	46%	18%	64%
How effective is the board in planning for CEO succession?	3%	5%	23%	47%	22%	69%

Table 1.2.   To Whom Are Boards Responsible?

As a Board Member, How Responsible to the Following Groups Do You Feel?	Owe No Duty To		Owe Some Duty To		Owe Most Duty To
Long-term shareholders	0%	0%	7%	31%	62%
Institutional investors	1%	2%	18%	54%	24%
Employees	0%	1%	19%	55%	25%
Government/regulators	1%	10%	31%	40%	19%
Communities where company operates	1%	13%	41%	35%	10%
Top management team	0%	10%	31%	40%	19%

Table 1.3.   Top Management Participation in Board Meetings

How Often Do the Following Nondirectors Attend Board Meetings?	Never	Rarely	Sometimes	Often	Always
Chief counsel	1%	3%	4%	7%	85%
Business unit heads	0%	4%	22%	43%	31%
Head of HR	6%	19%	35%	22%	19%
CFO	0%	0%	1%	8%	91%
CIO	8%	28%	40%	15%	9%
Head of marketing	10%	29%	37%	15%	9%

Board Composition and Participation

The average size of U.S. boards is 10.6 members. The average number of inside directors is 2.2 and the average number of outside directors is 8.4. Despite the emphasis in recent reforms on increasing director independence, the size and composition of the average board has not changed significantly from 2001. While the average large U.S. company board included only one other company executive besides the CEO, members of the top management team regularly participate in board meetings, with the CFO and chief counsel most likely to attend (see Table 1.3 above).

The reforms are having an impact on the ability of boards to recruit new members (see Table 1.4). Over one-third of the directors said that it is more difficult to recruit qualified directors and over half of the boards reported significantly broadening their search for individuals to serve as directors. Thirty percent of the directors also suggested that they are now considerably more hesitant to sit on a board. A growing percentage of

Table 1.4. Recruiting Directors

As the Result of the Changes in Corporate Governance, to What Extent is Each of the Following Statements True?	To a Very Small Extent	To a Small Extent	To Some Extent	To a Great Extent	To a Very Great Extent
It is more difficult to recruit qualified directors	14%	14%	35%	28%	9%
Boards are broadening their search for individuals to serve as directors	1%	7%	38%	44%	10%
I am more hesitant to be on boards than I was before	21%	18%	36%	14%	12%
Does the board have an effective process for selecting new members?	2%	5%	19%	47%	27%

respondents (74%) feel their boards have an effective process for selecting new members, an increase from 62% in 2003.

Even though it is getting harder to attract qualified directors, companies are imposing more limits on who can serve on their boards. The large majority of boards surveyed (74%) have age limits for directors, and a few have term limits (82% report that they do not have term limits for directors). Although term limits are not a common practice, the number of Boards imposing them has more than doubled from 9% in 2000 to 18% in 2004. Interestingly, 36% of directors said that their boards had considered term limits and decided not to adopt them.

Imposing limits on the number of other boards on which directors can serve is still not a popular practice, but it is rapidly increasing. Fifty percent have limits on the number of boards CEOs can serve on, up from 28% in 2001. Thirty-seven percent have limits on the number of boards outside directors can serve on, which represents a major increase from just 3% in 2001. Among those who said they have no limits, the majority indicated that their board has never considered this practice for either the CEO or outside directors.

In addition to recruiting new members, the other way that boards can add to the capabilities of their directors is by investing in training and development. Interestingly, although director roles and responsibilities and governance requirements have been transformed in recent years, only 68% of the respondents said they have any form of regular training. Seventeen percent report they began the training in the last year (see Table 1.5).

Board Leadership

One of the main factors that historically distinguished U.S. corporate boards from their counterparts in most other countries is the much greater power that resides in the CEO, who also serves as chair of the board in the large majority of firms. While this concentration of power has not been directly challenged by recent U.S. governance reforms, we are witnessing significant shifts to providing greater independent leadership for the board as more firms split this role (29% have nonexecutive chair) or appoint an outside director to serve as a lead or presiding director (up from 21% in 2001 to 75% in 2004) (see Table 1.6). For those firms that have a lead or presiding director, our survey revealed that just over one-third of boards rotate this position. The most common roles played by lead directors are chairing executive sessions and communicating with the CEO between meetings, while they are much less likely to set the

Table 1.5. Board Composition and Capabilities

Please Indicate Whether the Board Currently has the Following Practices:	YES			NO		
	Yes, has for More Than a Year	*Yes, Have Adopted in the Last Year*	*Adoption is Currently Being Considered*	*No, Considered and Decided not to Adopt*	*No, Never Considered*	*No, had it and Decided to Eliminate*
Term limits for directors	16%	2%	1%	36%	43%	2%
Age limits for directors	74%	3%	2%	6%	14%	1%
A limit to the number of other boards on which the *CEO* can serve as an outside director	39%	11%	7%	14%	28%	0%
A limit to the number of other boards on which *outside directors* can serve	23%	14%	7%	20%	35%	1%
Regular education and training for directors	51%	17%	14%	4%	14%	0%

agenda, preside at board meetings or communicate with other leaders in the firm between meetings (see Table 1.7).

Our analysis of the data revealed that boards with a separate, nonexecutive chair or a lead or presiding director are significantly more likely to adopt a series of governance practices that help build board capabilities, including:

- Evaluations of the board and individual directors
- Training for directors on their role and the firm's strategy
- Annual strategic retreats and regular executive sessions
- Having board committees, rather than the CEO, control the selection of new directors and committee members

Committees

The growing time demands on boards resulting from the reforms have forced them to rely more heavily on committees (see Table 1.8). The vast majority of directors agree that committees are becoming more important (77%) and doing more work (84%) and in general they are very positive about the role these committees play. Nearly all directors believe their boards have the right committees in place (96%) and that committee assignments utilize the skills and experiences of board members (95%).

Time Spent on Board Matters

One of the most direct impacts of governance reforms and the new environment in which boards are operating is the increased time that directors are spending on board activities. The average estimated time directors spent on board matters (including review, preparation time, meeting attendance, and travel) was 188 hours in 2004, up from 156 hours in 2001. When asked to compare the time they spent last year with the previous year, 62% said it was more, 36% said it was about the same, and only 1% said it was less. As a consequence, directors are serving on fewer boards, with the average director serving on two public boards.

Board Information and Communication

One of the ways in which CEOs have historically attempted to control their boards is to limit the flow and timing of information they receive,

Table 1.6. Board Leadership

Please Indicate Whether the Board Currently has the Following Practices:	YES			NO		
	Yes, has for More Than a Year	Yes, Have Adopted in the Last Year	Adoption is Currently Being Considered	No, Considered and Decided not to Adopt	No, Never Considered	No, had it and Decided to Eliminate
Nonexecutive chair	23%	6%	1%	33%	30%	6%
An independent director who provides leadership to the board (e.g., lead director, presiding director)	65%	10%	3%	10%	11%	1%

Table 1.7. Roles of Lead or Presiding Directors

If the Board has a Lead Director, Presiding Director, or Nonexecutive Chair; Please Indicate What Role This Person Plays:	% Yes
Chairs executive sessions	64%
Communicates with CEO between meetings	55%
Leads the board in the event of a crisis	41%
Mentors the CEO	38%
Communicates with outside directors between meetings	35%
Communicates with other company leaders between meetings	22%
Sets the meeting agenda	22%
Presides at board meetings	12%
Represents the board in external communications with the media, shareholders, etc.	9%
Other	2%

Table 1.8. Board Committees

To what extent:	To a Very Small Extent	To a Small Extent	To Some Extent	To a Great Extent	To a Very Great Extent	% Favorable (% of Directors who Responded To a Great Extent/To a Very Great Extent)
Do committee assignments effectively utilize the skills and experience of board members?	0%	0%	5%	55%	40%	95%
Does the board have the right committee	0%	0%	3%	40%	56%	96%
Committees are doing more work	1%	2%	13%	47%	37%	84%
Committees are more important	3%	3%	18%	43%	32%	7%

often giving them a stack of materials just before a meeting, with insufficient time for directors to analyze it well and ask penetrating questions. This pattern of behavior seems largely to be a thing of the past, as directors generally expressed very positive views about the information that they receive from management (see Table 1.9). One practice that may have contributed to better informed directors is conducting an annual retreat in which the board and top management can discuss the company's strategy in much greater detail than is possible in a typical board meeting, a practice now adopted by two-thirds of Boards, including 11% that have held their first retreat in the last year. In addition, 65% of respondents said that board members and the CEO communicate between scheduled meetings to a "great" or "very great extent." Few boards, however, have gone the next step and developed channels of information about the company's operations and management that are independent of the CEO (only 27% of firms) or instituted a requirement that directors regularly visit company operations (46%).

Board and Individual Director Evaluation

We have argued for many years that conducting a regular evaluation of the board and its members is one clear mechanism for fostering the continuous improvement of governance within a firm (Conger, Finegold, & Lawler, 1998). At the end of 2004, NYSE's new governance rules went into effect, requiring boards listed on the Exchange to conduct a regular self-evaluation of the performance of the board and its committees. A significant majority of the directors (71%) responded favorably when asked to rate the effectiveness of the board evaluation process employed by their particular boards (see Table 1.10). Directors, however, are far less positive about the evaluation of individual directors. This may reflect the lack of a formal process for evaluating individual directors in most firms (only 19% had one in 2003), and the frequent reliance solely on self-evaluation among those firms that do individual director evaluations.

CEO and Board Performance Management and Compensation

Boards in the U.S. finally appear to be responding to the growing public and investor pressure to crack down on excessive CEO pay that is poorly linked to individual or company performance. The days of doling out large reward packages that are not benchmarked to clear performance targets may be numbered, as signaled by bell weather companies like

Table 1.9. Board Information

To What Extent:	To a Very Small Extent	To a Small Extent	To Some Extent	To a Great Extent	To a Very Great Extent	% Favorable (% of Directors who responded To a Great Extent/To a Very Great Extent)
Does the board receive sufficient information to carry out its responsibilities?	0%	0%	5%	45%	50%	95%
Does the CEO keep the board informed about significant matters affecting the company?	0%	0%	4%	33%	63%	96%
Is the board kept informed of key risks facing the company?	0%	0%	11%	43%	46%	89%
Do board members and the CEO communicate between scheduled meetings?	0%	6%	29%	43%	22%	65%
Does the board have independent information channels that provide useful information about company operations and management practices?	3%	24%	46%	20%	7%	27%

Table 1.10. Board and Director Evaluations

Overall, How Effective is the…	Very Ineffective	Ineffective	Somewhat Effective	Effective	Very Effective	Don't Have One	% Favorable (% of Directors who Responded Effective/Very Effective)
Board evaluation process?	1%	6%	22%	49%	22%	0%	71%
Evaluation of individual directors?	5%	13%	38%	34%	9%	19%	43%

General Electric, which announced in 2003 that it was replacing all stock grants and options in Jeff Immelt's compensation with "performance share units." These units vest in 5 years based on two metrics: 50% based on meeting or exceeding the overall shareholder returns of the S&P 500 and 50% based on average annual operating cash flow growth (exceeding 10%) (General Electric, 2004).

In our survey, 97% of directors reported that they have a formal process for evaluating the CEO's performance in 2004, up from 79% in 2003 and 67% in 2001. Furthermore, as shown in Table 1.11, when asked to rate the effectiveness of the CEO's compensation plan and the process for evaluating the CEO's performance, directors responded favorably (88% and 80% respectively). Directors were slightly less positive about the board's compensation plan (77% favorable rating), despite the fact that average compensation for an individual director has climbed to close $110,000 per year.

Director Independence

A common objective underlying all of the recent governance reforms has been to try to increase the power of boards relative to management. Our survey results suggest that most U.S. directors (93%) already feel that their boards were very independent from management (see Table 1.12), and that this independence has been growing, up from 86% in 2003. In addition, 87% of directors responded favorably when asked to rate the extent to which their board members act with courage and take appropriate action as needed, compared to only 70% who felt their board members voice opinions that conflict with the CEO's view. Through the nominating or governance committee, the board is now exercising greater control over the choice of new directors and committee chairs, although the CEO/chair has significantly more influence over the latter decision. One practice that has contributed to board independence is having regular executive sessions where only outside directors are present (a requirement in the reforms that 95% of firms had adopted by 2004) (see Table 1.13).

CHANGES IN BOARD DYNAMICS, PRACTICES, AND PERCEIVED EFFECTIVENESS

In addition to documenting the effects the corporate governance reforms are already having in U.S. boardrooms, we also asked directors their opinions of the likely impact that these reforms would or have had on board effectiveness (see Table 1.14). Those that were thought to be having the

Table 1.11. CEO and Board Performance Management

	Very Ineffective	Ineffective	Somewhat Effective	Effective	Very Effective	Don't Have One	% Favorable (% of Directors who Responded Effective/Very Effective)
Overall, how effective is the CEO performance evaluation process employed by the board?	0%	2%	17%	40%	40%	3%	80%
How effective is the company's compensation plan for its CEO?	0%	1%	10%	52%	36%	NA	88%
How effective is the board's compensation plan?	0%	1%	21%	55%	22%	NA	77%

Table 1.12. Board Independence

To What Extent:	To a Very Small Extent	To a Small Extent	To Some Extent	To a Great Extent	To a Very Great Extent	% Favorable (% of Directors who responded To a Great Extent/To a Very Great Extent)
Is the board independent of management?	1%	2%	5%	28%	65%	93%
Do board members act with courage and take appropriate action as needed?	0%	1%	11%	56%	31%	87%
Do board members voice opinions that conflict with the CEO's view?	1%	4%	25%	46%	24%	70%

Table 1.13.   Influence Over Board Staffing

Who has the Most Influence in Determining...	New Directors	Committee Chairs
Nominating/Governance committee	71%	43%
CEO	14%	30%
Full board	8%	8%
Nonexecutive chair/Lead director	5%	16%
Shareholders	1%	0%
Other	1%	2%

most positive impact were: having a majority of independent directors, having a financial expert on the board, and having only independent directors on the compensation and audit committees. In contrast, director perceptions of proposals to increase the ability of shareholders to nominate their own slate of board members were perceived to have a negative impact on corporate governance, perhaps not surprising since these would be replacements for the directors responding to the survey.

On the hotly contested issue of whether to separate the roles of chair and CEO, requiring a nonexecutive director was seen as likely to have a slightly negative effect on board and company performance. Directors felt it would reduce CEO power and make it harder to attract a good CEO.

In addition to wanting to identify the current trends that directors perceive will have the greatest impact on corporate governance, we also conducted a statistical analysis of which individual board practices and dynamics were most strongly correlated with having a more effective board. The following practices and processes were the most significantly related to greater board effectiveness:

- Requirement that outside directors visit company operations during the year
- Regular executive sessions for outside directors
- Requirement that directors purchase company stock
- Holding an annual strategic retreat
- Regular education and training for the board
- Independent legal counsel for directors
- Board has its own outside consultants/advisors
- Board has good process for monitoring nonfinancial performance of company

Table 1.14. Perceived Impact of Governance Reforms

How do you Think the Following Practices Impact Corporate Governance?	Very Negative	Negative	Neither Negative nor Positive	Positive	Very Positive	% of Directors who Responded Positive or Very Positive
Having a majority of independent directors	0%	1%	6%	28%	65%	93%
Having a financial expert on the board	0%	10%	19%	50%	31%	81%
Having only independent directors on the audit committee	0%	2%	12%	44%	42%	86%
Having only independent directors on the compensation committee	0%	1%	13%	46%	40%	86%
Increasing the ability of shareholders to nominate directors	16%	42%	33%	8%	1%	9%

- Board has "good information" (e.g., informed about key risks, maintaining independent communication channels with operating company)
- Leadership role of the chair (e.g., chair encourages "frank and open exchange of ideas during board meetings")
- Board has power relative to CEO (e.g., board influences meeting agenda and directors feel able to "voice opinions that conflict with the CEO's view")
- Board feels responsible to nonowner stakeholders (e.g., employees, communities, regulators, management)
- Board has power relative to CEO in making committee assignments and appointing new directors

As a second stage in the analysis, we combined these processes and practices in a regression. Together they explained over half (51%) of the variation in perceived effectiveness across boards. The most significant explanatory factors, in order of importance, were (1) the quality of information available to the board, (2) having consultants/advisors to the board, and (3) strong leadership from the chair.

CONCLUSIONS

Evidence from the 2004 board survey clearly indicates that regulators' efforts to increase the power of boards relative to management appear to be paying off. The changes in the boardroom—such as requiring a majority of independent directors, increased use of executive sessions, and mandating responsibility for director nomination to a committee comprised of independent Board members—are all contributing to greater board independence. Directors indicate, for example, that they have significantly greater influence over the meeting agenda and the nomination of new board members and committee chairs than they had in 2003.

The good news is that despite boards' greater influence and independence, a large majority of directors (70%) do not feel it is becoming more difficult to work in close partnership with management. Given the time and money being spent on complying with the new reforms, it is not surprising that directors rate their boards as far more effective at the monitoring function than in helping to shape strategy or plan for CEO succession. However, it is encouraging that perceived effectiveness in both of these areas has improved in the last year given their relative importance, suggesting that boards are now feeling comfortable in the area of *compliance* and are turning greater attention to the more critical aspects of *governance*.

The increased time demands and liability risks for directors, along with growing company efforts to limit the number of outside boards that their CEOs can sit on, however, are making it much harder to recruit new directors. Companies have responded by increasing director compensation and broadening their search criteria for new directors.

Ramifications for Consultants

Although the long-term effects of SOX and the other recent governance reforms in improving the effectiveness of U.S. corporate boards are still uncertain, one clear short-term, unintended consequence has been to generate thousands of new jobs for accountants and consultants. SOX might be aptly renamed "The Financial Service Job Creation Act of 2002," since it has created lucrative new lines of business in the design and implementation of new governance practices and director training for firms that specialize in working with corporate boards. Large public companies have spent between $5 to 8 million (on average) to come into compliance with the new regulations (Parker, 2005). Consultants have been spending thousands of hours putting in place and/or documenting existing systems and processes to detect any financial or ethical improprieties so that the CEO and CFO can personally certify that the audit of their firm is complete and accurate, resulting in an average increase of over 100% t in the audit revenues of the Big Four accounting firms. Executives, as noted, have a strong personal incentive to invest heavily in documentation of these practices, since they face personal imprisonment if unethical behavior occurs and adequate controls are later shown not to have been in place.

The area of board consulting that is likely to be the focus of the most controversy in the years ahead is executive compensation. The new SEC guidelines requiring full disclosure of the total rewards package given to the five highest paid individuals public companies (including pay, bonuses, stock grants and options, benefits and all perquisites) were intended to curb the huge growth in CEO pay in the United States, which has now reached 500 times that of the average worker, and to avoid some of the high-profile excesses that have filled the headlines in the last 5 years. However, at a recent corporate governance conference that brought together top academic experts, board members, investors and board consultants, the consensus was that the guidelines may have just the opposite of the intended effect—providing benchmarking data on what other top executives are receiving that could lead to a further ratcheting up of executive pay packages.

For compensation consultants, this situation creates opportunities, but also many potential land mines. In the vast majority of U.S. public companies, where the CEO is also the chair of the board, there is an inherent conflict when it comes to setting top executive pay and how it is determined. Consultants who take a strong stance in favor of designing reward packages that truly tie pay to performance and align CEO incentives with shareholder or broader stakeholder interests may find it difficult to obtain and retain clients. While those who perpetuate the upward spiral of CEO pay, may find they have more business, but have to deal with media scrutiny and a dissatisfied public and investor community. For those who wish to take a more principled, long-term perspective on this work, it will thus be vital to determine first whether the board and the compensation committee—who should be the client for the work—have the necessary independence from the CEO to act in the true interests of the firm and its owners.

REFERENCES

Conger, J., Finegold, D., & Lawler, E. (1998). Appraising boardroom performance. *Harvard Business Review, 76*(1), 136–148.

Conger, J., Lawler, E., & Finegold, D. (2000). *Corporate boards: Adding value at the top.* San Francisco: Jossey-Bass.

Finegold, D., Hecht, D., & Benson, G. (2007). Corporate boards and company performance: A review of the literature in light of recent governance reforms. *International Journal of Corporate Governance, 15*(5), 865–878.

Galbraith, J. Downey, D., & Kates, A. (2002). *Designing dynamic organizations,* New York: AMACOM.

General Electric Corporation. (2004). *GE Annual Report.* Crotonville, NY: Author.

Johnson, J., Daily, C., & Ellstrand, A. (1996). Board of directors: A review and research agenda. *Journal of Management, 22*(3), 409-38.

Mohrman, S., Galbraith, J., & Lawler, E. (1998). *Tomorrow's organization.* San Francisco: Jossey-Bass.

Parker, A. (2005, February 9). New rules help "big four' firms double fees." *Financial Times*, p. A1.

Zahra, S., & Pearce, J. (1989). Boards of directors and corporate financial performance: A review and integrative model. *Journal of Management, 15*(2), 291–334.

CHAPTER 2

THE INCREASING ROLE
PROFESSIONAL SERVICE
FIRMS PLAY IN
THE REFORM OF
SHAREHOLDERS' MEETINGS

Jose Luis Alvarez and Joan E. Ricart

In the first months of 2005, there were reports in the Spanish business press of the launching of several associations for the defense of shareholders' economic interests. While some of these associations were specific to particular large companies or sectors (most notably banking), others were open to minority shareholders of all companies and industries. Some of the reports revealed that the executive committees of these associations were led by lawyers who were partners of Madrid's most prestigious law firms, with the backing of some well-known executives, many of them retired. It seemed, then, that most big firms had their own association. Often, that sponsorship was not clear in the press and had to be uncovered by further inquiry.

The simultaneous public launching of these associations became so noteworthy that one of the most prestigious Spanish corporate

Board Members and Management Consultants: Redefining the Boundaries of Consulting and Corporate Governance, pp. 27–43
Copyright © 2009 by Information Age Publishing
27

governance experts published an article on the phenomenon in *Expansión*, the economic daily with the largest circulation. Because of their relevance, the first and last paragraphs of that article (Trias Sagnier, 2005) follow:

> The launching of associations for the defence of minority shareholders should be applauded, even if it is motivated more by the private interest of the associations' promoters than by genuine concern for the interests of shareholders. After all, Reason used an ambitious, unscrupulous character such as Napoleon to expand the idea of freedom and tear down the barriers of ignorance. So we should not be alarmed if some professionals look after their own interests in this arena. In doing so, they may breathe fresh life into our system of corporate governance. The problem is precisely that they may be too blinkered in their pursuit of short-term profit and avoid the main battle.
>
> Any initiative by third parties to favour these associations should be welcome, even if the motives of their promoters are less than altruistic. In fact, the same scheme has been working in other countries. So, this trend is no bad thing for the lethargic Spanish system of corporate governance. All the same, it is better to be transparent and call a spade a spade than to use the guise of shareholder associations to offer professional services. (p. 61)

Trias Sagnier (2005) exposed the artificial nature of these associations while ultimately accepting their usefulness, pointing to the beneficial public consequences of selfish private behavior. That these associations are a front for legal consulting is obvious, yet they have a very interesting distinctive peculiarity: together with the strictly legal advice that they provide, they also claim to—indeed they have to—develop the collective will of minority shareholders. That makes them a new and unusual type of consulting venture. What drives them to develop their practice in this direction is the very same circumstance that puts minority shareholders at the mercy of their agents—ownership dispersion.

Ownership dispersion leads to a deficit of information and a deficit of social connections, posing almost insurmountable challenges for collective action. These two deficits are linked—to compensate for a structural weakness in information, minority principals should act together, but their very dispersion makes collective action highly unlikely. They need help to become aware of common interests, develop the will to act, and detect and exploit action opportunities. This interaction is what defines social movements. Associations in defense of minority shareholders claim to be the catalysts of such movements. Obviously, shareholders with large shareholdings do not need to engage in collective action in the same way, because most often they are composed of a very small number of individuals or even just one. The kind of consulting they need is mostly in the traditional legal realm.

The purpose of this chapter is to analyze the role of consultants, professional service firms and, in general, knowledge intermediaries in articulating the collective action of shareholders. The regulatory background is the current proposals for the reform of General Meetings of Shareholders in Spain. General meetings are particularly revealing of shareholder activism, as they are the forum in which shareholders' actions can be most effective. This assessment and the arguments that follow appear, to a very large extent, equally applicable to other European countries, as these proposals have been put forward in Spain within the context of the wider governance reforms promoted by the winter report in Europe and other national and supranational regulatory efforts.

General Meetings, and the attempts to reform them, are a clear illustration of a fact that applies equally to other institutions of governance: business and the economy are always a few steps ahead of, and invariably are more complex than, whatever legal mechanisms are in place to promote good corporate governance. Legal reforms, including quasi-legal professional regulations such as those based on good governance codes, may guarantee a certain minimum level of control; but good decision making, which is the essence of good governance, cannot be prescribed by law. As this chapter will explore, the consulting needed for active and decisive shareholder meetings requires more than legal advice.

GENERAL SHAREHOLDERS' MEETINGS IN SPAIN: THE DISCONNECT BETWEEN THE LAW AND THE "REAL WORLD"

Under Spanish law, the General Shareholders Meeting is the forum for the expression of the will of the company's owners. It is corporations' supreme and sovereign body, and as such it has the power to alter the corporation's bylaws and to appoint and remove directors. The General Meeting is defined as a meeting of shareholders, called in due form to deliberate and decide by majority on important company matters, to approve the annual accounts, and to appoint directors. It is not a standing body, but General Meetings are held at least once a year, in ordinary session, while Extraordinary General Meetings may be held at other times, subject to certain requirements.

It is widely acknowledged by legal experts, management scholars, and the business press that the legal definition is at odds with the way General Meetings actually work in practice. For instance, in large listed companies in Spain, the General Meeting has gradually become ineffectual and has de facto ceased to act as a sovereign assembly, even for the most important issues. In practice, it is no longer a forum for debate but essentially a formality required by law to rubber-stamp the decisions of the company's board, which in turn may be influenced by the top management, to varying and company-contingent degrees. Accordingly, its decision-making function has become secondary and merely formal, and geared primarily towards confirming decisions that have already been taken. Over the years, the Annual General Meeting has turned into a megaevent held in a blaze of publicity, in essence little more than a show (Vives, 2005). External consultants specialized in media, communications, and event organization are already involved in staging these corporate shows. And, thus far, the vast majority of these consultants have been working for the same side—directors and executives (the agents), who are appointed not by the minority shareholders but by the control groups (the dominant principals). In Southern Europe, these dominant groups are often called the "hard core." They reinforce their power in General Shareholders' Meetings by profiting from the mostly unresolved challenge of democracy—political, corporate, or any kind of democracy—when large groups come together, especially large uninformed groups, and are often at the mercy of closely knit, well organized minorities.

Some Spanish authors writing on legal issues, such as Roncero Sánchez (1996), have openly acknowledged the problem as follows:

> The legal framework remains divorced from reality, particularly in large public companies whose shares are traded on the capital market ... and whose shareholders consist mainly of investors holding a small share of the company's equity, generally as part of a diversified portfolio, whose main concern is to earn a high return on their investment and who are uninterested in the company's business. Consequently, the General Meeting does not in practice perform the role assigned to it by law. As a result, decision-making power is concentrated in the hands of a small group of controlling shareholders and/or in the hands of the company's administrators, who act basically without any supervision. (p. 665)

It is surprising how long the current rules governing General Shareholders' Meetings have remained unchanged, despite the overwhelming evidence that the "real world" is quite different from the legal fiction—and not precisely for the good of corporate governance. This is all the more unfortunate if we bear in mind that the General Shareholders' Meeting *ought* to play a particularly important role in the internal or intraorganizational governance systems typical of continental Europe and Japan, where large banks are the chief source of finance and also have significant shareholdings in the main industries. In these business systems, it falls to the company's internal bodies—the General Shareholders' Meeting and the board of directors—to oversee the work of the company's management. Unlike the Anglo-Saxon model of external controls based mainly on market control, they tend to feature a high concentration of share ownership, a high participation of banks in company ownership, and a slow rate of transfer of controlling interests. It is also common to have the representative of the controlling shareholders sitting on boards of directors. Clearly, therefore, the General Meeting has a vital role to play in corporate governance in Spain (and other countries with analogous governance systems), as a balancing body of the often all-too-powerful dominant shareholder groups. In the Spanish context, as noted above, banks have traditionally been the main source of financing for large companies, and as a consequence the capital market system is still relatively small, in spite of the increasing presence of institutional investors in the past decade. Any reform proposal will naturally involve strengthening the participation of shareholders in the governance of companies through their representatives, in order to establish a balance within the structure of power and decision making.

The General Meeting was completely absent from early discussions on corporate governance in Spain. What little attention it had received in the corporate governance literature has focused on isolated and highly technical aspects such as proxy voting or the information provided to shareholders.

Corporate Governance Reform

The debate on General Meetings did not really get under way in Spain until the 1998 publication of the Olivencia Code (Olivencia, 1998) on the good governance of listed companies and the influence of the more demanding 2002 corporate governance legislation in the United States, the United Kingdom (Higgs, 2003), the European Union (Winter, 2002), and the publication in Spain of the Aldama Report (Aldama, 1993), which is part of a wider movement to reform corporate governance.

The 1998 Olivencia Code launched the first phase of corporate governance reform in Spain. It questioned the effectiveness of certain policies designed to strengthen shareholder participation in the General Meeting, noting that "the capacity of the shareholders' meeting of listed companies to act as a supervisory and decision-making body is subject to many structural limitations" (p. 51). The pessimist assumption of the Olivencia Code, and of similar codes in other European countries, that the supervisory role of the General Meeting could never be fully and effectively exercised, has been highly criticized by various authors. According to Ledesma (1999), this readiness to relinquish the authority of the General Meeting is particularly surprising in Spain, where company ownership is highly concentrated and there is good reason to strengthen the role of the General Meeting. It was precisely the recognition of the inability of the General Meeting to impose discipline that served to justify the Olivencia Code's decision to sideline the General Meeting in favor of the board of directors as the leading supervisory body.

The second wave of corporate governance reform in Spain, epitomized by the Aldama Report, officially published in January 2003 but whose results were already available at the end of 2002, likewise included numerous proposals to improve the effectiveness of boards of directors. These proposals, however, were assumed to be insufficient and, as a consequence, the report also included proposals for the reform of the General Shareholders' Meeting. The Aldama Report unlike the earlier Olivencia Code, maintained that one of the primary goals of corporate governance reform should be to reinforce the role of the General Meeting as the most important decision-making and supervisory body for protecting the welfare of the company and the interests of the shareholders. It proposed that listed companies should lay down rules of conduct for General Meetings, just as they do for the conduct of boards of directors. The procedures and powers of the Annual General Meeting of Shareholders should be subject to approval by that very same body as subject of corporate sovereignty, and always with constituent powers. These regulations should cover:

1. Advance and public call of meetings, agenda, proposed resolutions and information to be made available to shareholders during the preparation period:

    -   General Meetings must be called with sufficient notice to allow shareholders to gather information or issue voting instructions.
    -   The text of any proposed resolutions and a statement of the purpose for which the meeting is convened must be published on the company's Web site.

2. Proceedings at General Meetings:

    -   The Aldama Report recommended, but did not require, that mutual and investment funds, financial institutions and financial intermediaries, which increasingly represent large groups of individual shareholders or investors, should take a more active role in shaping the company's decisions. Moreover, they should publicly state their intention to participate or not in the decisions of the companies in which they invest.

- The regulations should contain rules governing procedures of the General Shareholders' Meeting, regarding chairmanship, information, Q&As, duration, order and number of speakers, attendance, and participation of the external auditor and chairs of board committees.
- Efforts should be made to standardize the documentation issued to shareholders to attend meetings.

3. The report proposed, as a matter for self-regulation rather than for compulsory compliance, that companies should determine the procedures allowing the announcement and debate of proposals not on the agenda put forward by the board, so that the board of directors may decide, state and justify its opinion as to whether the proposal should be included or not, justifying its decision if the proposal is rejected; and for introducing systems to calculate the quorum electronically. Other rules should deal with proxy voting, voting by mail or electronic voting, and other technical issues of participation of "high numbers" in decision-making.

The Securities and Stock Exchange Act of July 2003 made obligatory many of the measures just mentioned. The aim was to breathe new life into the General Meeting in listed companies and give it a new vitality. It also opened a huge opportunity for legal advisors, who jumped in to help companies comply with a wealth of complex new regulations. Many of these regulations, however, had a limited impact, as the case of Banco Santander Central Hispano, one of the largest banks in Europe and Latin America, illustrates. At the General Shareholders' Meeting of Banco Santander Central Hispano held on June 21, 2003 an interesting situation arose. The board of directors, following the recommendations of the Aldama Committee, included in the agenda, under item seven, a resolution to establish, precisely, a set of regulations for the General Meetings of the bank's shareholders. At the same time, the representative of a recently formed association of minority shareholders put forward an alternative set of regulations. The main differences between the two sets of regulations concerned: (1) adding items to the agenda and (2) shareholder rights to address the meeting.

First, in terms of adding items to the agenda, the regulations proposed by the shareholder association allowed shareholders holding a minimum number of shares to demand that new items be included on the agenda, after the call of the meeting, which the board's regulations did not allow.

Second, concerning shareholder right to address the meeting, the shareholder association proposed regulations that followed parliamentary tradition in setting limits to speeches, which should be of a reasonable length, no more than half an hour, although the chairman of the meeting could authorize an extension if considered appropriate. The shareholder association's regulations also included a five-minute right of reply by shareholders, with the chairman having the last word. In contrast, the regulations proposed by the board of directors allowed 5 minutes maximum for each speech, with the chairman having the option of granting a 5-minute extension. No right of reply for shareholders was envisaged.

In the end, the shareholder association's alternative regulations were rejected, despite the fact that Banco Santander Central Hispano likes to present itself as one of the champions of corporate governance reform in Spain.

Demand for Legal Advice

As the Banco Santander Central Hispano vignette illustrates, the new regulations increased the demand for legal advice in several regards. Like any more detailed regulation of an economic or social phenomenon, it draws in lawyers to deal with that increased legal complexity. In the field of corporate governance, the new regulations of shareholder meetings come on top of regulations in accounting and transparency. So, for legal firms already advising the top management and boards of corporations in the stock market—usually expensive, top notch, high-fee firms—these new regulations mean more business of a similar nature. Since the new rules also open up opportunities for litigation by minority shareholders, smaller and less prestigious, less expensive law firms may take on projects with a new angle: going against the corporate status quo. Even more, both types of law firms may go after a new type of client—associations of shareholders, which are able to pay by pooling resources, paying higher fees—on condition that those law firms also act as social organizers of those interests. This represents a new type of consulting activity that also includes the promotion of media impact of their class actions, and other actions aimed at gaining increased visibility and publicity in search for greater social pressure on corporations.

INADEQUACY OF REFORMS OF FORMAL PROCEEDINGS OF GENERAL MEETINGS: THE RELIANCE ON SOCIAL ACTORS

Even the advocates of reform of General Shareholders' Meetings admit that such reforms will not be sufficient on their own. Some economic actors (e.g., minority shareholders) will need to mobilize themselves to be able to restore the role of the General Shareholders' Meeting as the highest functioning body of corporate governance. Trying to improve the various channels of participation in the General Meeting will have no effect if shareholders are unwilling to take an active role, or if it is taken for granted that all shareholders want to play an active role, which is not always the case. As in politics, in corporate governance there could be a "silent majority." Hence there is a need to distinguish between different types of shareholders, depending on their capabilities for activism, whether they are individual, institutional or significant shareholders, and so forth.

Individual shareholders are individual investors who have acquired shares in different companies. Also known as minority shareholders, because of the small size of their holdings and dispersion, they need self-awareness, political organization, knowledge of rights and interests, and persistence of action. This activism cannot be enacted without the intervention of an agent as social organizer (Terrow, 1994).

Significant shareholders are normally companies or institutions that hold a significant proportion of the company's shares on a long-term basis, with the intention of supervising and having a say in shaping the policies pursued by the companies in which they have invested. In Spain, they tend to be banks or large industrial groups. Because they most often have seats on the boards, they can act on their own, and have the capability to form alliances with other significant shareholders and act in unison. They need more of the same type of external or even internal legal advice. They do not need external help to organize themselves, which is relatively easy for them because of their small numbers and experience. They have the advantages elites have.

Institutional shareholders are organizations whose business involves trading in the securities market. They include mutual funds and investment trusts, pension funds and insurance companies, securities firms, banks and credit institutions. They have access to a large volume of funds, which they diversify in different securities in order to ensure the highest possible return for their clients. Institutional shareholders are assumed to have more investment expertise than individual shareholders. The size of their shareholdings and professional acumen allows them to put more pressure on the management team. However, their focus on margin makes it expensive for them to exercise "voice," and rather prefer the solution of "exit" (Garrido, 2002; Pozen, 1994).

Another way of classifying shareholders is according to their motivation towards activism, whether they are active or passive. The purpose of this distinction, far from discriminating among investors, is to acknowledge each shareholder's differentiated contribution to the long-term welfare of the corporation, based on their legitimate interests. *Active shareholders* constitute a "monitoring group" and may, if they act in concert, exercise a more direct influence over the company's management. However, voices have been raised warning of the risk of conflicts of interest that may affect such monitoring activities by active shareholders. That is why in Spain, for instance, the Aldama Report recommends that companies should make public, in an annual good governance report, all information about commercial relations or other situations in which directors or major shareholders are involved and that the board of directors has considered noncontroversial or a benefit for the company.

Passive shareholders, in contrast, see the company as no more than a transitory, low-commitment investment opportunity and have no desire, and sometimes no capacity, to exercise any more direct control over company management beyond the simple "exit" option. The norm in the Spanish securities market is for companies to issue ordinary shares that carry certain financial, voting and other nonfinancial rights, including the right to attend General Meetings and vote on resolutions. The problem is what to do about passive shareholders who by law are also owners and have rights that they do not intend to exercise, and in practice never do, thus creating the opportunity for a power play to secure their proxy votes. While voters in a political system cannot, at least easily, leave that system (emigration being one possibility), it is much easier for shareholders to leave a corporation and invest in another business opportunity. The easiness of exit is one of the main differences between corporate and political democracies.

The importance of the distinction between passive and active shareholders requires criteria for differentiation. Relevant parameters for activism may include:

- *Ownership of a significant percentage of the company's shares*. As the size of an investor's investment increases, the difficulty of disinvesting may also go up and investors are therefore likely to tend towards a more active attitude. On this basis, ownership of a significant percentage of a company's shares could be regarded as a pointer to the nature of a shareholder's interest in the company.
- *Maintaining the investment for a certain period of time*. The fact of holding shares for a certain length of time could be taken as a sign that the investor is interested in becoming involved in the company, given the stability and constancy of a medium to long-term investment as opposed to a speculative short-term investment. Moreover, the stability of the investment may indicate the strength of the investor's desire to supervise the company's management, so as to ensure a satisfactory return and prevent substantial changes that could put his investment at risk.

- *A declaration of intentions on investment policies.* Another criterion that might help to measure the extent of an investor's willingness to participate would be an explicit declaration by the investor of its investment policy. The Aldama Report recommended that investment trusts, financial institutions and intermediaries publish a statement, as is standard practice in the United States, setting out their policies with regard to participation in the company's decisions, thus making a more active contribution to governing the company and assuming a more participative role. This recommendation, by encouraging investors to declare a policy of active participation in the company, is intended to discourage the "hands-off" attitude of some investors, who feel free to invest or disinvest whenever it suits them. However, it seems unlikely that much progress will be made in that direction in Spain or continental Europe as a whole. Merely drafting such declarations is a financially and legally risky exercise that investors will shy away from, and that in any case is costly and will demand much legal consulting (Garrido, 2002).

- *Regular exercise of rights with respect to General Meetings* (attendance and voting). Whether a shareholder exercises his rights or not is another criterion for assessing his role. Failure to exercise the right to attend and vote in General Meetings, either in person or by proxy, for a certain period may be construed as a sign that the investor is unwilling to participate. Attending and voting in General Meetings is time-consuming and will only be efficient from the investor's point of view if it has a favorable impact on his earnings. A shareholder's supervisory role is closely linked to expected earnings, so the greater the expected earnings, the more willing the shareholder is likely to be to shoulder the costs of supervision, including consulting fees.

Companies treat each type of shareholder differently. Listed companies have tended to give priority to significant and institutional shareholders over individual shareholders. This difference is reflected in the way, in true contingency-theory fashion, differentiated structures or units are set up to deal with different shareholders separately. Thus, Investor Relations departments tend to oversee intense and continuous relations with institutional and significant shareholders, while shareholder service offices, much more in a public relations mood, handle relations, often discontinuous and more superficial, with minority shareholders.

Institutional and significant shareholders have traditionally received preferential treatment, which is reflected in the quantity and quality of the information they receive. In Spain, as in other countries, the meetings or presentations by top management to analysts and investment funds, the so-called "road shows," are quite common.

Communicating with small shareholders, however, can be much more difficult, because of their sheer numbers. A wide range of tools is available to recruit and retain minority shareholders, including magazines or newsletters, shareholder clubs, bonuses and prizes, free gifts in the run-up to General Meetings, and even the offering of the company's products to shareholders at special prices. These are a whole variety of potential activities, to be provided by another whole variety of experts.

Respect for shareholders' right to information is crucial to build confidence in the capital markets. Disclosure and transparency is particularly important in corporate governance, above all in connection with General Shareholders' Meetings, as it can be a means of encouraging greater shareholder participation. That is why the reforms in Spain have tried to establish mechanisms to ensure that companies fulfill their duty to inform their shareholders. This duty is particularly strict in the stock market, where listed companies must meet certain minimum security and liquidity requirements, combined with information transparency.

As mentioned earlier, the different treatment given to the different types of shareholders has traditionally been reflected in the information they receive. The tendency today, however, particularly with respect to disclosure, is for a more uniform treatment, facilitated by the new technologies. As the Aldama Report suggests, corporate Web sites can be a channel (though with no guarantee of effectiveness) for informing and interacting with shareholders, offering fresh content and communication tools (e.g., chat rooms, e-mail, user registration, mobile Internet). The Aldama Report also gives a list of the information that companies should publish on their Web sites, as a basic minimum, which includes the rules governing General Meetings, the stable shareholdings held by different shareholders, directors' shareholdings, and details about the General Meeting.

These reforms, however, do not go as far as directly helping dispersed minority shareholders to organize their collective action. This is left to them; in essence, they are left alone. This is the void and the need that associations of shareholders sponsored by professional service firms try to fill.

ACTIVISM: THE CHANGING ROLE OF INSTITUTIONAL INVESTORS

Despite the regulatory reforms and other formal proposals concerning the holding of General Meetings, the regulators in Spain, as in other countries, have recognized the need to recruit the efforts of other social actors, other than the formal institutions of corporate governance, to help improve corporate governance practices. Specifically, it has turned to institutional investors to fill this role. Institutional investors are increasingly well represented among the shareholders of Spanish companies, as the extensive study by Trias Sagnier (1998) shows. Traditionally, in the Anglo-Saxon countries, public companies have gone to the stock market to raise capital, whereas in continental Europe the main providers of capital for large listed companies have been the banks. Whereas in the United States and the United Kingdom institutional investors hold more than 50% of all listed shares, in Spain and other countries in Europe the proportion is smaller. Nevertheless, since the mid-1990s institutional investors have become more important in Spain, partly due to foreign investment, which is largely institutional. For instance, foreign institutional investors currently own more than one third of Spanish shares. Foreign investors have traditionally maintained a hands-off attitude towards company management. In fact, the most significant characteristic of foreign investors is said to be their absenteeism and lack of participation.

Although institutional investors have traditionally shown no interest in exercising the influence that in theory they could have, given the size of their shareholdings, there have been few instances recently where they have shown signs of activism. A striking example was in 1999, when for the first time in Spain a group of institutional investors that included Société Générale and Beta Capital called for the resignation of the board of directors of the company Duro Felguera because they were dissatisfied with its stewardship. Their example has been followed by others such as Union Investment and DWS Investment of Germany, which at the last meeting of Telefónica shareholders declared that they were not interested in the distribution of 30% of the shares of the Spanish television channel Antenna 3 TV in the form of a special dividend. The General Meeting of Shareholders is becoming the channel of shareholder participation, as an alternative to the more direct involvement that comes with board membership, or with direct influence channels, such as those exemplified by on the road shows (Vives, 2005).

Given the increasing importance of foreign investment in Spain, the question arises of how foreign shareholders can exercise their right to attend and vote at General Meetings. This brings us to the complex issue of cross-border voting, which has been analyzed in several country comparative studies. A report published in 2002 titled "Cross Border Proxy Voting," published under the aegis of the International Corporate Governance Network, analyzed issues relating to proxy voting and attendance at General Meetings in five different countries—the United States, United Kingdom, Germany, Italy, and Japan.

As already mentioned, the shareholder structure of listed companies in Spain includes a contingent of significant shareholders, though institutional investors have been gaining in importance. This trend is most apparent in Spanish banks, such as the BBVA (Banco Bilbao Vizcaya Argentaria) group, 44.1% of whose shares are owned by institutional investors, or the BSCH (Banco Santander Central Hispano) group, with 56.11% of its shares in institutional hands.

Could institutional investors be the drivers of a revitalization of the General Meeting as a governing body? The growth and consolidation of institutional investment in Spain has drawn attention to these investors' traditional absenteeism. Unlike in the United States, where pension fund managers are required by law to exercise their right to vote in all the companies in which they own shares, in Spanish law there is no obligation for institutional shareholders to exercise their voting rights. This is a relatively recent issue in Spain and it remains to be seen how it develops in the light of future changes in the law aimed at encouraging greater participation.

What is Left for Small Shareholders?

The small investor seems to be left with few options to contribute to the improvement of corporate governance. The reforms in many countries fall short of really empowering shareholders so that they have the instruments to effectively control governance bodies. There has been an increase in transparency, more information is being provided through corporate Web sites, and most corporations even have a specialized unit to deal with shareholders interests. But the impact is still minimal.

In continental European countries, where ownership is quite concentrated, we have seen that controlling blocks and institutional investors are not always the keepers of shareholders' interests. An extensive "democratization of ownership" may surely change things as the market for corporate control can get more important. Steps have already been taken in countries like Spain, but they do not seem to be very definitive, as the stock exchange returns receded and money flowed very fast towards real estate again.

It is at least a curiosity to observe that the democratization of ownership has not yet developed into a real democratization of governance structures. The key question, then, is whether we can come up with ways to give shareholders greater voice and participation. We have seen that the current General Shareholders' Meetings are not fully effective for that purpose. As indicated there are some possibilities for improvement, for instance, technology plays an important role here, as it drastically facilitates the necessary information transparency, which is fundamental in order to move forward in this respect. Another step, if only a small one, might be the creation of a board-level committee to establish a dialogue with minority stakeholders. In the complex world we live in, we have no doubt that corporations could learn a lot from such interaction, difficult though it may be. In any case, we would get at least a more informed shareholder. Direct ways to participate could be established, for instance through electronic voting, or even voting directly on certain specific decisions. Some companies are already trying to implement electronic voting, but mostly as a way to support current governance.

If we establish an analogy with political systems, we can see that information—via the Internet, the media or both—and voting procedures are important instruments, but they are not enough. The voter is still too small, and too far away to have any real impact. True democracy requires some way of organizing the different views through different versions of shareholder associations. Yet, although we have witnessed such "interested" associations, it is still difficult to imagine small investors trying to organize when they can simply sell the stock. Firms may eventually get a lot from listening to small shareholders, but most CEOs have no interest in doing so. And government is unlikely to start financing associations of small investors when there are so many other, more urgent needs. We will have to wait for democracy to impact firm governance.

The Role of Professional Services Firms

To avoid this risk, the active presence of knowledge workers or professional service firms, such as consultants, seems increasingly important. Throughout the chapter we have identified several types of them, some already present in the field, which because of the new regulations will have more business. They include media, communication and public relations experts, so far working mostly for the status quo of corporate governance. Of course, in the same group are lawyers specialized in corporate law, now with a new client to add to their traditional portfolio (e.g., boards, chief executives), institutional investors, and perhaps also individual investors with substantial personal assets.

A new client is also emerging, disenfranchised shareholders, who legally, economically, and socially need to act collectively to efficiently pursue their interests. The same reasons—lack of information, coupled with isolation—that make these principals candidates for being exploited by their agents require that the experts helping them perform two tasks, one of judicial substance and the other of political process: organizing collective action.

Professional service firms can play an important role the organization of collective action placing themselves as the key element in the transformation of corporate governance aimed at improving the influence of shareholders in the General Assembly and, as a consequence, the overall management of the firm.

CONCLUSIONS

The main proposals of the Aldama Report, as in most continental European corporate governance reform efforts, summed up in this chapter, are aimed at giving the General Shareholders' Meeting a more useful role in corporate governance. It remains to be seen whether the adoption of these recommendations by listed companies and institutional shareholders becomes just another formality, given the existing power structure of the General Meeting and board of directors and the custom of holding purely formal, "rubber-stamp" General Shareholders' Meetings. These practices are deeply ingrained in Spanish business culture. Similarly, investment funds are accustomed to pursuing a flexible and independent approach to portfolio management, without any involvement in company affairs beyond what is strictly necessary to administer their assets.

To make the General Shareholders' Meeting an effective governing body with deliberative and decision-making power, a new format will need to be found, nothing like the overblown media spectacle to which we are accustomed. Shareholder associations and groupings of institutional investors may have a prominent role to play in this respect. Also, the new technologies may bring major changes to the existing system with the introduction of electronic voting. Other proposals might include setting up a shareholder committee, on an analogy with the various other committees of the board of directors, but made up of shareholders representing the entire body of shareholders on a proportional basis.

All these changes are aimed above all at making the General Shareholders' Meeting a more effective supervisory body. They are unlikely, however, to bring any substantial improvement to its strategic, decision-making function. There is even a danger that reforms based on stricter control and regulation of governance procedures will end up making the decision-making process more rigid. This is the old problem of direct or participatory democracy. Forcing it deteriorates its very essence. Laziness in participation is a democratic right. This is even truer in business polities, where exit is often much easier than from countries. Professional service firms can be the fundamental catalyzer for the emergence of real democracy in corporate governance.

REFERENCES

Aldama, E. (2003). *Informe de la comisión especial para el fomento de la transparencia y seguridad en los mercados y en las sociedades cotizadas* [Report from the special comission to encourage trasparency and secutiry to markets and listed companies]. Madrid, Spain: Ministerio de Economia y Finanzas.

Garrido, J. M. (2002). *La distribución y el control del poder en las sociedades cotizadas y los inversores institucionales* [Power control and distribution in listed companies and institutional investors]. Bolonia, Italia: Publicaciones del Real Colegio de España.

Higgs, D. (2003). *Review of the role and effectiveness of non-executive directors*. London: Slaughter & May.

Ledesma, A. C. (1999). El Papel de la junta general en el gobierno corporativo [The role of General Asembly in corporate governance] (pp. 615–706). In G. E. Velasco, L. F. de la Gandara, & M. Embid Irujo (Eds.), *El Gobierno de las Sociedades Cotizadas* [The governance of listed companies] (. Colección Madrid-Barcelona: Garrigues & Andersen.

Olivencia, M. (1998). *El gobierno de las sociedades cotizadas* [The governance of listed companies]. Madrid, Spain: Ministerio de Economia y Finanzas.

Pozen, R. (1994). Institutional investors: The reluctant activists. *Harvard Business Review, 72*(1), 140–150.

Roncero Sánchez, A. (1996). *Representación del accionista en la junta general de la sociedad anónima* [Shareholder representation in general assembly of listed companies]. Madrid, Spain: Mcgraw-Hill.

Terrow, S. (1994). *Power in movement: Social movements, collective action and politics*. Cambridge, England: Cambridge University Press.

Trias Sagnier, M. (1998) *Los inversores institucionales y el gobierno de las sociedades cotizadas* [Institutional investors and corporate governance]. Madrid, Spain: McGraw-Hill.

Trias Sagnier, M. (2005, March 23). Los Accionistas y sus asociaciones defensoras [Shareholders and associations for their defense]. *Expansión*, p. 61.

Vives, F. (2005, March 26). Las Juntas Generales: Sólo un espectáculo? [General Assembly: Just a show?]. *El País*, p. 16.

Winter J. (2002). *Report of the high level group of company law experts on a modern regulatory framework for company law in Europe*. Brussels, Belgium: European Union Publications.

CHAPTER 3

WHY DON'T MORE INVESTOR REPRESENTATIVES SIT ON THE BOARDS OF PUBLICLY-TRADED COMPANIES?

Harry Korine

In the start-up context, it is very common for major investors to sit on the board—venture capitalists and other lead investors—to watch over the use of their funds and to actively guide young companies. Once a company goes public, the propensity for representatives of invested capital to sit on the board goes down markedly, unless the capital is owned in large blocks by families (e.g., Michelin), corporate cross-holdings (e.g., Allianz), or restructuring specialists and raiders (such as Icahn in the United States or Ebner in Switzerland). In most legal frameworks, the ultimate responsibility for company strategy and control over management is vested in the board, where the decisions are made that determine the future of the company. Nonetheless, although banks, investment funds, insurance companies, and pension funds individually often hold significant proportions of the equity of a company and collectively may make up very large blocks, they rarely place representatives on the board of directors of publicly-traded companies. This is a paradox that appears to hold over

Board Members and Management Consultants: Redefining the Boundaries of Consulting and Corporate Governance, pp. 45–55
Copyright © 2009 by Information Age Publishing

recent history and across Organization for Economic Co-operation and Development (OECD) legal systems (with the aforementioned exception of the corporate cross-holdings that have been the norm for large companies in Germany and Japan).

CURRENT PRACTICE

The observation that investors do not sit on the boards of public companies holds across investor types, encompassing both indirect and direct investors. Whether capital is invested *indirectly* via fund managers in banks and investment funds or *directly* (e.g., pension funds, insurance companies, family offices, wealthy individuals), the very idea of sitting on the board appears foreign to most investors in public companies. The most obvious reason appears to be that sitting on the board would constrain investors' freedom to buy and sell. Indeed, board members are subject to very strict insider trading restrictions in most OECD countries and sitting on the board implies a de facto moratorium on trading. Since the ability to move in and out of companies quickly—anticipating sector, country, and other macroeconomic trends—represents the principal strength of banks and investment funds, it is not surprising that indirectly invested capital is not represented on the board of companies.

Directly invested capital, without the intermediary of a bank or an investment fund, however, is almost as unlikely to place representatives on boards as indirectly invested capital. Since the capital in question is often large and hence cannot be easily moved from share to share, the argument of trading restrictions alone cannot adequately justify why representatives of directly invested capital generally do not sit on the boards of publicly-traded companies. Of course, not all directly invested capital is equal. Indeed, there are significant differences in time horizons, return expectations, and risk profiles. This variety of interests helps to explain why sources of directly invested capital find it so hard to collaborate, but it does not explain why some sources of directly invested capital, at least, do not regularly place representatives on the boards of companies they invest in.

Of the investors who stay with an investment long enough to be considered for the board of directors, it would seem that the many value investors (e.g., value funds) and relatively few engaged investors (e.g., Relational Investors LLC in the United States, Hermes Pensions Management and Governance for Owners LLP in the United Kingdom) would be the most keen to seek board representation. After all, these are investors whose purpose it is to see companies realize their longer-term valuation potential, typically from investment starting points of relative undervaluation, and the board is precisely where long-term strategies are decided upon. *Value investors*, with large, diversified portfolios to manage typically adopt a passive approach to their holdings—no one holding is important enough to portfolio performance to warrant the time and energy necessary to get deeply involved. *Engaged investors*, in contrast, have more concentrated portfolios than value investors and make it their point of distinction to work directly with boards and management teams (Monks & Minow, 2001). The role of the engaged investor in a publicly-traded company conceptually resembles that of the venture capitalist in a start-up. And yet, even this latter type of investor is only very rarely found on boards.

In order to explain the investor-board paradox more generally, it is necessary to draw on arguments from both legal structure and established practice. From a legal point of view, insider trading restrictions and procedural roadblocks in getting on the election ballot for the board prevent most investors from access. In practice, investors are generally seen to be too narrowly financially focused to qualify as business experts and, as representatives of interested capital, have not benefited from the last 10 years' push for independent nonexecutive directors.

Legal Structure

The rules that prevent insiders from trading on privileged information clearly form the heart of any legal explanation of the investor-board paradox. Put in place to protect the majority of investors from unscrupulous exploitation by those "in the know," insider trading rules imply that investors must be outsiders whose primary interest lies in buying and selling under fair conditions. Yet, although buying and selling under fair conditions is certainly a necessary prerequisite for creating economic value, it is not sufficient. In fact, quite the contrary—by keeping most investor representatives off the board, even in contexts where investors can make important contributions (as illustrated below), insider trading rules actually put limitations on value creation. As it currently stands, very few investors are willing or able to lock away their market freedoms in exchange for a seat on a board.

Even those investors whose time horizons are long enough to consider giving up the freedom to buy and sell a particular stock for a relatively prolonged period are likely to be frustrated by the procedural difficulties of getting their representatives on the ballot for election to the board. Although the board of directors in public companies is formally elected by the shareholders in most, if not all, national and local systems of jurisdiction, the actual process of putting together the slate of candidates for election is typically tightly controlled by the existing board and management and only modifiable by an amendment to the company's constitution. This practice makes it very difficult and prohibitively expensive for outsiders to present themselves for consideration. In the United States, especially, regime changes are being proposed by the Securities and Exchange Commission that would make it easier for a limited number of investor representatives to get on the ballot, and some companies are even taking the lead by inviting investors to suggest board candidates, but the norm is still one of inside control of the candidate selection and election process.

Established Practice: Board Composition

The composition of boards of publicly-traded companies has increasingly come to reflect the institution's purpose—strategy and control. The board is a forum of experts, with the required personal skills sets being industry knowledge, executive experience, and connections for deal making with partners in business and government. In practice, the nonexecutive director (NED) slots that investor representatives might help fill are particularly skill/business connection dependent. Whereas investors or their representatives characteristically possess strong financial analysis or actuary backgrounds, the boards of public companies prize "real" business experience, best obtained through a leading position in industry, or, at a minimum, in consulting. The relatively technical and short-term world of investors, it is felt, has only little to offer to the deliberation of boards.

Interestingly, the wide-spread push for more NEDs on the board since the early 1990s taking its cue from the influential Cadbury Report (United Kingdom) have not had the effect of putting more investors on boards (Charkham & Simpson, 1997). In practice, the representatives of invested capital are not seen as fully independent. But what is the purpose of the NED—surely to provide a check on executive in the boardroom and a push for transparency and accountability in the pursuit of shareholder interests. One could argue that investor representatives are particularly well motivated to provide a check on executive power and are also, in most cases, truly independent of management and the rest of the board, because they serve different sets of interests and masters. Of course, the investor representative of invested capital is not a disinterested outsider, but why would it only be the disinterested outsider who can act as a check on the executive? At a minimum, it is worth considering another category of board member: the *interested nonexecutive* who represents one or several shareholder groupings. From the point of view of investors, at least, the current discussion about the "fully independent"

NED appears somewhat distant from the real-life concerns of financial markets, and the addition of an "investor chosen" NED would seem to have the potential to add value to boards.

IN WHAT INVESTMENT CONTEXTS *SHOULD* A LONG-TERM INVESOR SIT ON THE BOARD?

Quite apart from the fact that investors do not generally sit on the boards of publicly- traded companies and regardless of the legal and practical reasons for this state of affairs, it is worth specifying when investors might have a justified interest in seeking a board seat. With the limiting proviso of a long-term orientation, there are three conditions under which investors are likely to find board representation relevant and useful in furthering their objectives:

1. When the investor, alone, or in coalition, represents a *significant equity share*
2. When the investor has *rare knowledge* about business/strategy
3. When the company is facing *strategic transformation*.

The degree to which these three conditions obtain will vary with type of investment. The conditions of share significance and knowledge rarity are particularly germane in the small and mid cap sectors of the stock market, and less so in the large cap sector. Whereas significant holdings by individual investors or even groups of like-minded investors are relatively rare in large caps because of the sheer amount of capital involved, such positions are much more common in the small and mid cap sectors (e.g., the series of $20 Mio investments that a New York-based diversified Europe Value Fund makes in European stocks amounts is negligible in Nestlé but highly significant in a Swiss or German small cap). Moreover, since the boards of large caps typically enjoy a surfeit of world-class business and strategy expertise, the boards of small and mid caps are usually drawn from a pool which is both more local and built on a narrower skill base. In other words, it would seem particularly appropriate for investors with a long-term perspective to seek representation on the boards of small and midcaps. This is the segment where investors' input on boards can have weight and add substantial value.

The condition of strategic transformation is especially relevant to investors who get involved in deep turnarounds and reorientations. In such contexts, the board needs to take a very active role in the business, typically through the appointment of new management and the agreement of new plans. Without sitting on the board, investors who take a significant interest in strategic transformation cases risk being too far away from the action, unable to materially influence or adequately monitor the profound changes taking place. Again, and for similar reasons to those cited earlier, small and mid caps undergoing strategic transformation would seem to be particularly suited to investors on the board. If investors have rare knowledge about the industry and business changes implied by the strategic transformation, their presence on the board not only serves the purpose of monitoring implementation but actually has the potential to add considerable value. It is worth noting that investors' involvement in cases of strategic transformation can be likened to venture capitalists' involvement in start-ups. Like the start-up, the turn-around is in a "do or die" situation.

Quite independent of the particular context or the sector of the market, one can cite an additional condition under which investors might usefully seek representation on the board, namely when investors can help bridge the gap between different factions on the board for the good of the company. A board is a decision-making body. As such it has to deal with all the social and psychological challenges and difficulties inherent in the decision-making process. Often, boards are either (1) dominated by insiders or powerful individuals, (2) unable to think of fresh solutions or (3) deadlocked and unable to make decisions. In such situations, an investor can play a facilitating or mediating role that permits the unlocking of value. As above in the discussion of knowledge rarity, this argument, too, assumes that there might be investors with a long-term perspective who have the necessary facilitating or mediating skills and find it lucrative to apply them.

In general, one can say that investors should sit on company boards when they can add economic value. This value lies not only in business expertise, but also in the political role that can be played by a different type of board member who is able to build bridges between the market and the company and between different factions in the board that may be preventing value from being realized. Clearly, few financial investors are currently in a position to add true economic value to company boards; conversely, today's company boards are made up of seasoned business executives who often have a love/hate relationship with the financial markets. Indeed, the two worlds are often separated by outlook, training, and tradition, and the chasm is wide. Hence, the conditions for effective investor participation on company boards described in this section will only apply to a specialized group of investors, namely those with business experience outside the narrow confines of pure financial analysis and portfolio management.

Even if investors do have the necessary skills and the conditions for board membership are right, the process of actually getting onto a board may take a long time and lead to considerable acrimony over the breaking of established norms of board member selection and election. The acrimony engendered, in turn, may prevent the investor from having a salutary effect on company decisions and performance, once on the board. Therefore, the investor needs to carefully consider how best to exert influence—depending on the legal and practical context, it may be preferable for the investor to act behind the scenes, as a kind of shadow board member (without inside information, but with influence). This is a path that a number of long-term investors, who would otherwise have an interest in seeking a seat on the board, are increasingly following.

APPLICATION: ENGAGED INVESTMENT IN SWISS SMALL CAPS

The question of board membership always needs to be addressed on a case by case basis, but, for the sake of this chapter, here the focus is placed on the example of engaged investment in Swiss small caps. Although many of the remarks made below might also apply to German small caps, it is necessary to differentiate between Switzerland and Germany on questions relating to the board. With the unitary board system obtaining in Switzerland, the Swiss Verwaltungsrat resembles and indeed takes many cues from its Anglo-Saxon equivalents; the dual system in place in Germany with the legally mandated equal representation of labor in the Aufsichtsrat raises another set of questions which is not entered into here. As a general rule, engaged investors in Swiss small caps do not push for a place on the board, unless the strategy is to invest in a company that needs to go through a full-scale turn-around. For the reasons outlined in the previous section, in a turn-around situation, board membership is probably a necessity. Indeed, turn-around specialists, in Switzerland as much as in other countries, will often make board membership a condition for investing (i.e., Affentranger Associates' investment in Mikron and Anton Affentranger's accession to the position of chairman of the board).

Instead of seeking board membership, shareholder engagement funds investing in Swiss small caps work to obtain influence with the board of the company invested in. Influence is obtained by demonstrating alignment of investor interests with those of the company and the board, providing strategic value-added and, a necessary tactical element in a small, highly interconnected country like Switzerland, use of the investor's personal contact network. Why seek indirect influence over the board rather than board membership? The potential for indirect influence is high in the Swiss small cap context. Board members, as well as managers of Swiss small caps, are typically quite entrepreneurial, with a "push up the shirt sleeves, get your hands dirty" orientation. As such, they are highly skeptical of fee-based consultants, but will be more likely to respond positively to investors who take significant capital in hand to align their interests with those of the company. By the same token, board members and managers of Swiss small caps are rather operational, not strategic in business orientation and hence can appreciate the value-added of an investor that brings broad executive experience to the table. Having a strong contact network in a highly interconnected country also means that investors are never more than one personal link away from the board and hence can obtain access under very favorable conditions of introduction.

While the potential for indirect influence over the board is high in the Swiss small cap context, by contrast actually obtaining a place on the board is generally a very difficult undertaking. In addition to the broader reasons discussed above, the Swiss context contains specific practical and legal hurdles to board membership. Noteworthy Swiss practical hurdles include: (1) the fact that the typical 3-year term for board members is too extensive for most, if not all, investors (as it is associate with trading restrictions); (2) the notion of board membership as a reward for years of loyal corporate or government service (e.g., seats on the board are not for upstarts); and (3) the lingering negative reputation of activist investment associated with 1990s corporate raider Martin Ebner who made an aggressive, highly publicized push for board membership in a number of well-known Swiss large caps. Covering term, tradition, and reputation, these practical hurdles to board membership are very high indeed in Switzerland and require a great deal of perseverance to overcome.

At the same time, legal hurdles to board membership are also significant (Boeckli, 2004): (1) the need for majority approval at the general meeting; (2) the fact that there is no guaranteed right to a minority seat for different types of shareholders, only for different categories of shareholdings (in contrast to Germany, for example, where employees are guaranteed an equal number of seats on the board); and (3) the practice of staggered boards, with different running times for different members, making it highly impractical, though in theory possible, to get on the board through a cumulative, nonmajority voting process. Again, the investor must weigh the costs of obtaining board membership against the benefits. Corporate governance disasters and strategy failures in corporate Switzerland's recent past have made boards and managers more open to listening to outside voices—no Swiss board wants to become known as the next Swissair or the next Swiss life. On the other hand, the social barriers and legal impediments against investor access to board membership remain as high, if not higher than elsewhere in the developed world.

BOARDS AND INVESTORS: THE FUTURE

This chapter started with a paradox, the question as to why there are not more investor representatives on the boards of publicly-traded companies. Starting with a general discussion of legal and practical impediments, the chapter examined the specific conditions under which investor representation on company boards might provide added value and offered a more detailed, personal view of the relationship between investors and boards in Switzerland.

Although there can be an effective role for investors on the boards of publicly-traded companies under certain conditions, it does not appear that there is likely to be a more pronounced *formal* presence of investors on boards in the foreseeable future. The legal and practical hurdles are too high, and the worldviews are too far apart. The current push in the United States to make it easier to nominate new board members from outside the conventional selection process is an exception that, unless more broadly followed, only proves the rule. Since most investors will not or cannot sit on company boards, easing the nomination process is unlikely to put many more investors on boards.

A question that remains concerns the extent to which boards will have to worry about investor influence. The answer, to a large extent, depends on developments in the financial markets, on the progress of corporate governance in the boardroom, and on the relative success or failure of engaged investors such as Relational Investors, Hermes Pensions Management, and Governance for Owners.

As long as financial markets offer outstanding returns to investors who merely pick stocks or who trade volatility without regard to underlying company performance, investors as a whole will not be much interested in spending the extra effort involved in trying to work with boards, whether through formal or informal channels. Yet, if financial markets enter into a period of prolonged sideways movement or stagnation with low returns, then investors will want to become more involved in the fortunes of individual companies in order to obtain a source of out-performance (Korine & Hindle Fischer, 2003). In the last period of prolonged low equity returns—running roughly from the first oil crisis in 1973 until the advent of disinflationary forces in 1982—investors had to work harder to achieve good performance and there was a strong push in the direction of shareholder activism.

Investor interest in what is happening in the boardroom also depends on steps taken towards improved corporate governance (Gomez, 2002). Poor corporate governance, however defined and measured, costs investors money, either when the most poorly governed companies significantly underperform their better governed peers or when poor corporate governance implies fraud and companies implode. Under the impression of Enron, Worldcom, Parmalat, Mannesmann, and Vivendi Universal, among others, significant new corporate governance codes have been adopted in almost all developed market countries. It remains to be seen how these codes will work out in practice, but investors are watching closely and can be expected to take matters into their own hands through increased direct contacts with boards if further governance breakdowns occur.

The investment community will also be carefully monitoring the success of engaged investors to see if the extra effort involved in working with companies pays off through superior returns. To the extent that the engaged investment model has already had some notable long-term successes—Lens, Relational, and Hermes, to name three—this game of "wait and see" is already metamorphosing into a desire to join the party on the part of banks and investment funds. However, the specific skill mix needed for engaged investment, namely financial analysis and executive experience and strategy/governance analysis, remains a rare good in the investor community, which is one of the key reasons why there have not yet been many true followers of the engaged investment model. Yet, even the most passive portfolio investors are starting to think about how certain elements of engaged investment can be built into their business plans —closer monitoring of problematic stocks, more in-depth conversations with managers about strategy, and so forth.

No matter how the board-investor paradox plays out over the next few years, it is likely that the boards of publicly-traded companies will have to deal more frequently with investors and investor concerns than they have been used to. Not only do investors (especially pension funds) represent a larger proportion of capital than they did in the past, they have also become more willing to assert the power and responsibility that come with size (Drucker, 1976). Pushed by legal reforms starting in the 1970s, public sentiment for change in the way companies are governed, and the bad experience of corporate misconduct, investors as a group are more directly interested in corporate decisions and the actions of boards. Under these changed circumstances, the question of whether investors should formally sit on boards may turn out to be less important than whether or not investors can find ways to make their influence felt in the boardroom.

As an advisor to a shareholder engagement fund and as an academic with interests in corporate strategy and corporate governance, I can therefore only recommend that boards take the time to learn about and truly understand investor concerns. In fact, the ability to work with investors will be a hallmark of successful boards in the future. Working with investors also means recognizing the variety of investors out there. There is more to working with investors than glibly satisfying the short-term expectations of the markets, and boards will need to recognize that investors are a varied group of constituents with different time horizons, return expectations, and risk profiles, and need to be treated accordingly. Perhaps, working with investors will become so central to the task of the board of the future that companies will of their own accord propose to put selected long-term investors on their boards, reversing and resolving the paradox this chapter started out with (Gomez & Korine, 2005).

For management consultants, the implications of the developments described in this chapter are twofold: first, the lines that traditionally separated investors from boards and executives are becoming increasingly blurred and management consultants may hence find themselves on one *or* the other side of strategic debates between investors and companies; as a consequence, there is a need for management consultants to develop a keen understanding of the concerns of investors and boards, to go with their well-established knowledge of senior management issues. These implications translate into the opening of a new business field for management consultants. The opportunities for growth in bridging the gaps between investors and companies are considerable; taking advantage of these opportunities will require that management consultants diversify their skills and broaden their customer base. Boards and investors are potentially as interesting, as customers, as the executive market that management consultants have served in the past.

REFERENCES

Boeckli, P. (2004). *Aktienrecht* [Stock company law] (3rd ed.). Zuerich, Germany: Schulthess.

Charkham, J., & Simpson, A. (1997). *Fair shares: The future of shareholder power and responsibility.* Oxford, England: Oxford University Press.

Drucker, P. (1976). *The unseen revolution: How pension fund socialism came to America.* New York: HarperCollins.

Gomez, P. -Y. (2002). *La République des actionnaires* [A republic of shareholders]. Paris: Syros.

Gomez, P. -Y., & Korine, H. (2005). Democracy and the evolution of corporate governance. *Corporate Governance: An International Review, 13*(6), 739–752.

Korine, H., & Hindle Fischer, R. (2003). The silver lining of the "post-bubble" era. *Financial Times*, June 2, Fund Management Supplement, p. 6.

Monks, R., & Minow, N. (2001). *Corporate governance.* Cambridge, MA: Blackwell.

PART II

DEFINING THE BOUNDARIES OF THE NEW EXPERTISE

CHAPTER 4

HOW CAN CORPORATE DIRECTORS BETTER PROTECT THEMSELVES?

Lessons From Litigation in the United States

Xavier de Sarrau and Thierry Tomasi

The board of directors plays a role of critical importance in the context of the market-based American corporate governance model (Rehman, 2004). Whereas the daily operation of the company is generally delegated to the management, the board is expected to safeguard shareholders' interests by directing and overseeing the corporation's business.[1] Board duties are, therefore, twofold and typically include both a *managerial role* (reviewing the corporation's overall business strategy, selecting and compensating senior executives) and a *monitoring role* (evaluating the corporations' outside auditors, overseeing the corporation's financial statements and overall performance) (Romano, 1993, p. 163). In performing these duties, directors act as fiduciaries to the corporation and to shareholders (Pinto & Branson, 1999). State corporate laws require that they

Board Members and Management Consultants: Redefining the Boundaries of Consulting and Corporate Governance, pp. 59–87
Copyright © 2009 by Information Age Publishing
59

act in good faith, with reasonable care, and in the best interest of the corporation,[2] and although the formulation of this fiduciary duty may vary from state to state, it is generally construed as implying a duty of care, a duty of loyalty, and a duty to communicate honestly.

DIRECTORS' DUTIES

The *duty of care* requires a director to perform his or her duties "in good faith, in a manner that he or she reasonably believes to be in the best interests of the corporation, and with the care that an ordinarily prudent person would reasonably be expected to exercise in a like position" (American Law Institute, 1994, pp. 138–139, 155–156). State laws are not uniform as to the precise scope of the duty of care standard. In some states, this standard may only reach gross negligence,[3] and the particular circumstances of the director's position may influence a court's findings.[4] Moreover, the courts have elaborated the doctrine of the *business judgment rule*, under which directors' decisions will not be challenged when these are made without illegality, without conflict of interest, with adequate process, and with good faith.[5] Thus, broadly speaking, the duty of care essentially requires that directors seek all reasonably available material information and dedicate sufficient time and deliberation prior to taking a business decision.

The *duty of loyalty* focuses on the situation where the fiduciary has a conflict of interest with the corporation.[6] It requires that the best interest of the corporation and its shareholders take precedence over any interest possessed by a director and not shared by the shareholders generally. For this purpose, courts scrutinize the substance and the process of a conflict of interest transaction to determine if it is fair, and state laws generally impose that any such transaction be disclosed and submitted to the approval of either disinterested directors or minority shareholders.[7]

Disclosure has always been an important feature of the duty of care and the duty of loyalty. In some states, there exists an autonomous *fiduciary duty to communicate honestly* with the shareholders, and "directors who knowingly disseminate false information that results in corporate injury or damage to an individual stockholder ... may be held accountable" (*Malone v. Brincat*, 1998).

The directors' fiduciary duty should be approached in conjunction with federal antifraud rules, distributed throughout securities laws and regulations. Broadly speaking, these rules, embodied in the Securities Act 1933, the Exchange Act 1934 and the rules adopted by the Securities and

Exchange Commission (SEC), prohibit false or misleading statements and material omissions in the context of the offering or trading of securities, proxy solicitations, tender offers and reporting of corporate performance.[8] Typically, claims under federal antifraud rules can be brought against directors who participate in disclosure violations.

Increased Pressure on the Board of Directors

Concerns about the proper performance of their duties by corporate boards are not new (Berle & Means, 1932). Yet, prior to recent corporate scandals, directors at scandal-ridden companies were believed to be well insulated against liability when they were not directly involved in the alleged corporate wrongdoing.

The received wisdom was that reliance on market forces could ensure adequate corporate behavior better than litigation, and that the perspective of liability could have the unwanted effect of scaring independent directors from serving on corporate boards or hamper necessary risk-taking in the conduct of corporate affairs.[9] In practice, plaintiffs bringing duty of care claims were rarely successful (Pinto & Branson, 1999) due to the reluctance of courts to interfere with a board's exercise of its authority, to the general deference to the business judgment rule, and to the exculpatory provisions contained in the articles of incorporation of many corporations.

Recent examples of corporate wrongdoing, however, have triggered a dramatic change in the business community's attitude. Scandals at Enron, WorldCom, and the like have provided tangible evidence that the problems relating to board structure and performance are far more common, and the consequences of board failure more serious, than was believed. This conviction has prompted a strong demand for greater accountability of corporate directors, and the enactment of new regulations purporting to ensure effective oversight of American corporations.[10] These concerns have been echoed by many courts across the country, which seem to have adopted a more receptive stance towards claims for breach of fiduciary duties.[11]

In this context of increased pressure on corporate boards, the question arises as to how directors may curtail the risk of litigation and liability in the performance of their attributions. Although it is impossible to prevent altogether unwanted litigation, recent cases suggest that compliance with a set of clear behavioral rules, and the implementation of a series of protective mechanisms may greatly limit the risk of liability.

The purpose of this article is to present a selection of recent cases in which the liability of corporate directors has been sought, and to outline the basic behavioral rules and the protective mechanisms that may be put into place in order to minimize the risk and consequences of litigation.

EXAMPLES FROM RECENT LITIGATION

The members of the board have become a frequent target whenever shareholders or other interested third parties are disgruntled by the way in which a corporation has been managed, or certain transactions have taken place. We have chosen to focus on a few significant cases, which illustrate the vast array of circumstances in which the directors may face the risk of litigation.

Compliance: Abbot Laboratories

Between 1993 and 1999, the Food and Drug Administration (FDA) conducted several investigations in Abbott Laboratories' (Abbott) facilities, and warned the corporation's management that several products did not comply with FDA regulations. In 1999, the FDA filed a complaint for an injunction and Abbott agreed to pay a $100 million fine and to destroy certain diagnostic kits, thereby generating a loss for the corporation estimated at $250 million.

Several shareholders brought a derivative action against the corporation's directors, alleging inter alia that they had been repeatedly informed of the FDA notifications but had failed to take any action in order to ensure compliance. According to the plaintiffs, such conduct constituted gross negligence, in breach of the director's fiduciary duty.

The Seventh Circuit Court of Appeals, assuming for procedural reasons that the facts alleged by the plaintiffs were true, noted that failure to take any action to ensure compliance of Abbott's processes with FDA regulations despite repeated warnings constituted a "sustained and systematic failure of the board to exercise oversight." According to the Court, the facts characterized an "intentional" failure, "in that the directors knew of the violations of law, [and] took no steps … to prevent or remedy the situation" (In Re Abbott Laboratories Derivative Shareholders Litigation, 325 F.3d 795 (7th Cir. 2003)).

Applying Illinois law, the Court found that the facts presented by the plaintiffs constituted a breach of the directors' duty of care committed in bad faith. Thus, the directors were not entitled to the protection of the business judgment rule and of the exculpatory provision contained in the corporation's articles of association. The Court allowed the suit to proceed.

Management Compensation and Benefits: The Walt Disney Company[12]

In October 1995, the Walt Disney Company (Disney) hired M. Ovitz, a close friend of the CEO (chief executive officer) and chairman of the board, as president for an initial term of 5 years. Under the employment agreement, termination by Disney without cause triggered the payment to Ovitz of a $10 million severance indemnity, of his remaining salaries through September 2000, of $7.5 million for each remaining year, and the immediate vesting of 3 million stock options.

Serious difficulties quickly arose, and after only 14 months of employment, a nonfault severance agreement was negotiated, allowing Ovitz to enjoy a $140 million-severance package. This agreement was confirmed by the board of directors in December 1996.

Several shareholders then started a derivative action against the members of the board, alleging that they had breached their fiduciary duty in failing to inform themselves as to the details of Ovitz's employment agreement. In particular, the decision to hire Ovitz had been left to the CEO, and the board's compensation committee had approved the employment agreement without engaging in an analysis of its provisions or obtaining expert advice.

On May 28, 2003, the Delaware Court of Chancery, assuming for procedural reasons that the facts alleged by the plaintiffs were true, found that the conduct of Disney's directors was not "merely negligent or grossly negligent" but constituted a failure to "exercise any business judgment [or] make any good faith attempt to fulfill their fiduciary duties." The Court distinguished the alleged facts with the situation where directors "in a negligent or grossly negligent manner, merely failed to inform themselves or to deliberate adequately about an issue of material importance" to the corporation, and held that the directors "knew that they were making material decisions without adequate information and without adequate deliberation" (In Re the Walt Disney Company Derivative Litigation, C.A. N° 15452, 2003 Del. Ch., Lexis 52 (May 28, 2003).

Consequently, the Court decided that the directors were not protected by the business judgment rule, that they were not entitled to rely on the exculpatory provisions contained in the corporation's articles of incorporation, and allowed the suit to proceed.

Related Party Transactions: Hollinger International Inc.

In 2003, it appeared that several key executives of Hollinger International Inc.'s (Hollinger) were at the heart of a scheme designed to divert cash and assets from the corporation, and to conceal their self-dealing from the shareholders.[13] They were notably accused of funneling to themselves approximately $85 million through related party transactions involving noncompetition payments, organizing the sale of certain Hollinger newspaper publications at below-market prices to a privately-held company they owned, and investing moneys of Hollinger into a venture capital fund to which they were affiliated.

In December 2003, Cardinal Value Equity Partners, a shareholder of the corporation, brought a derivative action in the Delaware Court of Chancery against Hollinger's directors[14], alleging inter alia that they had breached their fiduciary duty by rubberstamping dozens of transactions decided by management, to the detriment of the investors they were bound to protect.

In particular, the plaintiff relied on the minutes of various board meetings according to which the board had approved the sale of newspapers owned by Hollinger to companies controlled by several top executives at below-market prices without asking for independent valuations, and the board's audit committee had granted important noncompetition payments to several top executives without any analysis as to the justification and amount of these payments (Rushe, 2004).

On May 3, 2005, Hollinger announced that several of its directors had entered into an agreement to settle the claim. The settlement agreement, which contained no admission of wrongdoing or liability, provided for the payment to Hollinger of $50 million to be funded by proceeds from the corporation's executive and organizational liability insurance policies.[15]

Repurchase of its Own Shares by the Company: Strassburger

In August 1994, Ridgewood Properties, Inc. (Ridgewood), a small publicly-held real estate company, repurchased 83% of its outstanding common stock from two of its largest shareholders: Triton Group Ltd. and Hesperus Limited Partners. In order to finance these repurchases, Ridgewood had to sell its principal operating assets. These transactions left the CEO and director of Ridgewood in a position of absolute majority control.

The repurchases had been negotiated by the CEO and director of Ridgewood, and since two of the three other directors of Ridgewood also served on the board of Triton, a special committee composed of the company's sole disinterested director had been formed and in order to advise on the Triton repurchase.

After the repurchases, a Ridgewood shareholder brought a derivative action against the corporation's directors, alleging that they had breached their duty of loyalty to the corporation and its shareholders by approving a self-dealing transaction that was unfair to minority shareholders, and by improperly expending corporate funds to repurchase stock to perpetuate control in a single member of the board.

Since three of Ridgewood's four directors had a conflict of interests, the Delaware Court of Chancery held that the transaction was subject to the "entire fairness standard," under which the defendants bear the burden of demonstrating that the transaction is entirely fair to the corporation and the minority stakeholders. As to the substance of the transaction, the Court found that the directors had breached their fiduciary by approving "an expenditure of corporate funds for the primary purpose of conferring and perpetuating control upon [the CEO]" (*Strassburger v. Earley*, 752 A.2d 557 (Delaware Chancery Court, 2000)).[16] As to the process followed by the board, the Court noted that the special committee had reviewed only limited information before approving the transaction, and had omitted to seek expert advice. Thus, the Court found that Ridgewood's directors had failed to ensure independent representation of minority shareholders in the decision-making process.

Accordingly, the Court held that Ridgewood's directors had committed a breach of their duty of loyalty, and ordered the partial rescission of the Triton repurchase and payment of rescissory damages by the conflicted directors.

Improper Accounting: WorldCom Inc.

In 2002, it appeared that some of WorldCom Inc.'s (WorldCom) top executives had set up a scheme designed to falsely portray the corporation as a profitable business during the year 2001 and the first quarter of 2002. By transferring certain costs to the corporation's capital account in violation of generally accepted accounting principles, and by omitting to disclose these transfers to investors, WorldCom executives had overstated the corporation's income by about $11 billion and its balance sheet by more than $75 billion. The loss to shareholders has been estimated at as much as $200 billion.

This accounting fraud caused WorldCom to file for bankruptcy.[17] Criminal and civil proceedings were started against the management and the corporation;[18] contemporaneously, a class-action lawsuit was brought by shareholders against the corporation's executives, members of the board, and various other defendants including the corporation's auditors and several investment banks.

According to the plaintiffs, the directors of WorldCom had committed several violations of federal securities laws[19] and breached their fiduciary duty. In particular, a report by the bankruptcy court examiner insisted that the board's audit committee "did not understand the company's internal financial workings or its culture, and they devoted strikingly little time to their role, meeting as little as three to five hours a year" (Coates, 2003). The audit committee had not obtained direct reports, unfiltered through senior management, from the internal audit department, and had not required the external auditors to detail problems. Further, the board had approved multibillion dollar acquisitions with little discussion and almost no inquiry.

On January 5, 2005, ten former WorldCom directors agreed to settle the class-action lawsuit for an unparalleled amount of $54 million. Of these, $18 million—that is, 20% of the net aggregate worth of the settling directors, excluding primary residences and retirement plans—were contributed by the directors personally. The balance was provided by several insurance companies.[20]

BASIC BEHAVIORAL RECOMMENDATIONS

Whereas a strong commitment to the highest ethical conduct is a necessary condition for sitting on a corporate board, the cases outlined above demonstrate that mere integrity falls short of the behavioral standard expected from directors. The duties of care and loyalty as well as state and federal antifraud rules require adherence to a set of strict behavioral rules, which includes competence, diligence, avoidance of conflicts of interests, and independence.

Competence

The precise duties of the board may vary according to various factors, including the specific structure of the corporation and the extent of the powers delegated to management. However, all boards have a number of basic responsibilities which require directors to possess certain essential skills.

Essential Director Skills

Directors should possess a number of personal skills which are necessary in order to effectively engage in boardroom activities. These include the ability to prioritize multiple and complex issues, good interpersonal communication skills so as to work efficiently within the collegial environment, and the ability to support and promote the decisions of the governing body.

In addition, proper oversight of the corporation's strategy and operation requires an intimate understanding of its goals and objectives, familiarity with the needs and objectives of the company's constituencies, and knowledge of the corporation's internal rules and procedures. Lack of understanding thereof may seriously hamper the efficiency of the board's activity, and ultimately expose directors to liability.[21]

Further, the proper performance of directors' attributions mandates understanding of, and experience with, the primary management aspects of corporate governance, for example, business plans, financial statements, performance goals, budgets, and strategic planning.[22] In this respect, directors' skills may vary, and some may be appointed because of their particular expertise in a given field. Yet, directors should not be appointed solely for their public prestige, or to fulfill a political agenda. The proceedings against the former directors of Hollinger illustrate that prestige does not guarantee the efficient performance of the board's duties, or insulate board members from litigation.

Board/Directors Evaluation

The skills of boardroom candidates should be evaluated prior to their appointment. This implies both an honest assessment of their own abilities by all prospective directors, and the existence of a clearly defined selection process within the company. This selection process should be transparent, address the specific needs of the corporation, and might include setting up a separate nominating committee composed of independent directors.[23]

In addition, the board may wish to organize evaluation programs designed to ensure that these skills remain effective and updated. Different methods may be adopted or blended, depending on the corporation's needs. In particular, the board may resort to quantitative surveys focusing on written responses on a selection of topics, qualitative surveys based on personal interviews, or qualitative group assessments based on collective working sessions.

Board/Directors Training

In response to ever more demanding shareholders' expectations and to rapid and substantial changes in technology, legislation, and knowledge, there appears to be an increased recognition that training at the board level is desirable.[24]

Among the most common approaches to training are: individual coaching (for short-term development needs, with a focus on the individual's performance), mentoring (for long-term development needs), and external courses. In any event, it is recommended that training programs be tailored to the specific needs of the directors, and emphasize team-building, lateral communication and transparency.

Diligence

The exercise of due care is at the heart of the directors' fiduciary duty. Based on the examples of board failure outlined above, it is suggested that the standard of diligence for corporate directors essentially revolves around three major ideas: the adequate information of the board, proactive directors, and the efficient organization of the board's activity.

Adequate Information of the Board

The board's managerial and oversight functions can only be achieved if there is an adequate and continuous flow of information between the board and the other constituencies of the body corporate. In particular, as the board stands on the frontline for reporting corporate wrongdoing,[25] directors should ensure that the "gate-keepers" appointed in order to monitor the corporation's compliance programs have direct access to the board, or to the board members designated for that purpose. Ideally, these gatekeepers should possess an ability to filter the concerns raised by the employees so that only real compliance issues reach the board level.

Further, oversight of the management requires that the board receive periodic and direct information—that is, unfiltered by senior executives—from the corporation's key employees and advisers. For instance, proper monitoring of the corporation's accounting practices mandates that the board, or the members of the audit committee, schedule regular meetings with the individuals in charge of the corporation's finances, and with the corporation's external auditor.

Finally, directors should obtain and review all material information reasonably available to them before making a business decision. This entails receiving and reviewing relevant materials in advance of the meeting.[26] To the extent possible, directors should receive substantially final versions of any proposed agreement, and if the board considers that it has not been provided with sufficient information, it should postpone its decision pending further information.

A Proactive Board

As a matter of principle, the board should be responsive in addressing the matters put to its consideration. As illustrated by the *Abbott* case, failure to act when a red flag is raised may be regarded as a demonstration of bad faith, and deprive the directors of the protection of the business judgment rule. For this purpose, the directors should ensure that the periodicity of the board meetings is adapted to the issues submitted to the board's attention. Similarly, the directors should take sufficient time for discussion and deliberation at board meetings before making a business decision.[27]

Beyond mere responsiveness, however, directors should be proactive, as failure to raise issues that may significantly affect the corporation could be considered as a breach of the duty of care. Broadly speaking, directors should adopt a critical stance towards the representations made by the management. This includes asking all relevant questions about important matters, even if those matters are not on the agenda, considering alternatives to the proposed courses of action, and consulting with experts where appropriate. For this purpose, it is suggested that the board engages the expert, rather than resort to an expert engaged by management.[28]

Organization of the Board's Activity

In order to ensure efficient performance of its duties, the board should structure its activity according to the corporation's particular needs. For this purpose, it is suggested that the board focus on the quality of the process rather than mere compliance. The board should set up the adequate number of committees.[29] Examples of such committees include audit (responsible for monitoring the corporation's accounting), remuneration/compensation (responsible for the remuneration of management and/or directors), and nomination (responsible for the appointment of new directors). These committees should function pursuant to a clear set of working protocols providing for their composition[30] and the nature and extent of the powers delegated by the board.

In addition, the board may wish to set up a process for communications between the board and the other constituencies of the corporation, particularly the shareholders.[31] Creating a formal process may limit the risk inherent to informal and unofficial communications.

Further, the board's decision-making process should be documented through adequate minutes, as these normally constitute primary evidence of the board's diligence. It is essential that board and committee meeting minutes reflect the deliberative process of the directors, and while a detailed account of questions asked and the issues discussed is not necessary, some indication of the length and nature of the discussion is warranted.

Finally, the board may wish to consult an experienced legal counsel in order to understand in advance the legal implications of material decisions, including the consequences of alternative courses of action. This may be done on a punctual or recurring basis, and increasingly, boards in large corporations have a legal counsel attend all meetings.

Avoidance of Conflicts of Interest

Most state corporate laws deal with interested director transactions and provide that such transactions are not void solely because of the existence of a conflict of interest.[32] However, as a matter of principle, it is advisable that directors avoid all transactions that may give rise to a conflict of interest situation. Alternatively, directors should ensure that such transactions are entirely fair, and the subject of full and truthful disclosure.

Avoidance of Conflict of Interests Transactions

A number of transactions between board members—or parties related thereto—and the company may give rise to potential conflict of interests.[33] Similarly, a conflict of interest may arise in cases where a director takes advantage of a business opportunity that the company could have taken for itself. These transactions may well be in conformity with the best interests of the company and of its shareholders, and they do not constitute per se self-serving behavior by the conflicted directors. Yet, beyond the substance of the transaction, the issue is also one of perception.

A conflict of interests transaction that does not raise particular concern at a time when the company's financial situation appears to be sound may well become the subject of intense scrutiny by disgruntled stockholders when difficulties arise. Accordingly, corporate directors should avoid, to the extent possible, to participate in transactions involving conflict of interests issues.

Ensuring the Entirely Fairness of the Transaction

In cases where conflicts of interest cannot or would not be avoided, directors should ensure that the transaction is entirely fair. The standard of judicial review under the "entire fairness" test may vary from one state to the other (Pinto & Branson, 1999, pp. 201–213). However, it is generally required that the transaction be fair as to both its substance and process.[34]

As to the substance of the transaction, directors should ensure that it is in the best interest of the company. For this purpose, a number of factors are of importance, such as the value of what is received; the market value; the value of the bargain compared to what [the company] could have obtained from others; the need for the property; the ability to finance the transaction; the quality of the disclosure; and the possibility of corporate gains being siphoned off by the directors. (Pinto & Branson, 1999, pp. 203–204)

As to the process, the board should ensure that the interests of the company and of minority shareholders are represented throughout. First, in an effort to limit possible discussions as to the arm's length nature of the transaction, it is advisable that the negotiations on behalf of the corporation be conducted by one or more disinterested directors.

Second, it should be ensured that the transaction is approved by a committee composed of unconflicted, independent directors, or ratified by the minority shareholders. For this purpose most state laws as well as federal antifraud laws require full disclosure of all material facts,[35] including the existence and extent of the conflict of interests, the details of the transaction (price, valuation method), and the process adopted by the board to approve the transaction.[36]

Third, the unconflicted directors carrying out the negotiations on behalf of the corporation or called to approve the transaction should have a precise understanding of their duties. In this respect, the Delaware Court of Chancery recently held that the unconflicted director's desire to achieve a transaction that would be fair to both sides raises serious doubts as to the fairness of the approval process.[37] It follows that the unconflicted directors should have the interest of the corporation as sole objective.

Independence

Recent scandals have prompted the belief that the directors' independence from the management is essential to an effective monitoring board. It is now accepted that a majority of the directors should be economically independent from the company, and that the influence of the management on the board should be mitigated.[38] However, directors should be aware that the independence requirement may, in some cases, be extended beyond mere economic ties.

Directors' Economic Independence From the Management

In an effort to enhance the corporate governance of public companies, the NYSE (New York Stock Exchange) and NASDAQ (National Association of Securities Dealers Automated Quotation) have adopted new listing standards under which a majority of the board of directors of a listed company must be independent, that is, free of any material relationship with the company.[39]

According to these standards, lack of independence is characterized where the director (1) is an employee of the company, (2) has an immediate family member who is an executive officer of the company, (3) receives significant compensation (excluding board and committee fees) from the company,[40] (4) is affiliated to the company's auditor, or (5) where there exists a significant business relationship between the listed company and a company of which the director is an executive officer or employee.[41]

Further, recent legislation imposes specific independence requirements on the members of the board's audit committee. Section 301 of the Sarbanes-Oxley Act and the SEC rule implementing that section prohibit audit committee members of listed companies from accepting, directly or indirectly, any consulting, advisory or other compensatory fees from the company, other than fees for being a director or an audit committee member.[42]

Although the independence requirements contained in the Sarbanes-Oxley Act, the SEC rules and the NYSE and NASDAQ listing standards essentially apply to public companies,[43] it is recommended that the "best practices" reflected in these initiatives be adopted by private companies, particularly those where the exists a separation between ownership and control.

Mitigating the Influence of the Management

In order to ensure that independent directors are not subject to the undue influence of the senior executives sitting on the board, the NYSE and NASDAQ listing standards require that independent directors regularly convene in executive session from which "inside" directors are excluded.[44] These meetings provide an opportunity to freely discuss subjects of potential concern, and may be material in building a cohesive group of independent and critical directors.

In the same vein, it has been suggested that there should be a separation between the roles of chair (responsible for running the board) and chief executive officer (responsible for running the business) (The Committee on the financial aspects on Corporate Governance, 2002; Organisation for Economic Co-operation and Development, 1998). De facto, in many of the companies involved in recent corporate scandals, the CEO also served as chairman of the board, and often appeared as an "imperial" manager who dominated the board. An independent chairman may help to counterbalance the influence of senior executives, and constitute a referent for independent directors.

Beyond Economic Independence

The approach retained by recent laws and regulations, essentially centered on the prohibition of economic ties between the directors and the company, has been criticized for its "one size fits all" logic and its stiffened definition of independence (Paredes, 2004).

Beyond mere economic ties, a number of factors may influence the directors' decisions, including the context of relationships among board members, and between the directors and the management. Thus, in some cases, the definition of independence may include nonfinancial ties. This was recently confirmed by a decision of the Delaware Chancery Court in a case involving several directors of Oracle Co.

Shareholders had brought a derivative litigation against certain directors of the corporation for insider trading. The special litigation committee appointed by the company, consisting of two purportedly independent directors, had moved to terminate the action. However, the Court refused to dismiss the action, and questioned the independence of the committee directors because of their relations with Stanford University, which received gifts from some of the defendants. While the directors met all the listed standards of independence, the Court, for the first time, looked beyond the easily quantified listed standards and toward the director's social relationships.[45]

It follows that in the context of the board's decision-making function, independence requires a case-by-case evaluation based on the facts and circumstances surrounding the subject before the board. Consequently, directors should be careful to preserve their independence from any interference, both of a financial and nonfinancial nature.

PROTECTIVE MEASURES

It is impossible to prevent unwanted litigation, and adherence to the above behavioral rules may not be sufficient to deter potential claims for liability. Thus, corporate directors should ensure that a number of protective devices are in place, which essentially include exculpatory and indemnification provisions, directors and officers insurance, and asset protection measures.

Exculpatory and Indemnification Clauses

Most states have adopted legislation allowing corporations to eliminate or limit the personal liability of directors for breach of fiduciary duties through exculpatory and indemnification clauses. However, these clauses are usually subject to a number of limitations, so that they are effectively limited to "good faith" duty of care violations.

Exculpatory Provisions

Many state laws permit corporations to include in their certificate of incorporation "a provision eliminating or limiting the personal liability of a director to the corporation or its stockholders for monetary damages for breach of fiduciary duty as a director" (Delaware General Corporate Law §102 (b) (7); also see NEW York Business Corporate Law Section 402 (b)).

However, some state laws expressly provide that the certificate of incorporation may not eliminate or limit liability "for any breach of the director's duty of loyalty to the corporation or its stockholders." (Delaware General Corporate Law §102 (b) (7)). Other limitations typically include acts or omissions not in good faith or which involve intentional misconduct or a knowing violation of law, transactions for which the director derived an improper personal benefit, and unlawful distributions to shareholders.

Directors should ensure that an exculpatory provision is included in the company's certificate of incorporation, and that it closely tracks the relevant statutory language, so as to exclude or limit the board members' liability to the fullest extent permitted by the applicable law.[46] In addition, directors need to be aware that this clause may be revoked, or substantially amended. Thus, in some case, directors may want to insist upon a special arrangement making the exculpatory language irrevocable.

Indemnification Provisions

Similarly, state corporate laws permit companies to include in their articles of incorporation a clause providing for the indemnification, by the company, of directors whose liability is sought for breach of fiduciary duties.[47]

The scope of these indemnification clauses is usually broad, and may include "any threatened, pending or completed action, suit or proceeding, whether civil, criminal, administrative or investigative … by reason of the fact that the person is or was a director … of the corporation" (Delaware General Corporate Law §145 (a); also see New York Business Corporate Law Section 722 (a)).

The company is generally afforded the possibility to indemnify the directors against expenses (including attorney fees), judgments, fines and amounts paid in settlement actually and reasonably incurred by the person in connection with the action. Further, the expenses, including attorney fees, incurred by directors in defending the claim may be paid by the corporation in advance.

Typically, however, indemnification may only take place when the director acted in good faith and in a way that he or she reasonably believed to be in or not opposed to the interests of the corporation, and, with respect to criminal proceedings, had no reason to believe that his or her conduct was unlawful. In this respect, it is usually provided that

> the termination of any action ... by judgment, order, settlement, conviction, or upon a plea of nolo contendere ... shall not, of itself, create a presumption that the person did not act in good faith and in a manner which the person reasonably believed to be in ... the best interests of the corporation, and, with respect to any criminal action ..., had reasonable cause to believe that the person's conduct was unlawful. (Delaware General Corporate Law §145 (a); also see New York Business Corporate Law Section 722 (b))

In addition, state laws generally distinguish between actions brought by or in the right of the corporation, and actions brought by or in the right of other interested parties. In case of an action brought by or in the right of the corporation, indemnification is often prohibited where a director has been adjudged to be liable to the corporation, unless a court of competent jurisdiction determines that in view of the circumstances, the director in question is fairly and reasonably entitled to indemnification.

Directors should ensure that the indemnification clause contained in the corporation's articles of incorporation provide for indemnification to the fullest extent permitted by the applicable law. Again, directors may wish to obtain a special contract making the indemnification language irrevocable.[48]

D&O insurance

Considering that important limitations apply to exculpation and indemnification clauses, the coverage provided by a D&O insurance policy performs an essential function among the protective devices available to corporate directors. All states permit corporations to purchase insurance policies covering their directors for losses that may not be indemnified by the corporation.[49] These policies, however, are often complex products, and directors should carefully review whether insurance arrangements provide adequate coverage.

Amount of Coverage

The appropriate dollar amount of coverage depends on the risk factors which may affect the directors' liability. It has been suggested that $15 million to $20 million in coverage is usually enough for a reasonable settlement and defense costs. However, in view of the amount of recent settlements involving corporate directors, "companies with larger market capitalizations, volatile stock prices or recent public securities offerings … should consider larger coverage limits" (Rains & Erickson White, 2003).

The amount of the retention should be reasonable with respect to the company's financial capability. Accepting to take on large retentions may significantly reduce premiums. However, litigation often strikes when the company's financial situation is at its worst, and it has been suggested that "a company should not retain a payment obligation larger than it can afford to pay in one quarter without materially hurting earnings or cash flow" (Rains & Erickson White, 2003).

In addition, many factors may considerably reduce coverage. In particular, when the policy provides for entity coverage, claims against the corporation may exhaust the policy limits. Directors should ensure that the policy provides for separate sublimits for the company and for directors and officers, or that payments are prioritized (Butler & White, 2003). Alternatively, directors may request the purchase of a separate primary or excess policy.

Scope of Coverage

The policy should cover all foreseeable losses. Accordingly, the definition of covered claims should include civil and criminal proceedings, securities claims, administrative or regulatory actions (including subpoenas and orders), investigations, notices of charges, and arbitration proceedings. Symmetrically, covered losses should include defense costs,[50] civil fines or penalties, punitive, exemplary and multiple damages regarding securities claims, and any settlement.

Directors should also seek to limit the exclusions contained in the policy. In particular, all policies have a "fraud" exclusion that excludes coverage for losses caused by dishonest or fraudulent acts or omissions, willful violations of law, and illegal profit or remuneration.[51] The policy should contain both a severability provision, under which the fraud committed by one insured cannot be imputed to other insured, and "final adjudication" language, preventing the insurer from withholding coverage in the wake of mere allegations of fraud.

Finally, directors should be aware of the statutory exclusions which may apply to the policy. For instance, some state insurance laws forbid director insurance for losses resulting from disgorgement or restitution to the corporation. These exclusions are broad, and may include payments as a result of some SEC consent actions, payments qualified as reimbursement or disgorgement under the Sarbanes-Oxley Act of 2002, and damages under Sections 11 and 12 of the Securities Act 1933.[52]

Efficiency of Coverage

A number of events may affect the efficiency of coverage. First, state insurance laws generally allow the insurer to rescind the policy when an insured has provided false information in the policy application. For this purpose, a misrepresentation made by one insured may be imputed to all the insured (Aronowitz, 2005; Cutlter & Buck, 2004). In order to mitigate this risk, directors should ensure that the policy contains full severability clauses, under which the knowledge of one insured cannot be imputed to the other insured.[53]

Second, the company's insolvency may hamper the directors' access to the policy's proceeds when the policy provides for entity coverage. These policies are more likely to be considered assets of the bankruptcy estate, and directors may be unable to access the policy's proceeds to pay defense costs unless and until the bankruptcy court approves such payments. This could significantly affect the ability of the defendant directors to properly defend claims against them. Thus, it is suggested that the policy contain clear predetermined allocation provisions, with specific amounts dedicated only to directors and officers.

Finally, the risk of insolvency of the insurer should not be overlooked. Directors should enquire as to the financial situation of the insurer, and in case of a doubt as to the insurer's solvency, additional arrangements should be made in order to protect the policy's proceeds from the insurer's bankruptcy estate.[54]

Asset Protection Measures

In view of the uncertainties inherent to the adjudication process, a broad indemnification clause and good D&O insurance often create a strong incentive for the settlement of suits against corporate directors.[55] However, recent examples of settlements requiring directors to contribute a significant portion of their assets highlight the importance of asset protection measures as a complement to indemnification mechanisms.[56]

Tools for Asset Protection

Some of the tools that may be used are relatively simple, and include family gift-giving or planning based on creditor exemptions available under state laws. Other techniques are more sophisticated, and essentially consist in the use of a family limited partnership, a trust established under the laws of the client's country of citizenship or residency, or a trust governed by the laws of a foreign country. These various techniques may be combined in order to achieve maximum protection.

Family limited partnerships provide an important element of protection. Most state laws provide that a creditors' remedy against a limited partnership interest held by a debtor is to obtain a charging order, which is a rather unattractive remedy. A charging order does not entitle the creditor to reach control of the debtor's assets held by the limited partnership, and under federal tax law, the creditor runs the risk of being taxed on all or a portion of the limited partnership's income, whether or not the limited partnership distributes any income to its partners (Engel, 2000).

Alternatively, corporate directors may wish to set up a self-settled spendthrift trust in the United States.[57] However, under the law of most states, a self-settled spendthrift trust may be ineffective as to the settlor's creditors.[58] In addition, "a domestic trust remains subject to the jurisdiction of the U.S. court; thus, it can be reasonably expected to be a target in litigation against the settler if it holds a corpus of any significance" (Engel, 2000).

By comparison, foreign-situs trusts usually provide better protection. Trust laws in a number of offshore financial centers are often permissive regarding self-settled spendthrift trusts, and generally allow the trustee to invest trust assets in any part of the world. In addition, protective trust laws, the absence of comity for the enforcement of foreign judgments, and favorable statutes of limitations for actions challenging asset transfers to the trust are dissuasive for creditors attempting to pierce foreign-situs trusts.

Efficiency of Asset Protection Measures

In order to be fully efficient, asset protection measures should comply with state and federal laws prohibiting the fraudulent dissipation of assets and tax evasion. In some cases, failure to repatriate assets pursuant to a court order may cause the debtor to be held in contempt of court. However, impossibility of performance is a complete defense to a civil contempt charge,[59] to the extent that the party claiming impossibility of performance is not responsible for creating the impossibility. Thus, a well designed trust should make it virtually impossible for the settlor to repatriate trust assets following an adverse judgment or a court order.[60] Further, there should not be any nexus in time between a court order and the transfer of the assets to the trust.[61]

Similarly, fraudulent conveyance laws generally protect present and subsequent creditors from transfers made by a debtor or foreseeable debtor. In this respect, a Florida decision has stated that transfers are permissible as to one's possible creditors, but not as to one's probable creditors, the test being whether the person making the transfer has any outstanding judgments or whether he has any litigations pending, threatened or expected.[62]

Finally, asset protection measures may not be used to dissimulate assets, or to evade taxes. Dissimulating assets would be inconsistent with the obligation of full disclosure on tax returns, and may result in criminal prosecution. Thus, tax neutrality will generally prevail in a well-designed asset protection plan.

CONCLUSION

Beyond the issue of the directors' protection against litigation and liability, recent examples of corporate failure prompt the question of how to ensure that the board is effectively a source of added value to the corporation. To a large extent, the guidelines outlined in this article constitute key elements of efficient board building. The changes brought about by new law and regulations and adherence to a set of best practices do require an important investment by both public and private corporations across America (Foley & Lardner, 2004). New corporate governance rules also require somewhat of a shift in mentality, as they prescribe to treat the board of directors as a corporate team member as opposed to a periodic and ritualistic gathering.

In spite of the satisfaction displayed by prominent officials (Balls, 2005), recent data suggests that the movement towards sincere adherence to a clear set of corporate governance best practices may turn out to be a slow and evolutionary process, as changes in culture and values have been relatively slow (Bostrom, 2003; Fram & Zoffer, 2005).

NOTES

1. Under Delaware law, for instance: "the business and affairs of every corporation organized under this chapter shall be managed by or under the direction of a board of directors" (Delaware General Corporate Law §141(a).
2. See *The Role of the Board of Directors in Enron's Collapse*, Report prepared by the Permanent Subcommittee on Investigations of the Committee on Governmental Affairs of the U.S. Senate, July 8, 2002, p. 5.
3. For instance under Delaware law, see *Smith v. Van Gorkom*, 488 A.2d 858 (Del. 1985).
4. Directors who are insiders are generally held to a higher standard of care; see *Bates v. Dressler*, 251 U.S. 524, 40 S. Ct. 247, 64 L. Ed. 388 (1920). Moreover, "if certain directors are placed on the board for their particular

skills, their performance may be tested by a different standard measured by their expertise" (Pinto & Branson, 1999, pp. 187–188).

5. Accordingly, the business judgment rule is inapplicable when the board's decision is irrational or creates a no-win situation for the corporation (see *Litwin v. Allen*, 25, N.Y.S.D.2d. 667, 1940).

6. The duty of loyalty covers a wide array of instances, including directors taking for themselves a business opportunity that the corporation may use to its own advantage, trading on inside information, or management and directors' compensation.

7. However, state laws on this matter are not uniform. Compare, for instance, DEL. GEN. CORP. L. §144, NEW YORK BUS. CORP. LAW Sect. 713, CAL. CORP. CODE Sect. 310(a). In addition, compliance with disclosure requirements does not necessarily preclude a further inquiry as to the fairness of the transaction. See *Cohen v. Ayers*, 596 F.2d 733 (7th Cir. 1979).

8. See, for instance, §14-8-C(e) of the Securities Exchange Act, 1934, which prohibits misleading statements or omissions in connection with tender offers; SEC Rule 10b-5, which prohibits material omissions and misleading statements in any form in the context of the purchase or sale of any security, and applies to both public and closely held private corporations; SEC Rule 14a-9, which prohibits misleading statements or omissions in all communications with shareholders.

9. The reaction to the decision of the Delaware Supreme Court in the case of *Smith v. Van Gorkom*, 488 A.2d 858 (Del. 1985), is emblematic of this approach. The board had spent little time in considering a merger transaction, had relied exclusively on the statements of the corporation's executives, and had failed to read the merger agreement before approval. The Court found that the directors had been grossly negligent, and were not protected by the business judgment rule. Consequently, they could be held personally liable for their breach of duty of care to the corporation. Shortly thereafter, the state legislature enacted a new provision allowing corporations to amend their articles of incorporation to exclude directors' liability for breach of duty of care.

10. Notably the Sarbanes-Oxley Act of 2002 and new SEC, NYSE and NASDAQ regulations.

11. In a string of recent decisions, the Delaware courts have insisted on the directors' duty to exercise good faith, suggesting that "a violation of the duty of good faith will be found where the board fails to apply minimum levels of diligence" (Morrison & Foerster LLP, "Boardroom 'Best' Practices are Changing: The Need to Demonstrate Good Faith," at http://library.findlaw.com/2003/Sep/26/133075.html). This emphasis on the duty of good faith in duty of care cases is important: the finding that a director acted in bad faith may deprive him of the protection of the business judgment rule and of the exculpatory provision contained in the company's articles of incorporation, and therefore be far more reaching than a mere failure to exercise due care. See *In Re Abbott Laboratories Derivative Shareholder Litigation*, 325 F.3d 795 (7th Cir. 2003); *In Re The Walt Disney Company Derivative Litigation*, C.A. N° 15452, 2003 Del. Ch. LEXIS 52 (May 28,

2003); *Pereira v. Cogan*, 2003 U.S. Dist. LEXIS 7818 (S.D.N.Y. May 12, 2003).

12. Traditionally, courts do not like to be involved in compensation decisions. In the case of *Heller v. Boylan*, 29 N.Y.S.2d 653 (Sup. Ct. 1941), the U.S. Supreme Court recognized the difficulty of determining reasonable compensation, and while acknowledging that courts will not allow waste or misuse of corporate assets, it placed the ultimate responsibility on the shareholders. However, many recent scandals involve issues as to key officers', and the role of the board in the approval of management compensation package has come under increased scrutiny.

13. Chief among these were C. M. Black and F. D. Radler, then respectively CEO and COO of Hollinger International Inc.

14. Among the "outside" directors of Hollinger were many illustrious individuals, such as Richard Perle, former defence advisor and President Bush confident, Henry Kissinger, a Nobel prize-winner, Alfred Taubman, then Chairman of Sotheby's, Richard Burt, a former American ambassador, and James Thompson, a former Illinois governor.

15. See "Hollinger International Inc. Announces Settlement by Certain of its Current and Former Independent Directors of Claims Asserted in Derivative Action Filed by Cardinal Value Equity Partners, L.P.," at http://news.findlaw.com/prnewswire/20050503/03may2005160723.html

16. Under Delaware law, the burden of proof under the entire fairness standard can shift to the plaintiff where minority shareholders ratify the transaction, or where a committee of disinterested, independent directors effectively represents the interests of the minority stockholders. In this case, however, the Court noted that the transaction had been negotiated by the CEO, and that the special committee formed of the only unconflicted director had only reviewed limited information. Thus, the burden of proving the entire fairness of the transaction rested on the defendants.

17. The corporation has since emerged from bankruptcy under the name of MCI Inc.

18. On the criminal side, former CEO B. Ebbers has been found guilty of securities fraud, conspiracy and filing seven false reports with the SEC in March 2005. On July 13, 2005, he has been sentenced to 25 years in prison. Five other WorldCom officers have pleaded guilty in the massive fraud. On the civil side, an action was started by the SEC against WorldCom for the violation of several provisions of the Securities Exchange Act of 1934 and of the Exchange Act Rules, which was settled for payment of $750 million by the corporation (see Opinion and Order of Justice Jed S. Rakoff, US District Judge for the Southern District of New York, July 7, 2003).

19. The plaintiffs notably sought to rely on Section 11 of the Securities Act of 1933, under which a director of the issuer may be liable if any part of a registration statement contains an untrue statement or an omission of a material fact (the court applies a regular negligence standard), and sections 15 of the Securities Act of 1933 and 20(a) of the Securities Exchange

Act of 1934, under which directors face liability as controlling persons when the controlled person commits a violation of federal securities laws.

20.   Further, on March 23, 2005, WorldCom's last "outside" director agreed to pay $45 million of his own money to settle his part of the suit. See "Final WorldCom Board Member Settles," Retrieved March 23, 2005, from http://www.insurancejournal.com/news/national/2005/03/23/52978.htm and B. A. Masters and K. Day, "10 Ex-WorldCom Directors Agree to Settlement," Retrieved January 6, 2005, from http://www.ft.com

21.   Hence the criticism expressed by WorldCom's bankruptcy court examiner, according to whom the Board's Audit Committee "did not understand the company's internal financial workings or its culture" (see *supra*, p. 11).

22.   In this respect, section 407 of the Sarbanes-Oxley Act of 2002 requires companies to disclose in their Form 10–K whether the audit committee is comprised of at least one member who is an "audit committee financial expert". In addition, NASDAQ and NYSE rules require all audit committee members to be financially literate, and at least one member to have accounting or financial management experience.

23.   The SEC has adopted a number of rules designed to foster the transparency of public corporations' nominating process, which include the obligation to make certain disclosures about the nominating process, the nominating committee's charter, and the independence of directors participating to the nomination. These rules, however, do not require that the board form a special nomination committee. See "Final Rule: Disclosure Regarding Nominating Committee Functions and Communications between Security Holders and Board of Directors, Securities Act Rel. No. 33-8340, Exchange Act Rel. No. 34-48825, Investment Co. Act Rel. No IC-26262," http://www.sec.gov.rules/final/33-8340.htm (Nov. 24, 2003). By contrast, the NYSE and NASDAQ listing standards require listed companies to have independent nominating committees.

24.   For instance, the Combined Code on Corporate Governance, which applies to all companies listed on the London Stock Exchange, recommends that "all directors ... should regularly update and refresh their skills and knowledge.... The company should provide the necessary resources for developing and updating its directors' knowledge and capabilities" (Combined Code on Corporate Governance, London Stock Exchange, 2003, Provision A.5). Also see Renton (2003).

25.   See the Sarbanes-Oxley Act (2002) Sect. 301, 302, 404, and the decision of the Delaware Court of Chancery in the case of *In re Caremark Int'l Inc. Derivative Litigation*, 698 A.2d 959 (Del. Ch. 1996).

26.   Including an agenda of the meeting, and copies of all relevant documentation.

27.   This issue was specifically addressed by the Delaware Court of Chancery in the Disney case. The Court held that if the board "had taken sufficient time or efforts to review its options, perhaps with the assistance of expert legal advisors" the business judgment rule might have protected the board's actions. See *In Re the Walt Disney Company Derivative Litigation*, C.A. N° 15452, 2003 Del. Ch. LEXIS 52 (May 28, 2003).

28. In this respect, see the comments of the Delaware Court of Chancery in the Disney case, *supra*, footnote number 27.

29. State laws generally permit corporations to establish committees which are given particular tasks and make recommendations to the board. In some cases, these committees are delegated the power to act for the board. See for instance DEL. GEN. CORP. LAW. §141(c)(1), and RMBCA §8.25.

30. For instance, it is essential that the audit and remuneration committees be composed of directors who are independent from management.

31. There exist some statutory requirements as to shareholder communications with the board in public corporations. For instance, the Securities Exchange Act 14a-8 provides for the inclusion of the shareholders' proposals in the company's proxy statements. In addition, the SEC rules impose some disclosure requirements when the corporation does have a process for shareholders to send communications to the board. See "Final Rule: Disclosure Regarding Nominating Committee Functions and Communications between Security Holders and Board of Directors, Securities Act Rel. No. 33-8340, Exchange Act Rel. No. 34-48825, Investment Co. Act Rel. No IC-26262," http://www.sec.gov.rules/final/33-8340.htm (Nov. 24, 2003). Similar provisions exist under the NYSE listing standards.

32. See for instance California General Corporate Law Section 310(a). However, in an effort to discipline conflict of interests transaction, section 402 of the Sarbanes-Oxley Act of 2002 provides that a company shall not "directly or indirectly, ... extend or maintain credit, [or] arrange for the extension of credit, ... in the form a personal loan" to its directors.

33. These typically include transactions between two corporations having common directors, purchases and sales of property or services provided by or to the directors.

34. See California Corporate Code Section 310(a), New York Bus. Corp. Law Section 713(b), Delaware General Corporate Code §144, and the decision of the Delaware Supreme Court in *Strassburger v. Earley, supra*, p. 10.

35. See the comments of the Delaware Chancery Court in the case of *Strassburger v. Early, supra*, p. 10.

36. For an example under the law of Delaware, see *Clements v. Rogers*, 790 A.2d 1222 (Del. Ch. 2001). For an example under federal antifraud laws, see the proceedings commenced by the SEC against Disney for failure to disclose certain related party transactions between Disney and its directors, in breach of sections 13(a) and 14(a) of the Securities Exchange Act of 1934 and SEC Disclosure Rules 13a-1, 12b-20 and 14a-3(a), available at http://www.sec.gov/news/press/2004-174.htm

37. See the comments of the Delaware Court of Chancery in *Clements v. Rogers*, 790 A.2d 1222 (Del. Ch. 2001).

38. The idea that corporate boards ought to consist of a majority of outside directors is not new. See M.A. EISENBERG, *The Structure of the Corporation*, Little, Brown, Boston, 1976. However, existing studies on the direct effects of the director's independence on corporate governance and performance have shown nuanced results. Compare M. Weisbach, "Outside Directors and CEO turnover", *20 Journal of Financial Economics*, 431 (1988), and B.

BAYSINGER & H. BUTLER, "Corporate Governance and the Board of Directors: Performance Effects of Changes in Board Composition," *1 Journal of Law, Economics, and Organization*, 101 (1985).

39. The NYSE listing standards are available at http://www.nyse.com/pdfs/finalcorpgovrules.pdf and the Nasdaq listing standards at http://www.nasdaq.com/about/RecentRuleChanges.stm

40. The threshold for payments received from the company is $100,000 under the NYSE listing standards, and $60,000 under the NASDAQ listing standards.

41. The threshold for a business relationship between the listed company and the director's company is the greater of 2% of the annual gross revenues of the director's company or $1 million under the NYSE listing standards, and the greater of 5% of the annual gross revenues of the director's company or $200,000 under the Nasdaq listing standards.

42. The NYSE and NASDAQ listing standards contain similar requirements.

43. In addition, listed companies in which more than 50% of the voting power is held by an individual, group, or another company, and listed companies that list only preferred or debt securities are exempted from some of the independence requirements under the NYSE and NASDAQ listing standards.

44. In the case of the NYSE, these sessions must take place at least once a year.

45. See *In re Oracle Corp. Derivative Litigation*, C.A. No. 18571, (Del. Ch., June 13, 2003; revised June 17, 2003). Also see *Beam v. Stewart*, 833 A.2d 961 (Del. Ch. 2003).

46. For instance, an exculpatory clause under the law of the state of Delaware may read as follows: "No director of the Corporation shall be personally liable to the Corporation or its stockholders for monetary damages for breach of fiduciary duty as a director; provided, however, that the foregoing clause shall not apply to any liability of a director (i) for any breach of the director's duty of loyalty to the corporation or its stockholders, (ii) for acts or omissions not in good faith or which involve intentional misconduct or a knowing violation of law, (iii) under Section 174 of the General Corporation Law of the State of Delaware, or (iv) for any transaction from which the director derived an improper personal benefit." Alternatively, it may simply be provided that "The liability of the directors of the Company for monetary damages shall be eliminated to the fullest extent under applicable law."

47. The relevant statutes are generally permissive or enabling, and not self implementing. However, some state laws provide for mandatory indemnification, by the corporation, for "any person who has been successful, on the merits or otherwise, in the defence of a civil or criminal action." See NEW YORK BUS. CORP. LAW Section 723 (a).

48. In smaller corporations, directors may be concerned about the company's ability to fund a judgment or a settlement. In addition to purchasing D&O insurance, alternative funding sources may be envisaged, such as a security interest in an asset given to a director by the corporation. See generally J.

P. CARLTON & M. G. BROOKS, III, "Corporate and Officer Indemnification: Alternative Methods for Funding," *24 Wake Forest L. Rev.*, 53 (1989).

49. See for instance NEW YORK BUS. CORP. LAW Section 726 (a), and RMBCA § 8.57.

50. With respect to defense costs, directors should be aware of the risk of insolvency of the corporation and seek advancement on a quarterly basis by the insurer.

51. Exclusions may result from applicable state laws. The law of New York, for instance, provides that "no insurance ... may provide for any payment, other than cost of defence, to or on behalf of any director or officer ... if a judgment or other final adjudication ... establishes that his acts of active and deliberate dishonesty were material to the cause ... so adjudicated, or that he personally gained in fact a financial profit or other advantage to which he was not legally entitled." See NEW YORK BUS. CORP. LAW Section 726 (b).

52. See Waller, Lansden, Dortch & Davis, 2004.

53. See *In re HealthSouth Corporation Insurance Litigation*, 308 F.Supp.2d 1253, 1285 (N.D. Ala. March 16, 2004). However, in the wake of recent corporate scandals, full severability has become increasingly unavailable, and most insurers insist on limited severability provisions, imputing the knowledge of the signer to all insureds. See D. BAILEY, "Return to Basics: D&O Lessons From Recent Claims," Retrieved from http://library.findlaw.com/2002/Jul/8/128780.html

54. These may include setting up a separate trust holding part of the policy's proceeds, with the interests accruing to the benefit of the insurer.

55. In this respect, a further incentive derives from the fact that court approval of the settlement of a shareholder claim estops other shareholders from bringing similar claims (see ROMANO, 1993, p. 171)

56. In the case involving the directors of WorldCom, the plaintiffs had required that directors contribute as much as $18 million, representing 20% of their cumulative net worth excluding primary residences and retirement accounts. See *supra* p. 11. In January 2005, eighteen former directors of Enron reached a $168 million settlement with shareholders. In this context, the Enron's directors agreed to contribute $13 million from their own assets, corresponding to a portion of the pre-tax profit earned on the sale of Enron stock prior to the company's collapse. See S. SHAPPELL, "Independent Directors Forced to Use Personal Assets to Settle Shareholder Class Actions" (2005), at http://www.aon.com/about/publications/issues/2005_directors_assets.jsp

57. A trust is self-settled if the settler is a beneficiary, controls the trust or has a general power of appointment over it.

58. Although, in an effort to attract U.S. trust business, some states have enacted statutory asset protection trust provisions. See the laws of Alaska, Delaware, Nevada, Rhode Island and, to a lesser extent, Colorado.

59. See *Federal Trade Commission v. Sol Blaine*, 308FD Supp. 932 (N.D. Ga. 1970).

60.   See *Federal trade Commission v. Affordable Media, LLC* 179 F3d 1228 (9th Cir. 1999).
61.   See *Hyman Goldstein*, 105 F2d 150 (2d Cir. 1939).
62.   See *Opal G. Hurlbert v. John Shackleton*, 560 So.2d 1276 (Fla. Dist. Ct. App., 1st Dist., 1990).

REFERENCES

American Law Institute. (1994). *Principles of corporate governance: Analysis and recommendations*. Philadelphia: Author.

Aronowitz, D. (2005). The new rescission rules for D&O Insurance Policies. *Review of Securities & Commodities Regulations, 38*(2), 13–25.

Balls, A. (2005). *Greenspan praises corporate governance law*. Retrieved May 15, 2005, from http://financialtimes.com

Berle, A. A., Jr., & Means, G. C. (1932). *The modern corporation and private property*. New York: Macmillan.

Bostrom, R. (from Winston & Strawn). (2003). *Corporate governance: Developments and best practices one year after Sarbanes-Oxley*. Retrieved June 20, 2005, from http://www.iflr.com

Butler & White, S. P. (2003). *Directors and officers-limiting your liability while maximizing your coverage*. Retrieved June 27, 2005, from http://www.howrey.com/practices/globallit/insurance/risk/fall2003/index.cfm?fuseaction=directors

Coates, R. (2003). WorldCom's Ebbers a "spectacularly unsuccessful" manager. Retrieved June 10, 2005, from http://networks.silicon.com/telecoms/0,39024659,10004583,00.htm

The Committee on the financial aspects on Corporate Governance (2002). *Cadbury Report*. London: Gee.

Engel, B. (2000). *Integrated estate planning with foreign-situs trusts*. Retrieved January 1, 2002, from http://library.findlaw.com/2002/Jan/1/241493.html

Foley & Lardner LLP. (2004). *Foley & Lardner Sarbanes-Oxley study finds cost of being public rose 33 percent for small and mid-sized companies in 2004*. Retrieved June 20, 2005, from http://www.foley.com/news/news_detail.aspx?newsid=1270

Fram, E. H., & Zoffer, H. J. (2005). *Are American directors still ignoring the signals?* Retrieved March 11, 2005, from http://web2.westlaw.com

Malone v. Brincat, 722 A.2d 5 (Del. 1998).

Organisation for Economic Co-operation and Development. (1998). *Principles for corporate governance, OECD Report*. Paris: Author.

Paredes, T. A. (2004). Enron: The board, corporate governance, and some thoughts on the role of the Congress. In N. Rapoport & B. Dharan (Eds.), (pp. 495–536). *Enron: Corporate fiascos and their implications*. New York: Foundation Press/Thomson West.

Pinto, A. R., & Branson, D. M. (1999). *Understanding corporate law*. Albany, NY: Lexis Nexus/Matthew Bender.

Rains, D. P., & Erickson White, A. (2003). *15 questions you should ask before buying D&O insurance*. Retrieved November 15, 2005, from http://library .findlaw.com/2003/Nov/1/133258.html

Rehman, S. S. (2004). Are new rules of law needed for U.S. corporate governance? *International Business Law Journal, 6,* 797–826.

Renton, T. (2003). Training of directors. In *Selected issues in corporate governance: Regional and country experiences* (p. 39). New York: U.N. Conference on Trade and Development.

Romano, R. (1993). *Foundations of corporate law*. New York: Oxford University Press.

Rushe, D. (2004). *The illustrious Hollinger board that never said no*. Retrieved January 4, 2004, from http://business.timesonline.co.uk/article/ 0,,9071-952496,00.html

Waller Lansden Dortch & Davis LLP. (2004). *Current issues in director and officer insurance*. Retrieved June 30, 2005, http://boardmember.com/ network/index.pl?section=1147&article_id=12074&show=article

CHAPTER 5

BOUNDING THE
ROLE OF THE DIRECTOR

Gavin J. Nicholson, Geoffrey C. Kiel, and Kevin P. Hendry

Despite the rising importance of boards of directors to corporate life, there remains a dearth of advice on how, practically, directors can manage the multiple roles they generally take on. This is leading to a growing groundswell of support for limiting the number of directorships directors can hold. In the United States, for example, the Council of Institutional Investors (2004) suggested that directors with a full-time job should not sit on more than two other boards and current CEOs (chief executive officers) should only serve on one other board. In the United Kingdom, the *Combined Code* (Financial Reporting Council, 2003) recommends that full-time executive directors should not take on more than one nonexecutive directorship in a FTSE 100 company, while in Australia the Australian Shareholders' Association has issued a policy limiting the number of directorships to five (Galacho, 2004; Moullakis, 2004).

We take a more theoretical approach to the problem and seek to understand the conflicts that may be caused by nonexecutive directors' part-time status. In particular, we establish how social identity theory can provide an insight into the conflicts that are central to good governance. The chapter begins by reviewing the academic and normative literature on

Board Members and Management Consultants: Redefining the Boundaries of Consulting and Corporate Governance, pp. 89–106
Copyright © 2009 by Information Age Publishing
89

the functions[1] of a board of directors (particularly nonexecutive directors), contrasting this with the significant legal emphasis on a director's *fiduciary duty* and *duty of care and diligence*. As part of this analysis, emphasis is placed on how the multiple roles that directors play (particularly nonexecutive directors) can lead to role conflict. Drawing on these dynamics, a set of guidelines is developed that seek to establish how boards can set boundaries for their directors to simultaneously maximize director input, while ensuring legal duties are met. The chapter concludes with a series of points for both practitioners and academics to consider, and reflections on the ramifications for the use of consultants at the board level.

CONCEPTUALIZING THE FUNCTIONS OF THE BOARD

The role and function of a board of directors can be examined from a range of different perspectives—academic research, practice and the law —each of which has a different emphasis and orientation.

The Academic Perspective

Despite a long tradition of investigating whether boards have a significant impact on corporate performance (e.g., Andrews, 1981; Mace, 1971; Vance, 1983), different researchers still conceptualize the board's function set in different ways (e.g., Hung, 1998; Johnson, Daily, & Ellstrand, 1996; Lipton & Lorsch, 1992; Zahra & Pearce, 1989). Initially, investigators believed boards played a largely ceremonial function, as indicated by their description as "ornaments on the corporate Christmas tree" (Mace, 1971, p. 90) or as the "parsley on the fish" (Irving Olds, former chairman of Bethlehem Steel, quoted in Leblanc & Gillies, 2003, p. 1). More recently, however, there has been growing recognition that the board is a key decision-making group in the organization as they are entrusted with ultimate corporate power (Bainbridge, 2003). Furthermore, boards have become more active in using this power as their responsibilities to government, shareholders and the community have grown (Nadler, 2004b).

Despite the difficulty in developing a definitive set of functions for boards, there is general agreement as to how boards add value. This largely derives from one of the earliest categorizations of the board's function set provided by Eisenberg (1969), who envisaged four functions: (1) providing advice and counsel to the CEO, (2) authorizing major corporate actions, (3) representing corporate stakeholders other than management, and (4) selecting, evaluating, and removing the CEO. Since this early categorization, researchers have largely elaborated and extended these four functions. Conard (1976), for instance, argued that the board's function was to respond to the CEO (see 1 above), represent the views of stakeholders (see 3 above), and to distinguish the interests of managers, shareholders and stakeholders (an amalgam of 2, 3, and 4 above).

These two early definitions of board functions highlight a problem that has plagued corporate governance to the present time—different disciplines (and even people within the disciplines) conceptualize what boards do in different ways. As Figure 5.1 illustrates, different researchers have focused on different aspects of what boards do.

What is instructive, however, is the commonality across these different perspectives. With the exception of Pfeffer and Salancik (1978), who concentrated on the function of the board in dealing with the external environment, all major integrative works on the role of the board recognize the control (including monitoring) function of the board (Boyd, 1994; Conard, 1976; Eisenberg, 1969; Hillman & Dalziel, 2003; Hung, 1998; Johnson et al., 1996; Pettigrew, 1992; Zahra & Pearce, 1989). The application of agency theory to boards (Fama & Jensen, 1983; Jensen & Meckling, 1976) has also helped to intensify focus on the monitoring function. Similarly, all major research streams (including Pfeffer & Salancik, 1978) recognize the function the board plays in providing service to the organization. While this function may also be classified as advice provision or counsel, there is unanimous support for the board as a resource on which management can draw.

A function that has near unanimous support in the academic literature is providing access to resources (by co-optation or just through access to information). In fact, recent research sees access to resources as one of only two major functions of the board (Boyd, 1990)—the other being the control function. While some researchers view this function as a subcategory of the service function (e.g., Zahra & Pearce, 1989), others believe it so important that they provide a taxonomy for the access to resources function that has several different dimensions that fulfill the definition (Pfeffer & Salancik, 1978). Therefore, we contend it is generally accepted that providing access to resources is a key function of the board.

The final function, which has wide (though not unanimous) support in the academic community, is that of providing the company with strategic direction. While Eisenberg (1969) recognized the importance of the authorization function, it has not been until the last 15–20 years that a shifting locus of power from the CEO's office to the boardroom has highlighted boards as a serious contributor to the strategy function. Thus, in their integrative model, Zahra and Pearce (1989) explicitly recognize the strategy function, Pound (1995) identified the board as a key mechanism to improve decision making in the firm, and the strategy function of the board has become an increasing focus of empirical work (e.g., Golden & Zajac, 2001).

In summary, while there is still no consensus on the exact classification of the functions of the board, there is widespread academic support for the functions of: (1) control; (2) service; (3) access to resources; and (4) strategy.

The Practitioner Perspective

Ambiguity in the academic literature is replicated in the normative advice on the function(s) of the board. For instance, the U.S. Business Roundtable (1978) and American Bar Association (1978) produced a similar (but not identical) set of responsibilities, duties, functions and

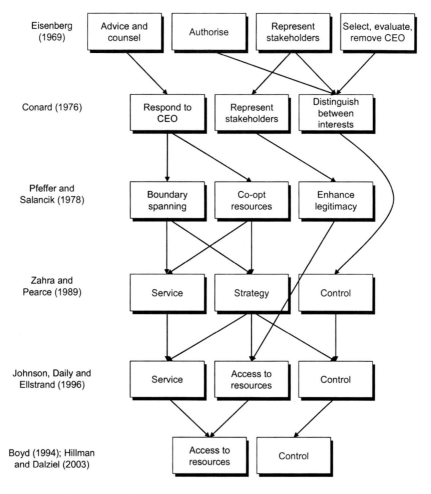

Figure 5.1.   Evolution of board functions.

composition suggestions for boards of directors. Both documents recognized the importance of the profitability and economic viability of the corporation as well as the importance of ensuring that corporate decisions comply with the norms and standards of society. As to particular functions, they foresaw the board's role as selecting, evaluating and removing senior officers, assuring compliance with relevant laws and approving corporate financial plans.

More recently, a plethora of expert opinion on the function of the board has emerged from the practitioner community. A summary of some of the key documents appear in Table 5.1. As Table 5.1 indicates, there is a significant overlap between academic interest and practitioner recommendations on the functions of the board, but a significant divergence in emphasis. Whereas academics have emphasized the monitoring and evaluation function of the board and the access to resources function, practitioners often emphasize the board's function in setting strategic direction. In contrast, the service or advice function of the board and access to resources function have not been major foci of practitioners. A final point of note is that access to resources is rarely mentioned by practitioners, with the notable exception of the board's function in maintaining relationships with investors, particularly institutional investors.

The Legal Perspective

In contrast to both the academic and normative views on the role of the board, much of the focus of legal scholars concentrates on the individual, rather than the board as a group (e.g., see Baxt, 2002). For example, under Australian corporation law, the function of the board is stated as a replaceable rule which should be placed in the company's constitution. According to the Corporations Act 2001 (section 198A), "The business of a company is to be managed by or under the direction of the directors." Should the shareholders wish, this collective power statement of the board's function can be modified, bearing in mind other requirements in the Act pertaining to directors and the general law on the function of the board. As a result, it can be argued that legislation on boards is largely silent on the role of the board. Instead (with the obvious exceptions of specific legislative requirements) the law concentrates on elaborating *how* directors should go about their role, often by setting boundaries on what they must not do.

The legal duties of directors in Western systems are largely common due to a shared philosophical basis—directors are there to serve the company and not their own interests. Thus, most jurisdictions provide for directors to owe a fiduciary duty to the company—they must act with

Table 5.1. Board Functions

Philosophical Function	Board Role	Australia			United Kingdom			United States	
		HIH Royal Commission	ASX Guidelines	Standards Australia	Cadbury Report	Hampel Report	Higgs Review	Business Roundtable	NACD
Control	Monitor and Evaluate	●	●	●	●	●	●	●	●
	Strategy	●	●	●	●	●	●	●	●
Access	Provide Service/Advice	◑	◑	◑	◑	◑	◑	●	◑
	Access to Resources	○	○	○	○	○	○	○	○
Sources		HIH Royal Commission (2003)	ASX Corporate Governance Council (2003)	Standards Australia, (2003)	Committee on the Financial Aspects of Corporate Governance (1992)	Hampel (1998)	Higgs (2003	Business Roundtable (2002)	NACD (2001)

Legend: Yes ●; Partially addressed ◑; No ○

"fidelity and trust" to another, and to the company (Baxt, 2002, p. 35). Although the precise understanding of what constitutes the company is highly technical (for example, in Australia it entails the current shareholders and sometimes future shareholders and creditors, but not employees), the key point is that directors are in a position of trust and must act accordingly. As a consequence, directors have a number of specific duties—generally to avoid a conflict of interest (including misusing their position and/or information) and to exercise due care and diligence. The conclusion is that the law is generally silent on what directors must do, concentrating instead on how they must do it.

The difference in focus of these streams of influence lead to an important potential conflict—the ability of a board to carry out its function effectively may lead its members to test the limits of their legal duties. To better explain how this conflict works, we turn to an emerging area of sociological research, social identity theory.

Social Identity Theory

Social identity theory (SIT) offers a social-psychological basis for the study of how people react to each other and various situations when they are members of groups or organizations. The area is a subfield of organizational identity, itself a topic that affects both the individual's satisfaction and an organization's effectiveness (Ashforth & Mael, 1989). SIT builds on the work of Tajfel and Turner (1985) and postulates that a person has multiple social identities derived from the membership of specific social groups such as a family, sporting club or, as we contend, a corporate board. These multiple roles that individuals play contribute to their overall sense of self (Hogg & Vaughan, 2002), including the searches for "meaning, connectedness, empowerment, and immortality" (Ashforth & Mael, 1989, p. 22).

Role and Organizational Identification: Benefits and Conflicts

SIT identifies that people involved in multiple roles will structure or combine them in various ways (Thoits, 1992). In a business setting, employees will identify with the organizations for which they work and with the roles they play. Thus, SIT (in an organizational context) has been defined as "the extent to which an individual defines and identifies working in terms of various roles such as task role, organizational role, product or service role and occupational role" (Meaning of Working

International Research Team, 1987, p. 57). Close association with an organization or work role is thought to have significant positive impacts on individual workplace behavior and workplace outcomes. The degree to which an individual identifies with an organization will affect their belief in the organization's goals, their willingness to exert themselves on behalf of the organization, and their desire to stay with the organization rather than seek membership of another organization (Mowday, Steers, & Porter, 1979).

Role identification (also called role embracement or intensity) "is the zeal with which one enacts a role" (Kossek, Noe, & DeMarr, 1999, p. 106). Role identification is dependent on the degree to which the individual defines him or herself by the role (Ashforth, 2001), such that greater role-identity will lead to a greater desire for expression of that role (Shamir, 1992). Therefore, those individuals who identify closely with an organization and/or role will perform better than those who are less committed and will have greater self esteem, since they will perceive membership in the organization as attractive (Dutton, Dukerich, & Harquail, 1994). It has also been suggested that this commitment may be an indicator of overall organizational effectiveness (Schein, 1970; Steers, 1975).

SIT is particularly important to the study of upper echelons, as executives and directors will identify much more closely with the organization than other workers (Tannenbaum, Kavcic, Rosner, Vianello, & Wieser, 1974). Since social identification is more likely to occur in directors and, further, that this is a key component of the individual's self esteem (Hogg & Turner, 1985), the application of SIT to directors is of special interest.

The concern, however, is that an individual's social identity may derive from other factors, such as the employee's work group, profession, age cohort and so on (see Albert & Whetten, 1985). Furthermore, identification with multiple roles will occur when the individual is a member of several organizations (such as for nonexecutive directors who sit on more than one board). This dynamic leads to the vexed issue of role conflict, because, while multiple roles may be rewarding for the individual (e.g., through increased status), they can lead to well documented problems such as role conflict, role strain, role ambiguity and role overload (e.g., Goode, 1960; Kahn, Wolfe, Quinn, Snoek, & Rosenthal 1964; Sieber, 1974).

Role conflict occurs when there are sets of expectations that are inconsistent with each other, leading to a conflict of loyalty or too little time to undertake the conflicting roles (Mui, 1992). In fact, role conflict (or the experience of competing or incompatible goals) is a well researched topic in areas as diverse as attempts by managers to satisfy competing stakeholders, balancing academic and sporting roles by student athletes, and the conflict of parents trying to meet both family and work commitments (Dumas, 2004).

Thus increased role identification has two outcomes. While it can lead to role conflict it can also lead to increased effort (Lobel & St. Clair, 1992), increased commitment, and increased time devoted to the role (Burke & Reitzes, 1991). Given these strong outcomes, it would seem reasonable that organizations would want strong identification between the director and the organization. Consequently, strong identification with an organization provides a dilemma for directors and the companies they serve. Strong identification is likely to lead to directors giving greater effort and commitment to their roles. Thus, strongly identifying directors will put greater effort into their specific functions of monitoring the company and overseeing the strategic direction of the company. Further, increased identification will lead to greater commitment, making it more likely that directors will use their networks (or social capital) to provide access to resources for the company, and provide advice to management. Finally, increased time commitment to the role is likely to improve the relationships between the director and management, leading to increased advice or counsel.

However, strong identification can also lead to increasing role conflict (e.g., see Greenhaus & Beutell, 1985 for a similar argument regarding the relationship between role salience and role conflict in work and family settings). This concern is exacerbated by the tendency for increased role identification to be associated with increased role integration. Given that this will lead directors to identify with their membership of the company at all times, it provides an obvious concern when they are, by law, required to separate out the directorial duties of the companies on which they serve.

Additionally, there is an issue of the relative level of role identification. Thompson and Bunderson (2001) contend that individuals will anchor their identity in a specific role that they undertake. This leads the individual to judge their actions (including desired outcomes) in terms of the anchored role, as this is a greater source of identity for that person. Consequently, when a non-anchor role leads to a discrepancy with the anchor-role, the individual will retreat to the anchor role.

This tendency is of particular concern to executive directors, who have two related but quite separate roles to play—a management role and a director's role. Given the management role will most likely be the culmination of a lifetime's effort, and the significant effort required of the management role and the part-time status of the directorial role, we would expect that most executive directors anchor themselves in their executive role rather than a directorial role. As a result, we would expect that when their directorial role requires them to act in a way that does not align with their executive role, they will tend to retreat from the directorial perspective and revert to the dominant managerial role identity. For instance, if as a senior manager they are seeking board approval for a substantial investment in their division, but as a board it is more appropriate to delay the investment, role-anchoring would predict that the executive director will find it difficult to cast off his or her managerial perspective.

Similarly, we would anticipate that directors who sit on multiple boards are more likely to anchor their identity in the board that provides greater meaning, influence or kudos. Thus, we would expect high-profile and influential boards would be the anchor point for nonexecutive directors. Possible negative consequences of an identity anchored in another board revolve around the idea that directors may favor action more suited to another organizational context. For instance, while policy and procedure may add great value to the governance of a large organization, a small start-up may benefit from a more culture-based governance system. Trying to impose the former on the latter may result in a significant disconnect.

Given the importance of avoiding conflicts of interest that are a focus of legislative intent, the potential impact of social identity and role conflict on directors can be profound. On the one hand, identification with the organization can lead to greater organizational loyalty and effort in fulfilling the board functions of a director. However, a director should leave his or her loyalty to other organizations at the boardroom door, as the decisions of directors should only account for the interests of the company the director serves. The view of the "perfect" nonexecutive director, then, is one who is committed to *an* organization, but does not identify with any other organizations on whose boards they sit. As such, the perfect executive director would not identify with their management position. Clearly, this is an impossible situation. The solution to overcoming this role conflict lies in role boundary management, an area of increasing interest to researchers addressing issues of multiple role enactment.

Role Boundary Management

To overcome the potential role conflict caused by holding multiple directorships, directors need to be able to manage the boundaries of the roles they fulfill. Boundary theory (Michaelsen & Johnson, 1997) is the term given to attempts by individuals to simplify and order their environment by creating and maintaining boundaries (Ashforth, Kreiner, & Fugate, 2000). These "mental fences" (Zerubavel, 1991, p. 2) that individuals erect create "slices of reality—domains—that have particular meaning for the individual(s)" (Ashforth et al., 2000, p. 474).

In a board of directors, where the individual has to reconcile their duty to serve the company with either their role as an executive (in the case of an executive director) or their role in other companies (in the case of nonexecutive directors), this is an especially important point. It is only by separating out the various roles that an individual can fulfill his or her fiduciary duties. The key problem is that when "switching cognitive gears" (Louis & Sutton, 1991, p. 55) between the roles, the individual is subject to potential role conflict.

In order to manage these difficulties, individuals are faced with a dilemma—do they integrate the roles or do they try to segment them? Dumas (2004) conceptualizes boundary management as a continuum ranging from integration to separation. Under integration, the boundaries between different roles are blurred leading to the situation where behaviors, resources, contacts and artifacts from different roles are located in the same time and space (Dumas, 2004; Nippert-Eng, 1996b). At its most extreme, there is complete integration such there is only "one way of being" or one identity (Nippert-Eng, 1996a, p. 568).

Thus, in a board setting, a director employing an integration technique may take a resource (such as information) located in one firm and use it in another firm.[2] In fact, this is precisely the behavior that the access to resources function of the board seeks to enact. Role integration can, therefore, assist the board in carrying out its function, particularly where there is a co-optation of resources issue, because it provides a framework to enable the mutual exchange process necessary for the use of social capital (Adler & Kwan, 2002).

At the other end of the spectrum, individuals can choose to compartmentalize or segment the roles to resolve the conflict (e.g., Merton, 1957). In this situation the individual centers attention on keeping the roles separate; this has the advantage of engaging fully in the separate roles while avoiding conflict between them. For example, an engineer who is also a member of a local choir may work late as the engineer to keep his or her weekends free for the hobby (Dumas, 2004). However, the problem is that maintaining rigid distinctions between the roles can be less efficient and more difficult (Nippert-Eng, 1996b).

The key problem for boards is to define when directors need to draw the line between the various roles with which they identify. Role integration simplifies the transition process between roles, but blurs the line between roles; role segmentation has the opposite effect (Ashforth et al., 2000). In fact, even within the integration process there is a significant difference depending on the overlap between roles.

Given the significant overlap between directing and managing that is intrinsic in an executive director, we would anticipate it being harder to transition between these roles. Thus, executive directors may experience confusion and anxiety about which role identity is most salient, particularly if there are conflicting objectives for the roles (e.g., see Dorsey, 1994). Furthermore, executive directors are highly likely to experience interruption to their roles (Hall, 1990)—for instance, they may be asked to answer a question as an executive when taking part in a board meeting. Just as home-based workers carve out work-home boundaries (Ahrentzen, 1990; Mirchandani, 1998), so too executives could be encouraged to have specific markers that enable them to clearly delineate between the two roles. Without such boundaries, workers lacking clear spatial and temporal boundaries will often change their behavior (Ashforth et al., 2000) to contrive boundaries that result in suboptimal performance (e.g., nannies have been shown to disparage their employers; see Macdonald, 1996).

The key contextual factors that influence the integration or separation decision of the individual are thought to be: (1) the level of role identification; (2) the situation or social strength of the role; and (3) the culture within which the role operates (Ashforth et al., 2000). Thus, a key determinant of the role integration is the importance society and the culture puts on the role, and how much importance the individual puts on the role. The prestige with which directorships are held means that, in general, there will be a strong tendency to integrate directorial roles. The major contingency factor will be the importance that the individual places on the directorship in question. Directors who value their role on the board will be more likely to integrate this social identity with their other roles than directors who do not.

BOUNDING THE ROLE OF THE BOARD: A PATH FORWARD

In order to provide an environment that encourages directors to be the best they can, there are a number of steps that companies can take in order to minimize the negative effects of role conflict on the board. Nippert-Eng (1996b) has shown that boundary management can be influenced by the structural characteristics of the role in question. Thus, the physical environment, the organizational policies and procedures, the group norms, and so forth can all act to aid individuals to better manage their multiple roles. In this section we provide a number of practical steps that boards and individual directors can take to bound their roles so as to take advantages of strong role identification while also minimizing role conflict.

The key problem in managing role boundaries is that "the cost of segmentation (high role contrast) is the benefit of integration (low role contrast), and the benefit of segmentation (low role blurring) is the cost of integration (high blurring)" (Ashforth et al., 2000, p. 482). Consequently there is a constant tension between where boards and directors should draw the boundary lines.

We argue that the most important step in board role delineation is establishing a support system that ensures directors assume the correct role at the correct decision point. This tactic recognizes that there is no one best strategy for boundary management (Bailyn, 1993; Kossek et al., 1999). Thus, at some times and in some functions (such as when drawing on directorial experience to advise management or when networking to secure resources) integration will be more advantageous. However, at other times, such as when undertaking the monitoring management and controlling the organization function, directors need to distance themselves from their other directorial or management roles. In these latter instances, segmentation will be more appropriate.

Steps the Organization (or Board) Can Take

The first step the organization can take to minimize role conflict is to clearly delineate the expectations of directors. Establishing a policy framework that makes it clear what the organization believes is the role of a director (as opposed to the role that may apply in another organization or the role of an executive) will focus individuals on what they need to do in this context. Thus, it will be a starting point for a board to better manage the transition between the various roles its directors undertake outside the boardroom and their role on the board.

Second, the board needs to encourage group norms that support loyalty to the organization and have a policy that delimits the expectations of directors. While having a policy that delineates the role of the director is a good first step, this role then needs to be enacted. An excellent method for building these norms is to have the board work on a problem that is of particular concern to the particular organization (Herb, Leslie, & Price, 2001). A very useful initiative, for example, is to have the board work on a board charter (or policy manual)—by systematically working through the key items of how the board works, there is the dual positive effect of both clarifying the stated position on issues (such as what constitutes a conflict of interest), while also developing a board norm on these items.

The third area where boards may be in a position to dissipate the role conflict of directors occurs when establishing the corporate governance processes for the company. Governance processes should aim to separate out the work of this board/role and keep it separate from the individual's other activities. These processes can range from simple steps (such as scheduling meetings well in advance to minimize timing conflicts for the individuals fulfilling multiple roles) through to more subtle and complex initiatives (such as presenting of information (e.g., using letterhead and pro-formas) to reinforce the task at hand). Ideally these formats (such as a generic structure of a board paper) will have been agreed by the board so that it reinforces the previous point about addressing board norms.

As well as taking steps to encourage appropriate role segmentation, boards can work at ways to encourage loyalty and commitment to the organization. Key techniques that encourage buy-in include involving the board in the company's strategy process (an area where directors relish the challenge of thinking about the company's future) (Nadler, 2004b) and ensuring there is an appropriate induction process that connects directors to the organization and its key members. Providing these types of activities enables directors to build a more complete picture of the organization they govern, while also building social bonds that encourage loyalty and commitment (Nadler, 2004a).

Finally, it is important for the board to establish a regular review process. Since "[b]ehavioral psychologists and organizational learning experts agree that people and organizations cannot learn without feedback. No matter how good a board is, it's bound to get better if it's reviewed intelligently" (Sonnenfeld, 2002, p. 113), a key priority in maintaining ongoing role segmentation is a recognition of the importance of this area in the governance process.

Steps the Individual Director Can Take

Thus far, we have been concentrating on the role that the organization can play in minimizing role conflict. There are also a number of steps that individual directors can take as they seek to manage potential role conflict, namely establishing transition routines to minimize role conflict and establishing processes that ensure they apply themselves equally to their roles.

There is a well established literature documenting the role that transition routines play in assisting individuals move between different roles. Transitions are commonly referred to as rites of passage (Ashforth et al., 2000; Richter, 1990) and involve elements that assist individuals move from one role to another (Van Gennep, 1960) by signaling to the individual and others the passage across roles. Although normally associated with a change in macro-role, such as a promotion or termination (see Ashforth et al., 2000; Trice & Morand, 1989), transitions are also useful when seeking to transition between microroles, such as between directorships or between executive and directorial roles (Ashforth et al., 2000).

Generally, these role transitions act as a cue for the individual to signal that they are about to engage in a different activity. Thus, someone preparing to transition from a home to work role will generally follow a daily routine of showering, dressing in suitable attire, and perhaps reading the business section of the paper over breakfast (Ashforth et al., 2000). These actions help to ready the individual for the change in role. It is also interesting that institutions (such as organizations) do not generally support the transition process and so much of the structuring task falls to the individual (Kossek et al., 1999).

In much the same way, directors at risk of role conflict can construct a routine that encourages them to change over to the correct role. In particular, directors can adopt rituals that include reviewing the company's Web site, board papers, and other materials prior to a board meeting. As well as physically preparing them for the role, the routinized approach to activities can lead to a greater focus and role separation for the individual. Thus, we would expect that a managing director who moves from an operational activity straight into the boardroom will experience greater role conflict than one that has a clear set of procedures that they follow. These procedures allow the individual to adopt an appropriate cognitive framework (e.g., they are a director of company A, not company B) and an appropriate level of arousal. Interestingly, changing time and space (such as through a commute) appears to provide a valued method of buffering role identity (Hall, 1990; Kluger, 1998). As a result, boards seeking to improve role separation may benefit from holding board meetings outside traditional domains if they have a significant number of executive directors.

Similarly, ritualistic mechanisms can be put in place to facilitate role entry. Just as entering a bar and exchanging greetings with other patrons can signify entry to the leisure role (Oldenburg, 1997), having a brief, ritualistic social cup of coffee or meal prior to a board meeting can be used to signify entry to the board role. These activities also have the advantage of building social ties between directors and building the norms of the group.

CONCLUSIONS

This chapter focused on the impact of role identity on a director's role execution. Each director has multiple identities (often as an executive with the company or as the director of another organization). These identities can act as a positive force on a director's key function (e.g., a director can draw on experience in one role when carrying out the service function in another company) or they can be a negative force on a role (e.g., the role of executive is widely believed to impact negatively on the individual's ability to monitor the organization).

To overcome this difficulty, we have argued that boards and individual directors need to establish routines, policies and procedures that better allow them to manage their role identities and transition from one role to another. In particular, we outlined the benefits and costs of role integration (where there is low distinction between roles and permeable boundaries between them) and role segmentation (where there is a significant distinction between roles and clear boundaries between them) and detailed a number of strategies for boards and individuals to better manage the transition between their roles.

In short, if a successful board requires the execution of a number of different functions, we anticipate there will be a constant tension between the various roles with which directors identify. It is important, therefore, for us to recognize this fact and develop a series of routines and support mechanisms that allow directors to do the best jobs they can.

NOTES

1. To avoid confusion over the use of the term "role" as it applies in social identity theory, we use "function" to describe the roles a board of directors must fulfill, such as the monitoring role.

2. We should clearly point out that we do not envisage this to necessarily be a conflict of interest nor breach of a director's confidentiality requirements. Instead, there may be general or nonsensitive information that the individual discovers on one board that can be applied to another. Similarly, facilitating a partnering or financing deal may be to the mutual benefit of two companies that a director serves.

REFERENCES

Adler, P. S., & Kwon, S.-W. (2002). Social capital: Prospects for a new concept. *Academy of Management Review, 27*, 17–40.

Ahrentzen, S. B. (1990). Managing conflict by managing boundaries: How professional homeworkers cope with multiple roles at home. *Environment and Behavior, 22*(6), 723–752.

Albert, S., & Whetten, D. A. (1985). Organizational identity. In L. L. Cummings & B. M. Staw (Eds.), *Research in organizational behavior* (Vol. 7, pp. 263–295). Greenwich, CT: JAI Press.

American Bar Association. (1978). Corporate director's guidebook. *Business Lawyer, 33*(5), 1591–1644.

Andrews, K. R. (1981). Corporate strategy as a vital function of the board. *Harvard Business Review, 59*, 174-176, 180-184.

Ashforth, B. E. (2001). *Role transitions in organizational life: An identity-based perspective.* Mahwah, NJ: Erlbaum.

Ashforth, B. E., & Mael, F. (1989). Social identity theory and the organization. *Academy of Management Review, 14*(1), 20–39.

Ashforth, B. E., Kreiner, G. E., & Fugate, M. (2000). All in a day's work: Boundaries and micro role transitions. *Academy of Management Review, 25*(3), 472–491.

Bailyn, L. (1993). *Breaking the mold: Women, men, and time in the new corporate world.* New York: Free Press.

Bainbridge, S. M. (2003). Director primacy: The means and ends of corporate governance. *Northwestern University Law Review, 97*(2), 547–606.

Baxt, R. (2002). *Duties and responsibilities of directors and officers* (17th ed.). Sydney: Australian Institute of Company Directors.

Boyd B. K. (1994). Board control and CEO compensation. *Strategic Management Journal, 15*(5), 335–344.

Boyd, B. K. (1990). Corporate linkages and organizational environment: A test of the resource dependence model. *Strategic Management Journal, 11*(6), 419–430.

Burke, P. J., & Reitzes, D. C. (1991). An identity theory approach to commitment. *Social Psychology Quarterly, 54*(3), 239–251.

Business Roundtable. (1978). The role and composition of the board of directors of the large publicly owned corporation: Statement of the Business Roundtable. *Business Lawyer, 33*(6), 2083–2113.

Conard, A. F. (1976). *Corporations in perspective.* Mineola, NY: Foundation Press.

Council of Institutional Investors. (2004). Corporate governance policies. Retrieved February 3, 2004, from www.cii.org/dcwascii/web.nsf/doc/policies_index.cm

Dorsey, D. (1994). *The force.* New York: Random House.

Dumas, T. L. (2004, August). *When to draw the line: Effects of identity and role boundary management on interrole conflict.* Paper presented at the Academy of Management, New Orleans, Louisiana.

Dutton, J. E., Dukerich, J. M., & Harquail, C. V. (1994). Organizational images and member identification. *Administrative Science Quarterly, 39*(2), 239–263.

Eisenberg, M. A. (1969). The legal roles of shareholders and management in modern corporate decision making. *California Law Review, 57*(1), 1–181.

Fama, E. F., & Jensen, M. C. (1983). Separation of ownership and control. *Journal of Law and Economics, 26*(2), 301–325.

Financial Reporting Council. (2003). *The combined code on corporate governance.* London: Author.

Galacho, O. (2004, December). Serial directors put under siege. *Courier-Mail, 23*, 29.

Golden, B. R., & Zajac, E. J. (2001). When will boards influence strategy? Inclination × power = strategic change. *Strategic Management Journal, 22*(12), 1087-1111.

Goode, W. J. (1960). A theory of role strain. *American Sociological Review, 25*(4), 483–496.

Greenhaus, J. H., & Beutell, N.J. (1985). Sources of conflict between work and family roles. *Academy of Management Review, 10*(1), 76–88.

Hall, D.T. (1990). Telecommuting and the management of work-home boundaries. In J. Abramson, A. Basu, A. Gupta, D. T. Hall, R. Hinckley, R. Solomon & et al. (Eds.), *Paradigms revised: The annual review of communications in society—1989* (pp. 177–208). Nashville, TN: Institute for Information Studies.

Herb, E., Leslie, K., & Price, C. (2001). Teamwork at the top. *McKinsey Quarterly, 2*, 32–43.

Hillman, A. J., & Dalziel, T. (2003). Boards of directors and firm performance: Integrating agency and resource dependence perspectives. *Academy of Management Review, 28*(3), 383–396.

Hogg, M. A., & Turner, J. C. (1985). Interpersonal attraction, social identification and psychological group formation. *European Journal of Social Psychology, 15*(1), 51–66.

Hogg, M. A., & Vaughan, G. M. (2002). *Social psychology* (3rd ed.). Harlow, England: Prentice Hall.

Hung, H. (1998). A typology of the theories of the roles of governing boards. *Corporate Governance: An International Review, 6*(2), 101–111.

Jensen, M. C., & Meckling, W. H. (1976). Theory of the firm: Managerial behavior, agency costs and ownership structure. *Journal of Financial Economics, 3*(4), 305–360.

Johnson, J. L., Daily, C. M., & Ellstrand, A. E. (1996). Boards of directors: A review and research agenda. *Journal of Management, 22*(3), 409–438.

Kahn, R. L., Wolfe, D. M., Quinn, R. P., Snoek, J. D., & Rosenthal, R. A. (1964). *Organizational stress: Studies in role conflict and ambiguity.* New York: Wiley.

Kluger, A. N. (1998). Commute variability and strain. *Journal of Organizational Behavior, 19*(2), 147–165.

Kossek, E. E., Noe, R. A., & DeMarr, B. J. (1999). Work-family role synthesis: Individual and organizational determinants. *International Journal of Conflict Management, 10*(2), 102–129.

Leblanc, R., & Gillies, J. (2003). The coming revolution in corporate governance. *Ivey Business Journal, 68*(1), 1–12.

Lipton, M., & Lorsch, J. W. (1992). A modest proposal for improved corporate governance. *Business Lawyer, 48*(1), 59–77.

Lobel, S. A., & St. Clair, L. (1992). Effects of family responsibilities, gender, and career identity salience on performance outcomes. *Academy of Management Journal, 35*(5), 1057–1069.

Louis, M. R., & Sutton, R. I. (1991). Switching cognitive gears: From habits of mind to active thinking. *Human Relations, 44*(1), 55–76.

Macdonald, C. L. (1996). Shadow mothers: Nannies, au pairs, and invisible work. In C. L. Macdonald & C. Sirianni (Eds.), *Working in the service society* (pp. 244–263). Philadelphia: Temple University Press.

Mace, M. L. G. (1971). *Directors: Myth and reality.* Boston: Division of Research Graduate School of Business Administration Harvard University.

Meaning of Working International Research Team. (1987). *The meaning of working: An international view.* London: Academic Press.

Merton, R. K. (1957). *Social theory and social structure.* New York: Free Press.

Michaelsen, S., & Johnson, D. E. (Eds.). (1997). *Border theory: The limits of cultural politics.* Minneapolis: University of Minnesota Press.

Mirchandani, K. (1998). Protecting the boundary: Teleworker insights on the expansive concept of "work." *Gender & Society, 12*(2), 168–187.

Moullakis, J. (2004, December). Director workloads questioned. *Australian Financial Review, 14*, 8.

Mowday, R.T., Steers, R. M., & Porter, L. W. (1979). The measurement of organizational commitment. *Journal of Vocational Behavior, 14*(2), 224–247.

Mui, A. (1992). Caregiver strain among black and white daughter caregivers: A role theory perspective. *The Gerontologist, 32*(2), 203–212.

Nadler, D. A. (2004a). Building better boards. *Harvard Business Review, 82*(5), 102–111.

Nadler, D. A. (2004b). What's the board's role in strategy development? Engaging the board in corporate strategy. *Strategy and Leadership, 32*(5), 25–33.

Nippert-Eng, C. E. (1996a). Calendars and keys: The classification of "home" and "work." *Sociological Forum, 11*(3), 563–582.

Nippert-Eng, C. E. (1996b). *Home and work: Negotiating boundaries through everyday life*. Chicago: University of Chicago Press.

Oldenburg, R. (1997). *The great good place: Cafés, coffee shops, community centers, beauty parlors, general stores, bars, hangouts and how they get you through the day*. New York: Marlowe.

Pettigrew, A. M. (1992). On studying managerial elites. *Strategic Management Journal, 13*(Special Issue: Fundamental Themes in Strategy Process Research), 163–182.

Pfeffer, J., & Salancik, G. R. (1978). *The external control of organizations: A resource dependence perspective*. New York: Harper & Row.

Pound, J. (1995). The promise of the governed corporation. *Harvard Business Review, 73*(2), 89–98.

Richter, J. (1990). Crossing boundaries between professional and private life. In H. Y. Grossman & N. L. Chester (Eds.), *The experience and meaning of work in women's lives* (pp. 143–163). Hillsdale, NJ: Erlbaum.

Schein, E. H. (1970). *Organizational psychology* (2nd ed.). Englewood Cliffs, NJ: Prentice-Hall.

Shamir, B. (1992). Some correlates of leisure identity salience: Three exploratory studies. *Journal of Leisure Research, 24*(4), 301–323.

Sieber, S. D. (1974). Toward a theory of role accumulation. *American Sociological Review, 39*(4), 567–578.

Sonnenfeld, J. (2002). What makes great boards great. *Harvard Business Review, 80*(9), 106–113.

Steers, R.M. (1975). Problems in the measurement of organizational effectiveness. *Administrative Science Quarterly, 20* (no. 4): 546-558.

Tajfel, H., & Turner, J. C. (1985). The social identity theory in intergroup behavior. In S. Worchel & W. G. Austin (Eds.), *Psychology of intergroup relations* (pp. 7–24). Chicago: Nelson-Hall.

Tannenbaum, A. S., Kavcic, B., Rosner, M., Vianello, M., & Wieser, G. (1974). *Hierarchy in organizations*. San Francisco: Jossey-Bass.

Thoits, P. A. (1992). Identity structures and psychological well-being: Gender and marital status comparisons. *Social Psychology Quarterly, 55*(3), 236–256.

Thompson, J. A., & Bunderson, J. S. (2001). Work-nonwork conflict and the phenomenology of time: Beyond the balance metaphor. *Work and Occupations, 28*(1), 17–39.

Trice, H. M., & Morand, D. A. (1989). Rites of passage in work careers. In M. B. Arthur, D. T. Hall, & B. S. Lawrence (Eds.), *Handbook of career theory* (pp. 397–416). Cambridge, England: Cambridge University Press.

Vance, S. C. (1983). *Corporate leadership: Boards, directors, and strategy.* New York: McGraw-Hill.

Van Gennep, A. (1960). *The rites of passage* (M. B. Vizedom & G. L. Caffee, Trans.) Chicago: University of Chicago Press.

Zahra, S. A., & Pearce, J. A., II. (1989). Boards of directors and corporate financial performance: A review and integrative model. *Journal of Management, 15*(2), 291–334.

Zerubavel, E. (1991). *The fine line: Making distinctions in everyday life.* New York: Free Press.

CHAPTER 6

EXPECTATIONS OF A CONSULTANT IN CORPOPRATE GOVERNANCE

David Risser

Corporate governance is under important changes. The latest corporate failures have given birth to new regulations, and more and more countries, following the United Kingdom's leadership, have developed corporate governance guidelines. Shareholders are also important actors in this process. As a consequence of the wealth destroyed, more and more investors are expressing their concerns about corporate governance.

In the quest for more effective corporate governance systems, boards are central elements. In fact, boards are so important that a set of tools has been put forward to contribute to better board functioning. Board committees, for example, are considered as a "must have" and board composition (largely in terms of "insiders" versus "outsiders," relative dependence) has been heavily questioned. Boards should not only be able to effectively monitor management but also to stand against them when corporate interests are not followed. Thus boards are asked to be less directly involved with management, and an increasing number of independent nonexecutive directors (independent NEDs) are being asked to sit on boards.

Board Members and Management Consultants: Redefining the Boundaries of Consulting and Corporate Governance, pp. 109–134
Copyright © 2009 by Information Age Publishing
All rights of reproduction in any form reserved.

Executive directors bring to the board their inside knowledge of the business and the nature of its markets, while outside directors bring their experience, knowledge, and independence of judgement. Independent NEDs are expected to stimulate true discussion and debate between members. As such, a lot is expected from independent NED—and considering the range of new tasks and responsibilities, NEDs do not hesitate to ask corporate governance consultants to help them focus on their job.

As more and more is expected from NEDs, it is important to fully understand the NED role. By clearly defining this role, the portrait of a NED should be easier to draw. From the consultant's perspective, however, there is more than one unique portrait that can be drawn.

An important starting point in understanding this role is to distinguish between NEDs and independent NEDs. A director can be a nonexecutive, but at the same time be a former company CEO (chief executive officer) or have a close relationship with the company. As boards composed of executives, nonexecutives, and independent nonexecutives are becoming increasingly common, this is an important distinction. Sir Cadbury (2002) prefers the term "outside director," as used in the United States, to NED because it is a "more precise description of their position and of the attributes which they bring to a board." The key difference is what is meant by the term "independence."

Although there is not a unique definition of independence, it is useful to draw on those used by the New York Stock Exchange (NYSE) and the European Union (EU) Commission.[1] The NYSE definition is the most important definition if we consider the number and the size of assets concerned. This definition of independence concerns not only U.S. companies listed on the NYSE but also companies with American Depositary Receipts (ADRs: Level 2 & 3). The EU Commission's definition is also primordial because it is the primary reference in Europe. Those definitions principally insist on direct/indirect material and nonmaterial relationships with the company. Independence, however, is not only a matter of relationship, it is also and, above all, a matter of independence of judgement and the ability of having free speech.

The proportion of outside directors who are independent has risen, encouraged by requirements to have independent directors on board and committees, more and more active investors, and by the behavior of peers. Yet, while there is a need for an increasing number of independent NEDs, less and less talented independent NEDs are keen on assuming the job due to the function's new responsibilities, or at least, the perceived responsibilities. Black, Cheffins, and Klausner (2005), for example, note that "outside directors already greatly overestimate the likelihood that they will have to pay damages out of their own pockets." Even if such a risk is small, the fact that former outside directors of WorldCom and

Enron have agreed to pay substantial sums out of their own pockets in groundbreaking U.S. settlements of class action lawsuits might make it more difficult to find good people willing to sit on boards. Would the rise of responsibilities carried by a director, and particularly a NED, lead to an adverse selection effect? The proportion of good directors would be smaller, benefiting directors with fewer abilities—or will this problem lead to a new full-time job? If so, what are the implications for the role played by a consultant in corporate governance?

In our search to define the "ideal" profile of the independent board member, we will first focus on board duties as a way of identifying the qualities required to be an effective board member. We will see that adding value to the board should be the main selecting criteria and that diversity is one way of achieving this goal. And if corporate governance consultants are privileged witnesses of the changing role of NED, they also have to constantly adapt their way of working to that change. The chapter concludes with an assessment of the role that consultants can play in helping directors add value to their boards and organizations.

BOARDS AT WORK: THE DUTIES OF A DIRECTOR

To assess what one can expect from an independent NED, we logically have to start with the tasks of the board and then turn to tasks of the director to assess how an independent NED can add value. This way of proceeding is opposed to traditional and too often common practices where a director selection process starts with the individual's name rather than the position's tasks and responsibilities.

According to Tricker (1994), boards and especially NEDs have two key roles, which he refers to as "performance" and "conformance" roles. *Performance roles* refer to those roles that should contribute to the overall performance of the company, and include roles such as contributing know-how, expertise and external information as well as networking, representing the company and adding status. *Conformance roles* are intended "to ensure that the company conforms to policies, procedures and plans determined by the board" (p. 99), and include judging, questioning and supervising executive management, as well as the watchdog and safety valve roles.

Board Duties

One concrete way to see what a board is supposed to do is to look at board charters. For example, UBS (Union Bank of Switzerland), the global financial services firm, discloses its articles of association and board of directors' charter, where its board duties are presented. The articles of association present, in quite general terms, the duties of the board:

> *Article 23—Duties and powers*: The Board of Directors has ultimate responsibility for the management of the Corporation and the supervision and control of its executive management. The Board of Directors may also take decisions on all matters which are not expressly reserved to the shareholders in General Meeting or to another corporate body by law or by the Articles of Association.

These duties are completed by the board of directors' charter:

> *Authorities and Duties*: Among the duties defined in the Articles of Association, the Board shall primarily focus on defining the Company's strategic development, assuming ultimate responsibility for the management of the Corporation, for succession planning and for supervising its executive management. The Board appoints and removes the Group CEO and the members of the Group Executive Board, and the Head of Group Internal Audit.

The majority of the board members are nonexecutive and fully independent. The chairman and at least one vice chairman are executive directors who also assume supervisory, leadership and business responsibilities.

The board's main duties are ensuring corporate strategic development, supervising management, and organizing board member nomination and replacement. Although it appears that all important duties are presented, the Board's assessment of its own functioning and performances is not highlighted. This is, as we will see, a key task where a corporate governance consultancy can add value. Having a set of duties does not necessary mean that a board will be able to follow them. Boards are unfortunately quite often stuck in day-to-day business and do not have the time and/or culture to work on long-term strategy. And this is true even when directors complain about the lack of their strategic role. Within this context, the role of governance consultants is not to set the strategy instead of the board, but rather to help the board put the right structures in place that will enable directors to focus on their core functions.

The Board as a Bridge Between Shareholders and Executives

The board's function is to act as the bridge between the shareholders and the executives. The board is appointed by the shareholders (and in few countries, like Germany, partially by employees) and it is accountable to them for company performance and actions. Boards should work toward an appropriate balance between the interests of the shareholders and the aims of the executives, when the two are not identical. In order to ensure this bridge function and to understand the main board tasks, one has to make a clear distinction between direction and management. As Sir Cadbury (2002, p. 36) underscores,

> direction is the task of the board and management is the task of executives.... It is the job of the board to set the ends, that is to say, to define what the company is in business for, and it's the job of the executives to decide the means by which those ends are best achieved.

From this distinction, one can set the following board tasks.

Set the Company's Mission

The board represents the interests of the shareholders by setting the company's aims and by monitoring their achievement. It is, therefore, the function of the board to define the purpose of the company. It can be defined in terms of the products or services the company will offer, the markets the company will enter, the financial targets the company will attempt to meet, or a combination of these objectives.

Agree on Strategies and Policies for Achieving That Mission

The board has to ensure that the company does not miss opportunities and keeps looking ahead to where those opportunities can be best found. It needs to determine not only the company's short- and long-term goals, but also the way they are achieved. The board is therefore responsible for the strategy of the business and for agreeing on the plans and targets required to turn the strategy into action. NEDs, as well as the board as a whole, should ensure that the recommended strategy is credible, will lead to return above the cost of capital, and will increase total shareholder returns at an acceptable rate compared to its peers. NEDs should also be able to require and understand a review of alternative strategies. The Board sets the company's standards and promotes its values through policies. Such policies relate to the manner in which the company is managed and the impact its actions will have, both within the company and on the outside community. As the company and its surrounding community are continually evolving, boards need not only to agree on policies but also to keep them up-to-date. It is also part of the board's task to ensure that company policies are followed.

Appoint and Dismiss Senior Management and Prepare Succession Planning

Appointing the right executives to the right positions is a key to making sure that the board's thinking and decisions are turned into practice. A critical board role is to appoint the chief executive and to ensure that he or she continues to measure up to the requirements of the job in a fast changing word. Appointing, and when necessary, replacing the chief executive are not only crucial board functions but they are difficult and extremely demanding ones. NEDs should control the nominating committee that considers new directors, as well as review development plans for key managers and ensure that compensation policies and program will attract and retain the desired management skills—while still being fair to shareholders.

Directors focus on appointment and performance monitoring (discussed below) but often forget to prepare a succession plan. A well prepared plan can help to avoid a succession war, and it can also ensure that the outgoing CEO will let the new CEO be entirely free to manage the company. To perform this task, governance consultants help directors build the framework that will lead to a successful succession. The consultants, of course, should not choose any successor—that is the role of the directors. The consultant's role is to remind the board of the importance of a good succession plan, guide its development, and help to design the steps in the process. Consultants should not complete tasks intended for directors, but rather assist the board in assessing its needs and helping to prepare tailor-made solutions that will help directors perform their job to the best of their ability.

Monitor and Assess Company Performance and the Executive Team

Boards appoint and compensate chief executives who are directly accountable to the board. Reviewing the performance of executives is thus a direct consequence of appointment. NEDs have a particular contribution to make when it comes to assessing the performance of company senior executives (usually the executive directors). Their status of independence gives them this special role. They are able to stand back from day-to-day activities and objectively view the aims and achievements of the company from the outside. They then can assess, with a nonbiased view, the extent to which the company has achieved the objectives set by the board.

In many reports (e.g., Hampel, 1998), it is stressed that in order to monitor executives effectively, non executives have to be independent and unbiased. However, nonexecutives also have to rely on the information CEOs provide to them to do their monitoring and advising jobs. That is while nonexecutives are expected to operate independently from interested parties, including managers, in practice they are unable to do so because the information they need to do their job is provided by those same managers (and the CEO in particular). Hence, this situation creates two paradoxical situations.

The first addresses the issue of who is responsible for the company (legally the board of directors) and who actually has the power in the company (the executives). The second involves judgement (requiring in-depth knowledge) and independence (requiring a more detached attitude). In both paradoxes, access to information and knowledge is crucial.

Higgs (2003) examines nonexecutives' responsibilities in judging the information they receive and providing feedback regarding this information. First, he suggests that "good non-executive directors will also satisfy themselves that they have appropriate information of sufficient quality to make sound judgements. NEDs should not hesitate in seeking clarification or amplification where necessary" (p. 51). Furthermore, he argues that it is:

> important that non-executive directors give constructive feedback on the value of material provided and guidance on what is required. Where information is not appropriate this should be clearly signalled through the chairman. It should be part of the annual evaluation of the board's performance to examine whether the information provided to the board meets directors' expectations and requirements. (p. 51)

Working with boards over a number of years makes one realize that directors are not necessary aware of the quality and quantity of information they get. In fact, only experienced directors are. Directors who do not have several board experiences or are simply not sufficiently involved in their job generally consider that they get adequate information. "Good" directors are often those who complain about information. Usually they do not want more information as they sometimes get too much, but they want more *actionable information* that will help the board follow all aspects of corporate performance as well as market trends and corporate risks. Only then will the board be able to assess whether the firm is able to reach the targets and the strategy approved by the board.

It is important for governance consultants to work closely with directors and to keep in touch as often as possible. Companies are pluralistic and so are directors. They do not have the same needs nor follow the same ways of doing things. Consultants cannot bring a "one-size-fits-all" solution, which is why they must listen to directors, accumulate their experience, practices, and concerns, and then use all that knowledge accordingly. Banks for instance improved considerably their governance over the last 5 years. Boards tend to have now a 12 or 18 months rolling agenda with a cycle of business unit presentations to the board. The aim of those presentations is to ensure that the board has a different view of major risks and at the same time a visibility, not just of the "top 10" senior managers but also of the "second tier" of managers. Boards in other sectors are not necessarily aware of such practices and would definitively benefit from implementing them.

Assessing the Board's Own Functioning and Performance

Board efficiency is influenced by its composition, the quality of its members, and by the way the board works and is organized. Assessing board members, especially in terms of how they work together, what each person brings to the board, is important. A related task is the assessment of the broader institutional framework in which the board evolves and how its work is structured. All that has been written above concerning boards and board members duties would be useless with a malfunctioning board. The U.K. Hampel Committee highlighted this issue saying that "performance appraisal by board was an interesting development which boards might usefully consider in the interest of continuous improvement" (Hampel, 1998, p. 27). Continuous improvement is the key. Evaluation will add value to the board *if* it helps its members to learn from their past mistakes and malfunctions. A sole assessment without any perspective (e.g., comparing its evolution over time or against peers) will not accomplish much, with the exception of better "box-ticking." The ongoing improvement of a board is critical to maintain its competitive edge and to meet shareholders expectations. TIAA-CREF (Teachers Insurance and Annuity Association–College Retirement Equities Fund) (2000)[2] has captured this role in its corporate governance guidelines that:

> the board should have mechanisms to evaluate and improve its performance in representing the shareholders in governing the corporation. At a minimum, there should be an annual review by the board of its performance overall, including the effectiveness of its committees, measured against criteria defined in committee charter.

Merril Lynch (2003), for example, has responded to this requirement and gives a precise description of how the board shall carry out such evaluation and assessment (see Appendix 6C).

Given the array of functions that a board is supposed to complete provides us with a general understanding of directors are expected to do. Yet, the range of these activities and responsibilities makes it difficult, if not impossible, to create a profile of the "ideal" independent NED. As we will see, beyond certain intrinsic qualities, the key appears to be what a specific NED can bring to the whole board.

SELECTION CRITERIA: ADDING VALUE TO THE BOARD

Today a requirement for boards is to appoint directors who can add value to board process and governance. Industry knowledge, leadership capabilities, management and international experiences are "must have" qualities. But a lingering question is how outside directors, who typically meet only 6 to 10 times a year for a day at a time, can offer anything of real value to senior management teams that are these days working 24/7.

Director Qualities

Much greater attention is paid to selecting directors on the basis of a range of criteria based on ethical standards, merit and the performance requirements of the board and the organization. For example, Goldman Sachs (2003), in its corporate governance guidelines dedicated to board composition and size, stresses that:

The Board's Corporate Governance and Nominating Committee shall be responsible for identifying and recommending to the Board qualified candidates for Board membership, based primarily on the following criteria:

- Judgment, character, expertise, skills and knowledge useful to the oversight of the company's business;
- Diversity of viewpoints, backgrounds, experiences and other demographics;
- Business or other relevant experience; and
- The extent to which the interplay of the candidate's expertise, skills, knowledge and experience with that of other board members will build a board that is effective, collegial and responsive to the needs of the company.

In its proxy guidelines, Lockheed Martin (2007, p. 8) advances that "Board seeks a diverse group of candidates who at a minimum possess the background, skills, expertise and time to make a significant contribution to the Board, Lockheed Martin, and its stockholders." The company, however, adds that potential criteria against which candidates may be measured may include the following (which are reassessed annually):

- meets bylaw age requirement;
- reflects highest personal and professional integrity;
- meets NYSE independence criteria;
- has relevant educational background;
- has exemplary professional background;
- has relevant past and current employment affiliation(s), board affiliations and experience;
- is free from conflicts of interest;
- is technology-proficient;
- has demonstrated effectiveness;
- possesses sound judgment;
- brings a diverse background;
- has adequate time to devote to board responsibilities; and
- represents the best interests of all stockholders.

This is a long list that emphasizes education, experience, and professional background, moral qualities, and technical skills. One has to keep in mind that one cannot expect to find the same qualities among all directors. From one country to another, from one sector to another, from a small company to a big firm, directors are pluralistic—and have to be. Even within the same board, directors have to bring different qualities. Of course, one finds common features, mainly relating to ethics and moral qualities. Experience is also a very important criterion. A director with significant retail or marketing experience, for example, can sit on a board of a telecom company provided that other directors have telecom experience. In return, he or she can usefully contribute "sell-side" expertise.

The trend toward greater board diversity presents an opportunity for governance consultants. As boards are becoming more diverse, the same applies to the consultants who advise the directors. Consultants have to face very different situations, or for similar situations interact with very different people. It is the job of a governance consultant to ensure that such accumulated experience is shared across the board. Directors are very keen on benefiting from shared experience. In addition to a networking purpose, the flourishing number of institutes of directors is a perfect illustration of this need.

Talent is Important—But it May Not be Enough

Besides the intrinsic qualities of a director, a board needs to be well balanced to have a chance to perform well. Like on a football (soccer) team, one needs to have and retain the best at each position. Having a team composed only of strikers, even the world's best, will not lead the organization very far. Just as a football team needs defenders, midfields and forwards, it also needs them to play together as a real team—it is the same for boards.

As Hilmer (1998) notes, "while board composition is important, so is the quality and ability of each individual on the board." Expanding further, he contends that

> effective board membership requires high levels of intellectual ability, experience, soundness of judgment and integrity. There is also the question of the collective capacity of the board in terms of the mix of abilities, experiences and personalities that best make up the board as a collective body.

Major investors who are active in term of corporate governance are aware of the importance of board diversity. Corporate governance reform campaigns by investors, such as TIAA-CREF, have targeted specific companies for shareholder proposals aimed at increasing board diversity. The Investor Responsibility Research Center's (1993) survey on voting by institutional investors on corporate governance issues indicated that "39 per cent of respondents noted that their guidelines require them to withhold their votes in cases where there is a lack of women or minorities on a board" (see Bilimoria & Wheeler, 2000, p. 139).

The Right Mix

As a group, a board of directors should combine a mix of competencies and capabilities. Boards have traditionally been viewed as a homogenous group of elites who have similar socioeconomic backgrounds, hold degrees from the same schools, have similar educational and professional training, and, as a result, have very similar views about business practices.

The idea of board diversity reflects the fact that we are now a much more multicultural, and ostensibly, gender sensitive society, and that personal backgrounds are also diverse. Within this context, companies today face a far more complex economy, which demands more sophisticated talent with global acumen, multicultural fluency, technological literacy, entrepreneurial skills, and the ability to manage increasingly de-layered, disaggregated organizations (Chambers, Foulon, Handfield-Jones, Franklin, & Michaels, 1998). Boards have begun to realize that they can benefit from diversity, that they need to move away from corporate monoculture and boardroom uniformity, and think about whether they have the right composition to provide the diverse perspectives that today's businesses require.

As an example, in the European banking sector[3] industry knowledge is a key criterion for selecting NEDs. But boards are also opened to managers coming from other industries or services (see Figure 6.1). In our banking sample (10 top European banks, with ADR level 2 or 3, part of the FTSEurofirst 300 index), the average director is around 58 years old, a man 9 times over 10, and a national citizen in 85% of cases.

With corporate governance, the concept of diversity relates to board composition and the varied combination of attributes, characteristics, and expertise contributed by individual board members in relation to board process and decision making. In the widest sense, the various types of diversity that may be represented among directors in the boardroom include age, gender, ethnicity, culture, religion, constituency representation, independence, professional background, knowledge, technical skills and expertise, commercial and industry experience, career and life experience (Milliken & Martins, 1996). As an illustration of such diversity, the General Electric pension fund "endeavours to have a board representing diverse experience at policy-making levels in business, government, education and technology, and in areas that are relevant to the company's global activities" (General Electric Governance, 2005). Similarly, Verizon's pension fund adds in its corporate governance proxy guidelines "in assessing the appropriate composition of the Board, the Corporate Governance Committee also considers demographic factors that promote diversity" (Verizon, 2004).

Governance consultants can provide useful assistance to boards and nomination committees in profiling board composition of relevant peers, assessing gaps with the current board composition. Working with numerous boards of directors provides consultants with knowledge of board composition, balance, and culture that individual directors do not necessary have. Thus, they can assist nomination committees in drawing profiles of "missing" directors. Head hunters are then usually asked to find directors according to the designed profile.

Why Diversity?

Boards can be seen as a potentially important strategic resource for organizations, especially in linking the firm to external resources, such as providing a linkage to a nation's business elite, access to capital, connections to competitors, and/or market and industry intelligence (Ingley & van der Walt, 2001). Diversity in this context argues for a broader range of backgrounds among external directors in providing this resource. In management terms, to increase diversity is to provide a rich

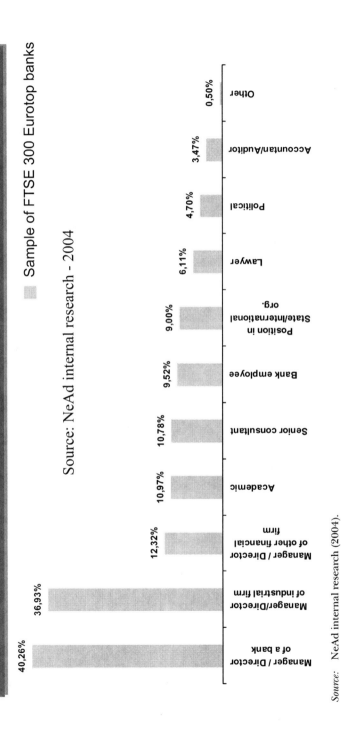

Industry experience

■ Sample of FTSE 300 Eurotop banks

Source: NeAd internal research - 2004

Manager / Director of a bank	40,26%
Manager/Director of industrial firm	36,93%
Manager / Director of other financial firm	12,32%
Academic	10,97%
Senior consultant	10,78%
Bank employee	9,52%
Position in State/International org.	9,00%
Lawyer	6,11%
Political	4,70%
Accountan/Auditor	3,47%
Other	0,50%

Source: NeAd internal research (2004).

Figure 6.1. Current professions of NEDs in European banks. (Sample of 10 banks belonging to the Eurofirst 300 index).

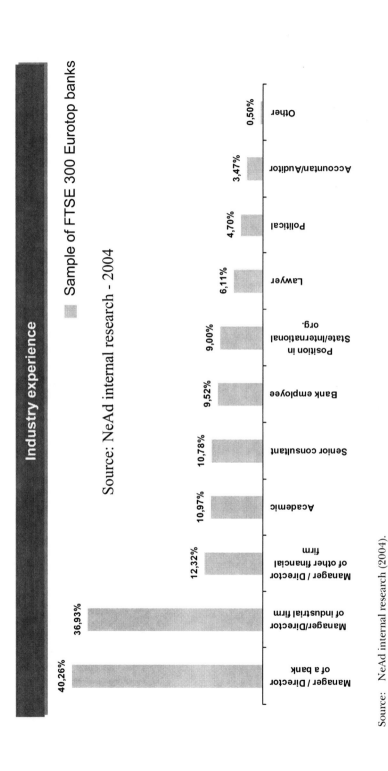

Industry experience

■ Sample of FTSE 300 Eurotop banks

Source: NeAd internal research - 2004

- Manager / Director of a bank: 40,26%
- Manager/Director of industrial firm: 36,93%
- Manager / Director of other financial firm: 12,32%
- Academic: 10,97%
- Senior consultant: 10,78%
- Bank employee: 9,52%
- Position in State/International org.: 9,00%
- Lawyer: 6,11%
- Political: 4,70%
- Accountan/Auditor: 3,47%
- Other: 0,50%

Source: NeAd internal research (2004).

Figure 6.2.   Current professions of NEDs in European banks. (Sample of 10 banks belonging to the Eurofirst 300 index).

source of innovative ideas and practical resources for dealing with difficult policy issues, to enlarge the basis on which policy develops, and to expand the issues over which negotiation will take place (Jones, Pringle, & Shepherd, 2000, p. 364) argue that "a concept of multi-voiced international discourse on issues of difference in organizations is a better model than 'knowledge transfer,' with its implications of passing on the latest advances in knowledge and practice."

In the boardroom context, diversity is purported to assure a broad base of wisdom, so that boards composed of qualified individuals who reflect a diversity of experience, gender, and ethnicity can take advantage of their differences to work successfully together on behalf of the organization. Thus, appointments with different backgrounds and bases of expertise offer different experiences and can make a valuable contribution to board decisions by providing unique perspectives on strategic issues.

Consultants also need to be diverse and understand different cultures. A real value added is to the ability to create a bridge between investors' expectations and a firm's culture. History and culture matter and can explain different corporate governance arrangements. In this regard, consultants can help companies explain those governance particularities and to adapt the corporate governance system to regulatory and market needs. Again, if corporate governance presents common features, those are in a sense "cosmetic." The reality of corporate governance goes far beyond the strict number of independent directors or which committees assist the board in its work. One has to look inside and assess how the entire governance system works.

THE CORPORATE GOVERNANCE CONSULTANT: A NECESSARY EXTERNAL COMPLEMENT

Among all board functions we have listed, corporate governance consultants are positioned to add value compared to independent NEDs in helping the board become more efficient. A corporate governance consultant per se may not be the most appropriate person to hold a directorship position, but he or she can be a useful complement. He has no vocation to decide but to contribute to directors' decision making process. The corporate governance consultants can assist the board in the completion of its duties, contributing their knowledge and expertise *and* their objectivity and impartiality. It is common practice, for example, that governance consultants attend board meetings and assess board efficiency on an ongoing basis. Discussions follow with the chairman.

Most investors express concerns about boards hiring consultants (not only governance consultants) at the company's expense. Because boards have more and more NEDs, these individuals are expected to bring value to their board and company—typically in lieu of a consultant. However, NEDs are not expected to be experts in all areas. They should, however, be able to understand the problems and solutions that consultants bring to the table. Directors sitting on remuneration committees, for example, do not necessarily need to be compensation experts; specialized consultants can be brought in for that purpose. But it is important that they understand the issues involved and the implications raised by the proposed solutions. In essence, working with governance consultants, directors fulfil their tasks, not necessarily by being experts in all fields, but understanding the stakes, focusing on the right questions and, thus, concentrating on their job and the decisions that need to be made.

Governance Consultants and Board Evaluation and Assessment

Governance experts can be useful in helping boards develop effective process and "know how" for their tasks. Selecting the "right" directors, in essence, building a balanced board composed of a mix of personalities, experiences and business knowledge, is a necessary but not a sufficient condition. One has to make sure that board is also functioning in the "right" way. It is difficult to be impartial, objective and independent in your evaluating one's own processes. One cannot be both judge and actor. Related to the problem of independence is the *dual nature* of evaluation. Evaluation should be both "absolute" and "relative": *absolute* refers to the performance of the board and evaluation of its members; *relative* benchmarks the absolute performance evaluation with other peers or best practices. A corporate governance expert is in an ideal position to both evaluate board performance and to enrich this assessment with benchmarking information.

Although such board evaluation is a complex task, there are specific steps that are recommended. A thorough board assessment should consider the functioning of the board itself and the performance of individual board members. Board powers and responsibilities, board structure in terms of its committees, board independence, board competence, and board engagement are ingredients that are necessary for a competent and engaged board.

The review agenda may start with defining the precise role of the board. Do board members agree on this role? Are executives conscious of this role? Is the board well balanced between strategic and operational tasks? Do board members, with a particular focus on independent NEDs, receive the information they need (in terms of both content and format)?

Once the role of the board is reviewed, the organization itself should be examined, especially in accordance with the previously defined board role. Among the factors to be considered include: the size of the board, its (un)balanced composition, independence, time involved, number of meetings, interlocking positions and competing commitments, duration of appointments, nomination process and board retirement practices, confidentiality provisions that protect board deliberations, and board financial resources.

A board review should then turn to important structural issues, such as defining exact committee functions, ensuring that the various committees and their members fully understand their duties. The board review could adequately end with questions related to the NEDs' perception of the board. This would provide the board a map of what directors think of the board and its functioning. This focus could include such areas as risk perception, internal control efficiency, strategy understanding, and board accountability. This type of evaluation can prove to be of significant benefit to board members, raising problems that board might not have previously been aware.

Individual member review can also prove to be of value to board members and to the board as a whole, even if directors are quite often reluctant to this type of evaluation. When an independent NED does not actively participate in board deliberations, he or she diminishes the value of the board as a whole. Thus, the level and quality of participations are important issues. These individual reviews can provide feedback and direction as to how directors can improve their role and how they might be able to receive more satisfaction from their board membership. This type of personal assessment, however, implies that the board already has a long culture of assessment.

Besides helping the board to assess its own functioning, corporate governance consultants brings and external view to the board, a broader look from outside and the knowledge of other board practices. Although this perspective is also what it is expected from independent NEDs, governance consultants are typically in a position that NEDs are not, especially in terms of being able to update the board on peer board best practices, on what their investors expect from them, and where the board stands in comparison to these practices and expectations. Consultants can also provide a broader picture of how different boards work, drawing on their insights from director interviews, contacts, and company analyses. In essence, consultants are in a position to accumulate knowledge that directors are not able to accumulate—which is all the more true now that directors are asked to hold a limited number of directorships. In the end, this type of knowledge provides a meaningful service to directors and boards. But one should keep in mind that a consultant has a contractual relationship with the company and such, will never be considered as independent.

CONCLUSION

A board playing its "performance" and "conformance" roles is essential, but not sufficient, for healthy corporate governance. In the same vein, independent NEDs are essential but not sufficient. Sound corporate governance is a complex mix of a number of different ingredients, all of which have to be well balanced. Board effectiveness, the right incentives, comprehensive and reliable information, and respect for shareholder rights, among others are all elements that contribute to sound corporate governance. Corporate governance consultants can help board achieve the "right" mix and balance of good ingredients at all corporate levels. While making the system work is one of the board's primary tasks, governance consultants can help to ensure ensuring that the company has an appropriate corporate governance system and structure.

NOTES

1. These definitions are presented in Appendices 6A and 6B.
2. Nestor Advisors has compiled and developed the most extensive database on investors' expectations in term of corporate governance. Analysis is based on sources coming from the top 500 global pension funds and from the top 500 global asset managers.
3. This information is based on a sample of 10 banks part of FTSEurofirst 300 index. Those banks also have ADRs level 2 or 3.

APPENDIX 6A

NYSE Independence Definition

SECTION 303A .01 & .02

In order to tighten the definition of "independent director" for purposes of these standards:

  (a) No director qualifies as "independent" unless the board of directors affirmatively determines that the director has no material relationship with the listed company (either directly or as a partner, share-holder or officer of an organization that has a relationship with the company). Companies must identify which directors are independent and disclose the basis for that determination.

(b) In addition, a director is not independent if:

I. The director is, or has been within the last 3 years, an employee of the listed company, or an immediate family member is, or has been within the last 3 years, an executive officer, of the listed company.

Commentary: Employment as an interim chairman or CEO or other executive officer shall not disqualify a director from being considered independent following that employment.

II. The director has received, or has an immediate family member who has received, during any 12-month period within the last 3 years, more than $100,000 in direct compensation from the listed company, other than director and committee fees and pension or other forms of deferred compensation for prior service (provided such compensation is not contingent in any way on continued service.

Commentary: Compensation received by a director for former service as an interim chairman or CEO or other executive officer need not be considered in determining independence under this test. Compensation received by an immediate family member for service as an employee of the listed company (other than an executive officer) need not be considered in determining independence under this test.

III. (A) The director or an immediate family member is a current partner of a firm that is the company's internal or external auditor; (B) the director is a current employee of such a firm; (C) the director has an immediate family member who is a current employee of such a firm and who participates in the firm's audit, assurance or tax compliance (but not tax planning) practice; or (D) the director or an immediate family member was within the last three years (but is no longer) a partner or employee of such a firm and personally worked on the listed company's audit within that time.

IV. The director or an immediate family member is, or has been within the last 3 years, employed as an executive officer of another company where any of the listed company's present executive officers at the same time serves or served on that company's compensation committee.

V. The director is a current employee, or an immediate family member is a current executive officer, of a company that has made payments to, or received payments from, the listed company for property or services in an amount which, in any of the last 3 fiscal years, exceeds the greater of $1 million, or 2% of such other company's consolidated gross revenues.

Commentary: In applying the test in Section 303A.02(b)(v), both the payments and the consolidated gross revenues to be measured shall be those reported in the last completed fiscal year of such other company. The look-back provision for this test applies solely to the financial relationship between the listed company and the director or immediate family member's current employer; a listed company need not consider former employment of the director or immediate family member.

Contributions to tax exempt organizations shall not be considered "payments" for purposes of Section 303A.02(b)(v), provided however that a listed company shall disclose in its annual proxy statement, or if the listed company does not file an annual proxy statement, in the company's annual report on Form 10–K filed with the Securities and Exchange Commission, any such contributions made by the listed company to any tax exempt organization in which any independent director serves as an executive officer if, within the preceding 3 years, contributions in any single fiscal year from the listed company to the organization exceeded the greater of $1 million, or 2% of such tax exempt organization's consolidated gross revenues. Listed company boards are reminded of their obligations to consider the materiality of any such relationship in accordance with Section 303A.02(a) above.

General Commentary to Section 303A.02(b): An "immediate family member" includes a person's spouse, parents, children, siblings, mothers and fathers-in-law, sons and daughters-in-law, brothers and sisters-in-law, and anyone (other than domestic employees) who shares such person's home. When applying the lookback provisions in Section 303A.02(b), listed companies need not consider individuals who are no longer immediate family members as a result of legal separation or divorce, or those who have died or become incapacitated.

In addition, references to the "company" would include any parent or subsidiary in a consolidated group with the company.

APPENDIX 6B

EU Independence Definition

EUROPEAN UNION COMMISSSION

13.1. A director should be considered to be independent when he is free from any business, family or other relationship—with the company, its controlling shareholder or the management of either—that creates a conflict of interest such as to jeopardize exercise of his judgement

13.2. A number of criteria for assessment of the independence of directors should be adopted at national level, taking into account the guidance provided in Annex II, which identifies a number of situations reflecting the relationships or circumstances usually recognized as potentially leading to the presence of material conflict of interest. The determination of what constitutes independence is fundamentally an issue for the (supervisory) board itself to determine. The (supervisory) board may indeed consider that, although a particular director meets all of the criteria retained at national level for assessment of independence of directors, he cannot be held to be independent owing to the specific circumstances of the person or the company, and the converse also applies.

13.3. Proper information should be disclosed on the conclusions reached by the (supervisory) board in its determination of whether a particular director should be regarded as independent.
13.3.1. When the appointment of a nonexecutive or supervisory director is proposed, the company should disclose whether it considers him to be independent; when one or several of the criteria retained at national level for assessment of independence of directors is not met, the company should disclose its reasons for nevertheless considering this director to be independent. Companies should also disclose annually which directors they consider to be independent;

13.3.2. When one or several of the criteria retained at national level for assessment of independence of directors has not been met throughout the year, the company should disclose its reasons for considering this director to be independent. To ensure the accuracy of the information provided on the independence of directors, the company should require the independent directors to revalidate their independence periodically.

Profile of Independent Nonexecutive or Supervisory Directors

1. It is not possible to list comprehensively all threats to directors' independence; the relationships or circumstances which may appear relevant to its determination may vary to a certain extent across Member States and companies, and best practices in this respect may evolve over time. However, a number of situations are frequently recognized as relevant in helping the (supervisory) board to determine whether a nonexecutive or supervisory director may be regarded as independent, even though it is widely understood that assessment of the independence of any particular director should be based on the substance rather than the form. In this context, a number of criteria—to be used by the (supervisory) board—should be adopted at national level.

Such criteria, which should be tailored to the national context, should be based on due consideration of at least the following situations:

(a) Not to be an executive or managing director of the company or an associated company, and not having been in such a position for the previous 5 years;
(b) Not to be an employee of the company or an associated company, and not having been in such a position for the previous 3 years, except when the nonexecutive or supervisory director does not belong to senior management and has been elected to the (supervisory) board in the context of a system of workers' representation recognized by law and providing for adequate protection against abusive dismissal and other forms of unfair treatment;
(c) Not to receive, or have received, significant additional remuneration from the company or an associated company apart from a fee received as nonexecutive or supervisory director. Such additional remuneration covers in particular any participation in a share option or any other performance-related pay scheme; it does not cover the receipt of fixed amounts of compensation under a retirement plan (including deferred compensation) for prior service with

the company (provided that such compensation is not contingent in any way on continued service);

(d) Not to be or to represent in any way the controlling shareholder(s) (control being determined by reference to the cases mentioned in Article 1 §1 of the Seventh Council Directive of 13 June 1983 on consolidated accounts);

(e) Not to have, or have had within the last year, a significant business relationship with the company or an associated company, either directly or as a partner, shareholder, director or senior employee of a body having such a relationship. Business relationships include the situation of a significant supplier of goods or services (including financial, legal, advisory or consulting services), of a significant customer, and of organizations that receive significant contributions from the company or its group;

(f) Not to be, or have been within the last 3 years, partner or employee of the present or former external auditor of the company or an associated company;

(g) Not to be executive or managing director in another company in which an executive or managing director of the company is nonexecutive or supervisory director, and not to have other significant links with executive directors of the company through involvement in other companies or bodies;

(h) Not to have served on the (supervisory) board as a nonexecutive or supervisory director for more than three terms (or, alternatively, more than 12 years where national law provides for normal terms of a very small length);

(i) Not to be a close family member of an executive or managing director, or of persons in the situations referred to in points (a) to (h);

2. The independent director undertakes (a) to maintain in all circumstances his independence of analysis, decision, and action, (b) not to seek or accept any unreasonable advantages that could be considered as compromising his independence, and (c) to clearly express his opposition in the event that he finds that a decision of the (supervisory) board may harm the company. When the (supervisory) board has made decisions about which an independent nonexecutive or supervisory director has serious reservations, he should draw all the appropriate consequences from this. If he were to resign, he should explain his reasons in a letter to the board or the audit committee, and—where appropriate—to any relevant body external to the company.

APPENDIX 6C

Merrill Lynch Governance Guidelines

MERRILL LYNCH GUIDELINES (2003)

9. Annual Evaluations

A. Board Self-Evaluation. The Nominating and Corporate

Governance Committee of the Board will lead the Board in an annual self-evaluation process to determine whether the Board and its committees are functioning effectively. The Nominating and Corporate Governance Committee is responsible for receiving comments from the Board, reviewing them and reporting annually to the Board an assessment of the Board's performance. The Board will discuss the evaluation report annually. The assessment will focus on the Board's contribution to the Corporation and emphasize those areas in which the Board believes a better contribution could be made. The Nominating and Corporate Governance Committee will establish the criteria to be used in such evaluations.

B. Review of Board's Core Competencies and Composition

The Nominating and Corporate Governance Committee is also responsible for reviewing with the Board, on an annual basis, the skills and characteristics of the Board of Directors and the composition of the Board as a whole. This assessment should include an analysis of the Board's core competencies, including understanding of the financial industry, financial expertise, integrity, wisdom, judgment, commitment to excellence, business experience and acumen, skills, diverse perspectives and availability. As a result of this assessment, the Nominating and Corporate Governance Committee will determine whether the Board is lacking any of the core competencies deemed essential to its effectiveness and whether consideration should be given to any change in the Board's membership.

C. Committee Self-Evaluation

Each of the Audit Committee, the Management Development, and Compensation Committee and the Nominating and Corporate Governance Committee will perform an annual review of such

Committee's performance, including a review of the Committee's compliance with its respective Charter. Each such Committee shall conduct such evaluation and review in such manner as it deems appropriate and report the results of the evaluation to the entire Board of Directors.

REFERENCES

Bilimoria, D., & Wheeler, J. V. (2000). Women corporate directors: Current research and future directions. In R. J. Burke & M. C. Mattis (Eds.), *Women in management: Current research issues* (Vol. II, pp. 138–163). London: SAGE.

Black, B., Cheffins, B., & Klausner, M. (2005). Why directors' damages may harm investors. *Financial Times.* Retrieved January 19, 2005, from http://search.ft.com/ftArticle?query-Text=Why%20directors%27%20damages%20may%20harm%20investors&y=5&aje=true&x=17&id=050119008382

Cadbury, A. (2002). *Corporate governance and chairmanship: A personal view.* Oxford, England: Oxford University Press.

Chambers, E. G., Foulon, M., Handfield-Jones, H., Franklin, S. M., & Michaels, E. G., III (1998). The war for talent. *The McKinsey Quarterly, 3*, 44–57.

General Electric. (2005). *General Electric Governance Principles.* Fairfield, CT: Author.

Goldman Sachs. (2003). *Goldman Sachs governance guidelines.* New York: Author.

Hampel, R. (1998). *Committee on corporate governance: Final report.* London: Gee.

Higgs, D. (2003). *Review of the role and effectiveness of non-executive directors.* London: Department of Trade and Industry.

Hilmer, F. G. (1998). *Strictly boardroom: Improving governance to enhance company performance (*2nd ed). Melbourne, Australia: Business Library.

Ingley, C. B., & van der Walt, N. T. (2001). The strategic board: The changing role of directors in developing and maintaining corporate capability. *Corporate Governance: An International Review, 9*(3), 174–185.

Investor Responsibility Research Center. (1993). *Annual survey voting by institutional investors on corporate governance issues.* Retrieved June 2006, from www.issproxy.com/

Jones, D., Pringle, J., & Shepherd, D. (2000). Managing diversity meets Aotearoa/New Zealand. *Personnel Review, 29*(3), 364–380.

Lockheed Martin. (2007). Lockheed Martin 2007 proxy statement, *Notice of 2007 Annual Meeting of Stockholders.* Retrieved June 2007, http://www.lockheedmartin.com/data/assets/corporate/documents/2007_ProxyStatement.pdf

Merrill Lynch. (2003). *Merrill Lynch governance guidelines.* New York: Merrill Lynch.

Milliken, F. J., & Martins, L. (1996). Searching for common threads: Understanding the multiple effects of diversity in organizational groups. *Academy of Management Review, 21*(2), 402–433.

Teachers Insurance and Annuity Association–College Retirement Equities Fund. (2000). *TIAA-CREF Policy Statement on Corporate Governance. TIAA-CREF.* Retrieved June 2000, http://www.tiaa-cref.org/pubs/pdf/governance_policy.pdf

Tricker, R. I. (1994). *International corporate governance: Text, readings and cases.* New York: Prentice Hall.

Verizon. (2004). *Verizon corporate governance proxy guidelines.* Retrieved June 2004, from http://investor.verizon.com/financial/annual/2004/proxy04.html

PART III

"SUPER" MANAGER OR "SUPER" CONSULTANT? THEORIZING THE ROLE OF THE DIRECTOR

CHAPTER 7

KNOWLEDGE AND ACCOUNTABILITY

Outside Directors' Contribution in the Corporate Value Chain

Morten Huse, Jonas Gabrielsson, and Alessandro Minichilli

Considerable evidence has shown that boards of directors often act as management consultants rather than agents monitoring management on behalf of external shareholders (Lorsch & McIver, 1989; Mace, 1971). The seminal work of Mace more than 3 decades ago showed that it was a myth that board set objectives, hired, fired, and compensated the chief executive officer (CEO), and asked discerning questions. In reality, boards most often were only ornaments on the "corporate Christmas tree" or at best acted as consultants for the management. The gap between myth and reality was largely due to various institutional forces emerging from managerial and class hegemony.

Board Members and Management Consultants: Redefining the Boundaries of Consulting and Corporate Governance, pp. 137–153
Copyright © 2009 by Information Age Publishing
All rights of reproduction in any form reserved.

CONSULTANTS OR DIRECTORS: A VALUE CHAIN APPROACH

Despite recent developments and trends in corporate governance, boards seem still to function very much as consultants for the management. During the late 1980s and the 1990s, we experienced the evolution of the shareholder supremacy paradigm that led to the introduction of nominally independent board members. The expected role of these barbarian-like board members was to ratify important decisions and to create value for shareholders that in relation to the firm in most cases were distant and faceless—and sometimes also heartless. However, recent research has found that the observations by Mace (1971) are still true, and various institutional forces uphold a managerial hegemony (Ocasio, 1999; Westphal, 1998; Westphal & Khanna, 2003; Westphal & Zajac, 1994). Furthermore, we have seen a renewed attention of boards' contribution to value creation throughout the whole value chain, and not only to external stakeholders through value distribution (Monks & Minow, 2004; Taylor, 2001). In this situation, knowledge and accountability becomes important key concepts to understand and reflect upon.

This chapter is about the knowledge and accountability of outside directors, and their contribution to value creation. Accountability is about embedding actual board behavior in relation to board role expectations (Huse, 2005). The fiduciary duty of boards of directors in most constitutions is to do what is best for the company (Monks & Minow, 2004), and various stakeholders, including various groups of shareholders, may have different board role expectations (Blair & Stout, 2001; Huse & Rindova, 2001). Accountability means to balance and meet the interest of the various stakeholders. The consequence and responsibility for the individual board members will thus be to use their knowledge and skills to create value for the company and not only for certain stakeholders.

Our objective is to show through a value chain analysis how outside directors may contribute to value creation. The chapter also explores how outside directors, through responsible use of their knowledge and skills, may help align board role expectations and actual board task performance, and thus create accountability. The chapter contributes in various ways. First, we approach various board tasks from a value chain perspective, a novel approach as board tasks most often have been studied from contingency or stakeholder perspectives. A premise of the chapter is that outside directors simultaneously perform a variety of tasks. This gives direction with respect to the selection of board members and the structuring of the inner working of board. Second, we have a focus on how outside directors may contribute to value creation and not only to value distribution. The chapter illustrates how outside board members contribute through resource provision, knowledge, process mentoring, decision making, evaluation, and negotiation.

The chapter proceeds in four sections. In the first section, we position various board role theories and identify board tasks based on these theories. Main board tasks are split into six categories: output control, behavioral control, decision control, networking, advisory tasks, and strategic leadership. In the second section, the discussion turns to the fit between these various tasks and the different parts of the value chain. The value chain is divided into resource provision, operations, innovation, decision-making, implementation, and value distribution. The third section contains a presentation of obstacles for outside directors to make contributions on boards. Knowledge and competencies of the outside directors are linked to requirements across the value chain. In the fourth section, we present a board evaluation framework that is useful for developing the accountability of outside directors.

Board Task Typology

Board tasks can be examined from both external and internal perspectives. Board tasks from external perspectives are most often called *control tasks*, while the tasks from internal perspectives are referred to as *service tasks* (Forbes & Milliken, 1999; Huse, 1993; Mintzberg, 1983). The idea of distinguishing between external and internal perspectives has its background in the assumed conflict of interest between various actors, among which the conflict between external and internal actors has got the most attention (Jensen & Meckling, 1976; Kosnik, 1987). The emphasis on the various perspectives is less important when the conflict of interest is not obvious, which is one of the arguments from stewardship theory (Davis, Schoorman, & Donaldson, 1997).

The external perspectives are about how firm-external stakeholders can use or benefit from boards of directors. Boards are often seen as agents for external stakeholders, and their main task will then often be related to control (Fama & Jensen, 1983). However, sometimes it may be difficult to make clear distinctions between who are the actors external or internal to a firm. Shareholders are often considered to be the most important external stakeholders, but the list of external stakeholders may include customers, suppliers, competitors, the society, and various regulatory authorities and their representatives. Employees and unions are sometimes considered to be external stakeholders, in particular when there may be conflicts of interests between the employees, and the CEO and the executive team. Agency theory, including common agency theory and agency-stakeholder theory, has given the most contributions in understanding the board from external perspectives (Eisenhardt, 1989; Hill & Jones, 1992).

The CEO and the top management team are in most cases the main internal stakeholders. Boards are from internal perspectives considered to have service tasks. In the list of internal stakeholders, we may find the families of the executives, and others with close psychological and financial ties to the CEO and the top management team. It is also argued that employees, most often regardless of their relationships with the management, should have internal perspectives on the firm and the board. Furthermore, in many cases owners have internal perspectives as well. This is particularly the case in family firms, many small firms and firms with concentrated ownership. Various strategic management theories, including resource dependence theory (Pfeffer & Salancik, 1978) and the resource based view of the firm (Barney, 1991), contribute to understand board tasks from firm-internal perspectives.

In the board task typology we combine various focuses with the two perspectives, which are presented in Table 7.1. The three focuses used are firm-internal, firm-external, and strategic. The board may have a focus on how the firm relates to the external environment, what takes place inside the firm, and it may focus on decisions having an impact on the long-term and short-term development of the firm, which creates six main board tasks. The theoretical rationale and examples of empirical studies relating to each of these tasks are presented in Huse (2005).

- *Board output control tasks*. Boards acting on behalf of *external stakeholders* and having an *external focus* will most often concentrate on output control. The main interest of these stakeholders will be how firm outcomes meet their needs or objectives. Usually they will either be stakeholders or shareholders that use the markets for control, and the board members will spend limited time in board commitments. These stakeholders will abandon the firm if the firm outcome is unsatisfactory. The output control task also includes

Table 7.1.   Typology of Board Tasks

	Tasks	
Focus	*Firm External Perspective Control Tasks*	*Firm Internal Perspective Service Tasks*
External focus	Board output control tasks	Board networking tasks
Internal focus	Board behavioral control tasks	Board advisory tasks
Decision/Strategy focus	Board decision control tasks	Board mentoring tasks

how various stakeholders supervise and negotiate the distribution of values from the firm.

- *Board networking tasks*. Boards acting on behalf of *internal stakeholders* and having an *external focus* will often be involved in resource dependency tasks (Pfeffer & Salancik, 1978). These involve networking, lobbying, and legitimacy tasks. People controlling or influencing resources that are important to the firm may be co-opted or selected as board members.

- *Board behavioral control tasks*. These board tasks take place when *external stakeholders* use the board members to *control* top management behavior and firm-internal issues. This kind of control is more time consuming than output control. The focus is on how things are done or performed more than on the final outcome (Baysinger & Hoskisson, 1990).

- *Board advisory tasks*. Board members may be *consultants* to the management, and they may themselves provide various kinds of knowledge and competencies (Castaldi & Wortman, 1984; Gabrielsson & Huse, 2005). The inclusion in the boards of persons providing such resources may be a way to providing the firm sustainable competitive advantage. Resources should, however, be important, inimitable and nonsubstitutable. Offering board membership to these persons may be a way of binding resources to the firm.

- *Board decision control tasks*. From a *firm-external* perspective based on agency theory, it is advised to separate decision management from decision control (Fama & Jensen, 1983). Boards are, from this perspective, expected to *ratify* and *control* important decisions. Decision management, including decision formulation and implementation, is the responsibility of the management.

- *Board mentoring tasks*. From an *internal perspective* and a *decision* or *strategic focus*, board members are expected to mentor and stimulate the management in strategic decision making, including that of formulating and implementing important decisions. In strategic leadership the boards are not only ratifying decisions presented, but they also take part in raising the issues, developing the context and formulating the content of the decisions (McNulty & Pettigrew, 1999).

Board Tasks and the Value Chain

The recent literature has readdressed boards' contribution in the whole value chain, moving well beyond the final value distribution part (Huse,

2007). A main promoter of this perspective is Taylor (2001), who calls for a move from "corporate governance to corporate entrepreneurship." According to Taylor, the drive for short-term profits puts too much focus on value distribution rather than enhancing the prosperity of the business throughout the whole value chain (see Figure 7.1). In Figure 7.1, we also see how the various phases relate to the different board tasks presented above.

Figure 7.1, although very simplified, has merits for our purpose, illustrating that board members simultaneously need to balance both accountability and knowledge. The *accountability dimension* is emphasized through the need to balance and meet the interest of various stakeholders. The *knowledge dimension* is emphasized through the need to use their knowledge and skills to continuously and effectively support the creation of value. However, the concepts are not fully developed, and the relations between the value chain phases and board tasks are more complex than what is illustrated.

The first phase in the value chain concerns securing and providing resources. A firm depends on an array of different resources, which are to various degrees controlled by the external environment. Board networking tasks, including the whole range of managing resource dependencies, may be of particular importance in this phase. Board members may for example bring connections to valuable contacts and provide timely information and other critical resources through their personal networks. The second phase is operations. Operations may include production, sales and marketing, finance, law and general management. Board advisory or consultancy tasks may be of particular importance in this phase. Firm operations may for example be supported by the expert knowledge about the market and the industry provided by board members. The third phase is called innovation, which encompasses the development of products,

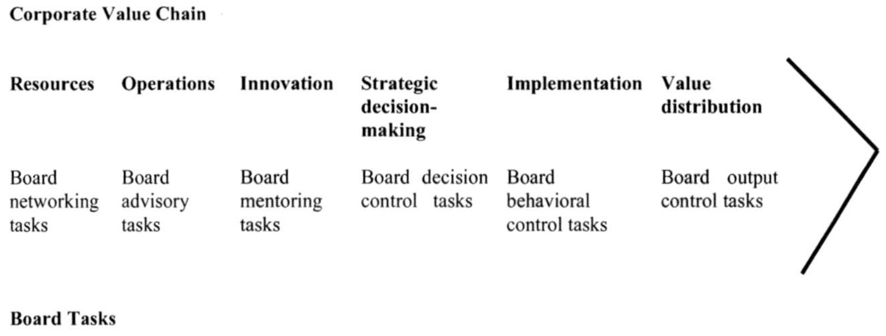

Corporate Value Chain

Resources	Operations	Innovation	Strategic decision-making	Implementation	Value distribution
Board networking tasks	Board advisory tasks	Board mentoring tasks	Board decision control tasks	Board behavioral control tasks	Board output control tasks

Board Tasks

Figure 7.1. Board tasks and the corporate value chain.

processes, the organization and markets. Board mentoring tasks may be particularly important in this phase. Mentoring provided by experienced board members may in this respect create a shared vision and mutual understanding of organizational goals in the upper echelon of the organization that coordinate action and enhance the quality of innovative efforts. Strategic decision-making involves making decisions that are important for the long-term development of the firm. In this phase, the boards have an important decision ratification and control task. By ratifying and controlling strategic decisions board members can for example ensure the future survival and success of the enterprise by providing external oversight and performing high-level reviews of strategic plans. With respect to implementation, the boards have a behavioral control task, including hiring, compensating, and firing the CEO. This behavioral control task include board members involvement in overseeing operating matters and holding managers accountable to the firm's various key stakeholders to protect the assets of the firm. Finally, we have the value distribution phase. This phase includes decisions of how corporate results or assets should be allocated to various stakeholders, including corporate social responsibility considerations. Board output control and negotiation tasks are important in this phase. Board members can communicate, coordinate and compromise with important groups of stakeholders to reduce transactions costs associated with value distribution decisions.

Understanding board tasks from a value chain perspective helps us understand that the board may fulfill several tasks at the same time. This goes beyond the arguments that board tasks primarily depend on firm contexts, such as the firm's life cycle, including experience of crisis (Huse, 1998; Lorsch & McIver, 1989; Lynall, Golden, & Hillman, 2003), company size (Gabrielsson & Huse, 2005; Huse, 2000), ownership structure, including ownership type and dispersion (Johannisson & Huse, 2000; Zahra, Neubaum, & Huse, 2000), industry and industrial environment (Huse, 1990), national, geographical and cultural differences (Aguilera & Jackson, 2003), and CEO tenure and characteristics (Shen, 2003). However, the context may have an impact on how the contribution in various phases should be balanced. The value chain approach is still novel, however, and requires empirical investigation.

Knowledge Requirements in the Value Chain

The discussion now turns to accountability and creating accountability. In this section, we focus on the lack of knowledge and competence as a limitation for outsiders to make contributions. Boards are often composed of inside and outside directors, although there are no clear or common definitions with respect to what is meant by an outside versus an inside director (Daily, Johnson, & Dalton, 1999). However, for our purpose, definitions should be compared to how we in the previous section presented internal and external perspectives. Usually an outside director is defined as a person who is not a member of the top management team of the firm. In the English vocabulary, we find the distinctions between executive and nonexecutive directors as terms relating to inside and outside directors respectively. Persons being financially or psychologically dependent of the top management team, including belonging to the families of the top management team members, are usually considered to be insiders. Outsiders are often also called independent directors, but not all outsiders are considered to be independent because being truly independent may set requirements to knowledge and information, incentives, and various power relationships.

The fiduciary duty of directors, under most legislation, is to do what is best for the company (Monks & Minow, 2004), which implies accountability on the part of outside directors. There are, however, a number of obstacles that hinder outside directors from fully contributing to effective board task performance. The lack of independence, for example, has been the main argument in agency theory (Eisenhardt, 1989; Kosnik, 1987). Lack of time has also been discussed by Mace (1971), Baysinger and Hoskisson (1990) as well as by others. Board members often serve on multiple boards in addition to their regular job, which gives them limited time for their various assignments which in turn risk lead to an insufficient board working style. In fact, insufficient working style in the boardroom is a major argument proposed by Demb and Neubauer (1992) and also to some extent by Forbes and Milliken (1999). These are all concerns or elements in the independence-detachment dimension.

The issue of "lack of knowledge" is an additional issue. Outsiders are often considered to bring in different kinds of knowledge, networks and perspectives than what already exist in the firm. Outside directors, however, do not always have sufficient expertise and firm-specific knowledge to understand and evaluate complex firm decisions (Baysinger & Hoskisson; 1990; Demb & Neubauer, 1992). Such lack of understanding can reduce the board's potential contribution to a minimum.

There are a number of obstacles that constrain board members' contributions along various parts of the value chain. It is thus a challenge to recruit and develop board members that as a team can use their knowledge and skills to align board role expectations and actual board task performance, which creates accountability. The general argument from a shareholder value point of view is that there is a need for independent and detached outside board members. But a value chain analysis would rather suggest that too many independent and detached outside board members risk damaging accountability. Its trade-off costs, in terms of lack of firm-specific knowledge, the lack of involvement and the lack of understanding that comes from the lack of such knowledge, may hinder the embedment of actual board behavior in relation to board role expectations.

Tasks and the Value Chain

Different knowledge and competencies are needed to make contributions in the various steps in the value chain and the corresponding board tasks. Based on our value chain analysis, we recognize needs for:

- Resource providers
- Advisors
- Mentors
- Decision makers
- Evaluators
- Distributors and negotiators

These roles can be played by different board members, and some board members may play more than one role. However, boards can only fulfill their full value creating potential by collectively securing that all these roles are simultaneously performed.

The *resource providers* contribute with various networking tasks, including legitimacy, contacting, and lobbying. The characteristics of the resource providers are discussed in the literature using resource dependence theory (Hillman, Cannella, & Paetzold, 2000). These board members should have (1) large networks among the groups being the most important for the firm and (2) enjoy credibility in these groups. Sometimes and for some firms it may be important to relate to financiers, including the banks, sometimes politicians and public authorities, and sometimes to customers, suppliers or competitors. The knowledge needed is more related to who they are than to what they do. The resource provision tasks can in some cases be obtained by external consultants, but often it gives more credibility and commitment when this competency is included among the board members.

The *advisors* may contribute to firm operations by giving advice on issues like finance, market, general management and leadership, law and technical issues (Castaldi & Wortman, 1984). The board members may, from a knowledge-based or resource-based perspective, through their personal and intangible skills and competencies, be valuable resources for the firm (Barney, 1991). There may be alternative ways of getting these resources (e.g., through consultants in the market or through employment in the hierarchy), which should be considered. However, including these resources on the board may sometimes contribute to securing resources that may be valuable, rare, nonsubstitutable, and inimitable in a way that may provide long term competitive advantage.

Board members may be *mentors* for the firm and the CEO, including being a sounding board and a discussion partner. This will involve outside board members who with openness and generosity share their experiences, knowledge and time with the CEO (Huse, Minichilli, & Schøning, 2005). Board members with diverse backgrounds and characteristics should be involved in creative processes, leading to innovative activities in relation to products, processes, organization, and markets. The board members may in this way contribute to, formulate and form the content and context of strategic decisions.

Board members are also *decision makers*, and the board members must understand the implications of the decisions they are to ratify. Boards will normally make decisions about issues that are important with respect to size and consequences for the firm. There are thus needs for board members that combine integrity, maturity, responsibility and risk-taking behavior on behalf of stakeholders, with both long-term and short-term perspectives.

The need for *evaluators* means that the firm must have board members with sufficient time, knowledge and independence to evaluate managerial performance. It may be difficult for outside board members, only having part-time involvement on the board and in the firm, to be sufficiently informed. However, routines should be developed that board-decisions and other external obligations are followed up, including ethical standards, accounting, and so forth. Board members should prioritize time to be informed about the main products and activities of the firm, major risks, the market situation of the firm, and organization culture among a host of other functions and factors. Board members should also have time and opportunity to meet regularly with the top management team.

Board output control tasks are important for value distribution. The board members will need to balance the stakes and interest of various internal and external actors. Often they have particular responsibilities to safeguard the interests of certain stakeholders or owners (e.g., various family branches in family firms, short-term versus long-term investors, managerial versus ownership perspectives, corporate social responsibility and employee issues). These tasks have implications for board members as *negotiators*.

This section of the chapter examined various requirements that are needed for outside board members to make contributions in the different phases in the value chain. Our focus has been that the lack of knowledge may be a major hindrance for the outside board members' ability to maximize the boards' full value-creating potential. The discussion now turns to board evaluation as a system that may make actual board task performance meet board role expectations.

Board Evaluations

It is often argued that it is necessary to have an evaluation of the accountability and knowledge of board members to maximize the boards' value creating potential (e.g., see Conger, Finegold, & Lawler, 1998). However, empirical studies have showed that board evaluations are far from common practice, and the process of evaluating the whole board is even scarcer than for that of evaluating individual board members (Gabrielsson & Winlund, 2000; O'Neal & Thomas, 1996). A board evaluation process can, in this respect, be helpful for defining how various board tasks contribute to value creation and to balance and meet the interest of the firm's various stakeholders.

Before starting a board evaluation process, three basic questions should be asked: Who does what, for whom, and how? A board evaluation system should thus consist of four elements (Minichilli, Gabrielsson, & Huse, 2007):

- The agents performing the evaluation (e.g., self-evaluation, consultants)
- The issues being evaluated (e.g., accountability, knowledge)
- The stakeholder behind the evaluation (e.g., internal stakeholders, external stakeholders, the board itself)
- The way the evaluation is performed (e.g., schemes, interviews, observations)

Together these four elements will help meet the purpose of an evaluation. The main elements of this board evaluation system are illustrated in Figure 7.2.

The stakeholders are presented on the horizontal axis, and the agents of the evaluation are presented on the vertical axis. Board-to-market evaluation has now become compulsory through various codes of best practices under the heading "comply or explain." To a large degree, it is a self-legitimizing approach. A main purpose for the market-to-market evaluation is transparency to meet accountability. Main objectives for market-to-board and board-to-board evaluations are to create accountability and effectiveness. This is done through the securing and development of the knowledge and skills of the board members. As it is the responsibility of the individual directors to use their

EVALUATOR

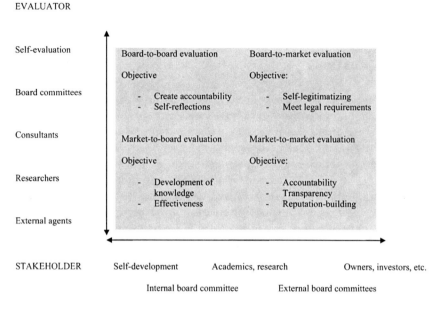

Source: Huse, Minichilli, and Schøning (2005).

Figure 7.2.   Board evaluation.

knowledge and skills to create accountability, this process may be promoted through a board-to-board evaluation. The design of board-to-board evaluation is often inspired by the will to assess the quality of board operations and to improve the decision making culture. Besides its potential, this evaluation system hides the risk of evaluation biases, and suffers of likely deficiencies of knowledge, tools and expertise for effective evaluations. With respect to this, a market-to-board evaluation will be of more help to evaluate the knowledge and skills of the board members than a board-to-board evaluation. Market-to-board evaluation is an external and market-driven system developed for internal purposes. It implies greater objectivity and more effective use of tools and techniques by external professionals, with the purpose to enhance board effectiveness and external accountability.

Figure 7.3 helps defining accountability and the creation of accountability (see Huse, 2005). Board role expectations are developed from various theories, including agency theory, stakeholder theory, resource dependence theory, and resource-based theory (Huse & Rindova, 2001). Different expectations may exist among various stakeholders, including various groups of shareholders. The board will need to balance these expectations. Board task performance is the role(s) the board in reality is performing. The challenge to creating board accountability is to align actual board task performance with board role expectations (Huse, 2005). Various interactions, knowledge and attributes of the board members, board structures and norms, and the board decision-making culture may hinder or secure this alignment. The board decision-making culture is a result of interactions, leadership style, and board structure and norms inside the boardroom (Huse et al., 2005). The interactions between external stakeholders, internal stakeholders, and the board members result in the definition of board role expectations. The leadership style the chairman adopts in the board meetings helps to improve board effectiveness and the use of knowledge and skills by board members. The board structures and norms allow that the board performs its tasks coherently with its role expectations, and contribute to develop an effective decision-making culture.

The creation of accountability thus includes selecting, motivating and developing board members and the decision-making culture through board leadership and structures. Figure 7.3 also helps us identify the main issues that should be included in evaluations of board accountability and knowledge. A major contribution of board evaluations is to structure the inner working of boards to align the knowledge and competency of the outside board members with the various parts of the value chain.

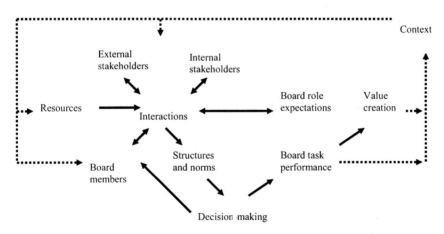

Source: Huse (2005).

Figure 7.3.   The content of board evaluation: Accountability and the inner working of boards

CONCLUSIONS

The objective of the chapter was to show how outside directors may contribute to value creation. Through a value chain analysis, the analysis focused on their potential contribution through various board tasks. We have shown how outside directors through responsible use of their knowledge and skills may help align board role expectations and actual board task performance, thus creating accountability.

The chapter contributes to our understanding of these dynamics in a number of ways. First, it approaches various board tasks from a value chain perspective. This is a novel approach as board tasks most often have been studied from contingency or stakeholder perspectives. The chapter illustrates how outside directors, at the same time, may have various tasks. This perspective gives direction with respect to the selection of board members and the structuring of the inner working of board. Second, it has a focus on how outside directors may contribute to value creation and not only to value distribution. We show how outside board members contribute through resource provision, advice and knowledge, mentorship, decision making, evaluation and control, and negotiation and distribution.

Boards and outside board members are accountable to the firm as well as to internal and external stakeholders in creating values throughout the whole value chain. This implies that consultants acting as board members or as consultants for boards need detailed and specific analyses of how boards can collectively contribute to value creation. Our analysis suggests that boards should be composed of persons who have knowledge and competency to create values in the different parts of the value chain. Board members should complement one another and secure the provision of expert knowledge and strategic information about firm operations and the industry, rather than serving only certain groups of stakeholders. This includes balancing board tasks from firm internal and external perspectives, among them various consultancy and advisory tasks, in order to enhance boards' value creating potential.

The requirements for board member knowledge and skills, however, are complex, and there are various hindrances that can make it difficult for outsiders to make contributions. Outsiders face a number of dilemmas with respect to knowledge and accountability, including balancing of independence and information, distance and closeness, and control and service. In a knowledge-based society, outside directors cannot limit their responsibility to just that of being consultants to the CEO. Board members have an individual legal and social responsibility to create value for the firm and at the same time balance the interests of shareholders as well as those of a broader set of stakeholders.

REFERENCES

Aguilera, R. V., & Jackson, G. (2003). The cross-national diversity of corporate governance: Dimensions and determinants, *Academy of Management Review, 28*(3), 447–465.

Barney, J. (1991). Firm resources and sustained competitive advantage, *Journal of Management, 17*(1), 99–120.

Baysinger, B. D., & Hoskisson R. E. (1990). The composition of boards of directors and strategic control: Effects on corporate strategy, *Academy of Management Review, 15*(1), 72–80.

Blair, M. M., & Stout, L. A. (2001). Corporate accountability: director accountability and the mediating role of the corporate board. *Washington University Law Review, 79*(2), 403–447.

Castaldi, R., & Wortman, M. (1984). Boards of directors in small corporations: An untapped resource. *American Journal of Small Business, 9*(2), 1–10.

Conger, J. A., Finegold, D., & Lawler, E. E. (1998). Appraising boardroom performance, *Harvard Business Review, 76*(1), 136–148.

Daily, C. M., Johnson, J. L., & Dalton, D. R. (1999). On the measurement of board composition: Poor consistency and a serious mismatch of theory and operationalizations. *Decision Sciences, 20*(1), 83–106.

Davis, J., Schoorman, F. D., & Donaldson, L. (1997). Towards a stewardship theory of management, *Academy of Management Review, 22*(1), 20–48.

Demb, A., & Neubauer, F. F. (1992). *The Corporate Board*. Oxford, England: Oxford University Press.

Eisenhardt, K. M. (1989). Agency theory: An assessment and review, *Academy of Management Review, 14*(1), 57–74.

Fama, E. F., & Jensen, M. C. (1983). Separation of ownership and control, *Journal of Law and Economics, 26*(3), 301–325.

Forbes, D. P. & Milliken, F. J. (1999). Cognition and corporate governance: Understanding boards of directors as strategic decision making groups, *Academy of Management Review, 24*(3), 489–505.

Gabrielsson, J., & Huse, M. (2005). "Outside" directors in SME boards: A call for theoretical reflections, *Corporate board: Roles, duties & composition, 1*(1), 28–37.

Gabrielsson, J., & Winlund, H. (2000). Boards of directors in small and medium sized industrial firms: Examining the effects of the boards working style on board task performance. *Entrepreneurship and Regional Development, 12*(4), 311–330.

Hillman, A., Cannella, A. A., Jr., & Paetzold, R. (2000) The resource dependence role of corporate directors: Strategic adaptation of board composition in response to environmental change. *Journal of Management Studies, 37*(2), 235–256.

Hill, C. W., & Jones, T. M. (1992). Stakeholder-agency theory. *Journal of Management Studies, 29*(2), 132–154.

Huse, M. (1990). Board composition in small enterprises. *Entrepreneurship & Regional Development, 2*(4), 363–373.

Huse, M. (1993). Relational norms as supplement to neo-classical understanding of directorates: An empirical study of boards of directors. *Journal of Socio-Economics*, 22(3), 219–240.

Huse, M. (1998). Researching the dynamics of board-stakeholder relations, *Long Range Planning*, 31(2), 218–226.

Huse, M. (2000). Boards in SMEs: a review and research agenda. *Entrepreneurship and Regional Development*, 12(4), 271–290.

Huse, M. (2005). Accountability and creating accountability: A framework for exploring behavioral perspectives of corporate governance. *British Journal of Management*, 16(1), 65–79.

Huse, M. (2007). *Boards, governance and value creation: The human side of corporate governance*. Cambridge, England: Cambridge University Press.

Huse, M., Minichilli, A., & Schøning, M. (2005). Corporate boards as assets for operating in the new Europe: The value of process-oriented boardroom dynamics. *Organizational Dynamics*, 34(3), 285–297.

Huse, M., & Rindova, V. (2001). Stakeholders´ expectation to boards of directors: the case of subsidiary boards. *Journal of Management and Governance*, 5(2), 153–178.

Jensen, M. C., & Meckling, W. H. (1976). Theory of the firm: Managerial behavior, agency costs and ownership structure. *Journal of Financial Economics*, 2(4), 305–360.

Johannisson, B., & Huse, M. (2000). Recruiting outside board members in the small family business: an ideological challenge. *Entrepreneurship & Regional Development*, 12(4), 353–378.

Kosnik, R. D. (1987). Greenmail: A study of board performance in corporate governance. *Administrative Science Quarterly*, 32(1), 163–185.

Lorsch, J. W., & McIver, E. (1989). *Pawns or potentates: The reality of America's corporate board*. Boston: Harvard Business School Press.

Lynall, M. D., Golden, B. R., & Hillman, A. J. (2003). Board composition from adolescence to maturity: A multi-theoretical view. *Academy of Management Review*, 28(3), 416–431.

Mace, M. L. (1971). *Directors: Myth and reality*. Boston: Harvard University.

McNulty, T., & Pettigrew, A. (1999). Strategists on the board. *Organization Studies*, 20(1), 40–74.

Minichilli, A., Gabrielsson, J., & Huse, M. (2007). Board evaluations: Making a fit between the purpose and the system. *Corporate Governance: An International Review*, 15(4), 609–622.

Mintzberg, H. (1983). *Power in and around organizations*. Englewood Cliffs, NJ: Prentice Hall.

Monks, R. A. G., & Minow, N. (2004). *Corporate governance*. Oxford, England: Blackwell.

Ocasio, W. (1999). Institutionalized action and corporate governance: The reliance on rules of CEO succession. *Administrative Science Quarterly*, 44(2), 384–416.

O'Neal, D., & Thomas, H. (1996). Developing the strategic board. *Long Range Planning*, 29(3), 314–327.

Pfeffer, J., & Salancik, G. R. (1978). *The external control of organizations: A resource dependence perspective*. New York: Harper & Row.

Shen, W. (2003). The dynamics of the CEO-board relationships: An evolutionary perspective. *Academy of Management Review, 28*(3), 466–476.

Taylor, B. (2001). From corporate governance to corporate entrepreneurship. *Journal of Change Management, 2*(2), 128–147.

Westphal, J. D. (1998). Board games: How CEOs adapt to increases in structural board independence from management. *Administrative Science Quarterly, 43*(1), 511–537.

Westphal, J. D., & Khanna, P. (2003). Keeping directors in line: Social distancing as a control mechanism in the corporate elite. *Administrative Science Quarterly, 48*(3), 361–398.

Westphal, J. D., & Zajac, E. J. (1994). Substance and symbolism in CEOs long-term incentive plans. *Administrative Science Quarterly, 39*(3), 367–390.

Zahra, S. A., Neubaum, D. O., & Huse, M. (2000). Entrepreneurship in medium-sized firms: Exploring the effects of ownership and governance systems. *Journal of Management, 26*(5), 947–976.

CHAPTER 8

THE QUESTION OF MOTIVATION OF NONEXECUTIVE DIRECTORS

Pierre-Yves Gomez and David Russell

On January 5, 2005, 10 former nonexecutive directors (NEDs) of Worldcom agreed to pay damages to plaintiffs out of their personal funds to settle a class action lawsuit that had been brought against members of the Worldcom board. The lawsuit was a follow-up to the debacle that had seen the collapse of the company and the loss of hundreds of millions of dollars to Worldcom shareholders. This move sent a shock wave through corporate boards as directors wondered whether they, too, could be held personally liable for mistakes and lack of vigilance, which took place during their watch. Both the corporate and academic communities reacted with apprehension to this surprising development, fearing the effects it would have on potential directors' desire to serve on corporate boards. At a time when calls for increased NED representation on boards are being heeded in the United States and throughout the world, this development runs the risk of making well qualified NEDs harder to find and increasingly reluctant to serve on corporate boards. The paradox is that NEDs have been seen as those actors in corporate governance most likely to

Board Members and Management Consultants: Redefining the Boundaries of Consulting and Corporate Governance, pp. 155–170
Copyright © 2009 by Information Age Publishing
155

represent the interests of diverse shareholders, and most able to hold management accountable for its actions (Gomez & Korine, 2005).

In light of today's fear that the increasing responsibilities and risks associated with being a NED will dissuade experienced and qualified individuals from serving as directors, the time has come to address an issue which has curiously remained unaddressed in corporate governance research—the motivation to serve as a NED. Daily and Dalton (2003) have stated that today, service as a corporate officer or director is more daunting a task than at any other time in business history. Much recent research in the area of corporate governance has focused on the rationale behind and the impact of the appointment of increasing numbers of NEDs to corporate boards. From the standpoint of the major theories that have informed corporate governance practice over the past decades, the anticipated benefits accruing to the firm from increased NED presence on corporate boards have been well spelled out. And yet scholars, the corporate community, and the business press are sounding an alarm over the possibility that well qualified individuals will be increasingly unlikely to seek service as a NED on a corporate board.

The chapter focuses on the motivation of the NED. Using theories of corporate governance, the discussion probes the essential question of what motivates an individual to become a NED, moving toward an integrative model of motivation. By better understanding what motivates a person to serve as a NED, we may be better able to confront the crisis of the dearth of individuals willing to serve in this important capacity.

THE PARADOX OF THE NED

The corporate governance literature is not lacking in research concerning NEDs. Most of this research, however, has dealt primarily with board structure. McNulty and Pettigrew (1996), identified the roles of directors in terms of three main perspectives: a governance perspective, concerned with the monitoring function of the board; a strategic perspective, concerning decisions enabling the firm to change; and the resource perspective, which is concerned with how the board links the firm to its external environment and enables it to acquire critical resources. NEDs are seen as playing important roles in each of these areas, and the board literature from each of these perspectives provides arguments for the increased presence of NEDs on boards (for the strategy perspective, see (Pass, 2004; for the governance perspective, see Baysinger & Butler, 1985; Daily & Dalton, 1994; and Waldo, 1985; for the resource perspective, see Boussouara & Deakins, 2000; and Hambrick & D'Aveni, 1992).

The emphasis on board structure in the research led to numerous studies of the impact of NEDs on firm performance (Finkelstein & Hambrick, 1990; Zahra & Pearce, 1989). Some studies found that higher numbers of NEDs on boards were associated with higher profitability (Ezzamel & Watson, 1993; Pearce & Zahra, 1992; Rosenstein & Wyatt, 1990) or with higher return on equity (Baysinger & Butler, 1985). One study (Brickley, Coles, & Terry, 1994) determined that, during takeover attempts, shareholders reacted more positively when more nonexecutive directors NEDs sat on a board. Yet, despite the findings of these studies, other empirical studies demonstrated that no clear link could be established between the number of NEDs present on a board and firm performance (Daily & Dalton, 1992; Wagner Stimpert, & Fubara, 1998; Wood & Patrick, 2003; Zahra & Stanton, 1988). Some studies even found a negative relationship between the number of NEDs on a board and firm performance (Bhagat & Black, 1999; Yermack, 1986).

Results of meta-analyses have not provided a conclusive answer, either. A meta-analysis carried out in 1998 of 54 studies of the relationship between board composition and firm financial performance could not find any link (Dalton, Daily, Ellstrand, & Johnson, 1998). A meta-analysis carried out in 2000 of 59 studies of this relationship (Rhoades, Rechner, & Sundaramurthy, 2000) could find only a very small link between board composition and firm performance. Thus, after considerable research studying the effects of NEDs on firm performance, the results were summed up by James Westphal (2002, p. 6) when he stated that nearly 2 decades of research found little evidence that board independence enhances board effectiveness.

The lack of conclusive evidence linking board structure to firm performance turned researchers' attention back to the black box of board processes, emphasizing the element of firm context in determining the role and value of the NED (Huse, 2005; Weir & Laing, 2001). This focus has enriched our theoretical insights into the major issues and problems of corporate governance (Hoskisson, Hitt, Wan, & Yiu, 1999). The perspective of board process and firm context in reference to NEDs has seen researchers concentrate on such issues as director competences and skills. A consensus has grown among researchers that NEDs must bring a variety of skills to their appointments, and NEDs must be sensitive to firm context (Kakabadse, Ward, Korac-Kakabadse, & Bowman, 2001; Tosi & Gomez-Mejia, 1994). In terms of the strategy and resource perspective, NEDs are seen as being able to link their firms to informal networks, provide contacts in new markets, and improve the credibility of the firm in new markets (Hambrick & D'Aveni, 1992). In an even broader context, NEDs have been called upon to provide guidance with regard to growth strategies, general problem solving, strategic planning, recruitment and staff development, and marketing (Boussouara & Deakins, 2000).

Research on the impact of NEDs as well as the competences and skills that are required of them has served to underline the potential benefits to a firm of increased NED representation on the board. The limitation of this work, however, is that each of these perspectives views the NED only from the point of view of the firm. Surprisingly little research has directly addressed what should be one of the most important issues concerning the NED—his or her motivation to become one. Some researchers have put forward rationales which may induce an individual to serve as a NED, including an increase in the individual's prestige, expansion of personal networks of influential contacts, and exposure to a wide range of business situations (Mizruchi, 1996). The downsides of service as a NED, however, are also apparent: service as a NED increasingly requires a significant personal commitment for comparatively little remuneration. Furthermore, the potential liabilities of service as a NED are increasing, to such an extent that one may wonder why anyone would become a NED (Hambrick & Jackson, 2000).

What corporate governance research is lacking is the incorporation of NED motivation into the corporate governance theoretical framework. We believe that research concerning boards, whether examining board structure or board process, is incomplete unless it also considers the motivation of the NED to accept this responsibility. As stated above, our purpose is to show how corporate governance theories can integrate this important issue of director motivation. We now turn our attention to the major theories of corporate governance in an effort to accomplish this task.

GOVERNANCE THEORY AND THE MOTIVATION OF THE NED

There are several theoretical frameworks that are useful to probe the question of NED motivation. This section draws on agency theory, the resource-based view of the firm, stewardship theory, social cognitive theory, and a commitment to corporate social responsibility to move toward an integrative motivational model for NEDs.

NEDs and the Alignment of Interests: Agency Theory in Question

The foundation of agency theory, which has been one of the dominant theories of corporate governance since the last quarter of the twentieth century, is Berle and Means' (1932) observations about the separation of ownership and control in the modern corporation. Agency theory sees the firm as a nexus of contracts (Fama, 1980). Therefore, the unit of analysis of the firm under agency theory is the contract. According to agency theory, the separation of ownership and control, which is one of the hallmarks of the modern corporation, will lead in many instances to firm managers using their firm-specific knowledge and managerial expertise to gain an advantage over the firm's owners, who are absent from the day-to-day affairs of the firm. Since the managers are in control of the firm, the risk is that they will pursue actions in their own self interest rather than in the interest of the owners (Jensen & Meckling, 1976).

Agency theory recognizes specific roles for the main actors in corporate governance, stipulating that it is up to top management to make strategic decisions, and that shareholders have the power to hold management accountable according to firm results obtained (Fama & Jensen 1983). It could be said that agency theory became the main theory of corporate governance in the 1980s, and that it defined corporate governance in terms of balancing the interests of the firm's principals—the shareholders—with the responsibilities and expertise of the firm's top managers.

Agency theory's validity and coherence depend upon the existence of mechanisms by which firm owners are able to monitor the performance of managers to verify that firm managers are using their own competences, and the firm's resources, to achieve the best returns for the principals (Fama, 1980). This perspective identifies the board of directors as the primary internal control mechanism that enables the firm's principals to monitor management behavior. According to the theory, one of the main tasks of the board is to specifically carry out the monitoring function on behalf of the firm's owners, acting to remove managers who misuse firm assets and participating in the formulation of strategic decisions, which have a considerable impact on shareholder investments (Fleischer, Hazard, & Klipper, 1988; Waldo, 1985). It is for this reason that advocates of corporate governance reform have long emphasized the independence of board members as being critical to their ability to carry out the monitoring function. Thus, according to agency theory (Baysinger & Butler, 1985; Waldo, 1985), increasing the number of NEDs on a board will increase the board's independence.

Agency theory identifies the actors in the governance of the firm as principals or agents, and holds the view that the essential problem of corporate governance is the alignment of interests between the principals and agents. According to the theory, the owners (or shareholders) are the principals, and the firm managers are their agents. But where does this leave the board of directors as the primary control mechanism? We believe that under agency theory, the board of directors in general, and

NEDs in particular, are a weak link in the corporate governance framework. Board members may also be considered part of the nexus of contracts, which go to make up the firm, and if their primary function is one of monitoring management, then board members, particularly NEDs, are also acting as agents of the firm owners. If this is so, then one must also consider the alignment of interests between the principals (firm owners), and their agents (NEDs). This brings us back to our basic question: what is the interest of an individual to serve as a NED?

While agency theory does an adequate job of describing the alignment of interests between firm owners and managers (Baysinger & Hoskisson, 1989; Gomez-Meija, 1994; Hoskisson & Turk, 1990; Zahra & Pearce, 1989), almost no research has been done to describe the alignment of interests between firm owners and NEDs. Very few studies in the agency theory framework indicate the interest in serving as a NED *from the NED's point of view*. A small number of studies has dealt with the issue of aligning the interests of NEDs with those of the firm owners, but these have largely seen increased shareholding on the part of NEDs as a solution to the problem of the alignment of interests (Hambrick & Jackson, 2000; Pass, 2004). While this addresses the issue from a mechanistic point of view, it presupposes that the NED has already agreed to serve and thus does not address the issue of an individual's motivation to serve as a NED in the first place.

While we consider the lack of research into the motivation of an individual to serve as a NED a flaw in the agency theory framework, we do recognize the difficulty inherent in researching "unobservables" (Godfrey & Hill, 1995). It has already been observed that carrying out research into human motives is fraught with difficulties (Hoskisson & Hitt, 1990). Nevertheless we believe that researchers should endeavor to enhance the agency theory perspective with insights from other research perspectives to arrive at an integrated model of motivation in the area of corporate governance.

Directors or Consultants? The Resource-Based View

Recent research in the area of corporate governance has followed a more general trend in the area of strategic management to consider more closely the black box of the firm, and to see the firm as a bundle of unique resources, which when used effectively can provide the firm with its competitive advantage (Barney, 1991; Grant, 1996). This has come to be known as the Resource-Based View of the Firm (RBV). Some corporate governance researchers have taken a view that it is an error to overemphasize the monitoring role of boards, and that more emphasis should be paid to the skills and other knowledge resources that directors, and particularly NEDs, can bring to the firm (Short, Keasy, Wright, & Hull, 1999). This perspective has coincided with other efforts in corporate governance research to increase the focus on firm context and board processes (Huse, 2005). With this increasing emphasis on issues of firm context and boardroom processes, and with certain weaknesses increasingly apparent in the agency theory view of the role of the NED, the RBV has provided supplementary rationales to support the widespread calls for increased NED presence on corporate boards. In contrast to agency theory, with its emphasis on managing conflicting goals between managers and shareholders within the firm, the resource based view underlines the role that the NED can play in bringing unique resources to the firm. According to this theory, it is the task of management to gather and deploy the unique assets of the firm so as to achieve competitive advantage (Wernerfelt, 1984).

Questions, of course, can be raised about RBV theory and the perceived role and expectations attached to the NED. Firms can learn in two ways: (1) through the knowledge of its existing members, and (2) by integrating new members who possess knowledge that the firm did not previously have. By recruiting NEDs, firms use a particularly efficient method of integrating knowledge. Researchers in the RBV perspective, when identifying the skills, which are the most important availing firms of a competitive advantage, cite functionally-based distinctive competencies (Hitt & Ireland, 1986), and a unique combination of business experience (Spender, 1989). Specifically, firms are increasingly seeking to recruit NEDs who will be able to provide them with knowledge assets, often coming from outside the firm itself. NEDs are also members of social networks, with access to critical knowledge, which can also be put to the service of the firm (Huse, 1998). Closely related to this is the belief that the presence of NEDs facilitates the development of relationships within an organization, and that this in turn fosters improved communication and the development of knowledge (Lewicki & Bunker, 1996).

While agency theory sees the role of the NED primarily in terms of monitoring, the current view of the NED is that he or she must bring a wide variety of competences to the firm, which can contribute to the performance of the company, including financial and marketing skills, business sector knowledge, links to the financial sector, experience leading change, and the ability to be a mentor (Kakabadse et al., 2001). In terms of the strategy and resource perspective, NEDs are seen as being able to link their firms to informal networks, provide contacts in new markets, and improve the credibility of the firm in new markets (Hambrick & D'Aveni, 1992). In an even broader context, NEDs have been called upon to provide guidance with regard to growth strategies, general problem solving, strategic planning, recruitment and staff development, and even marketing (Boussouara & Deakins, 2000).

While the RBV has provided important new insights with regard to corporate governance and the role of NEDs, we encounter the same situation concerning director motivation in the RBV framework as was encountered under the agency theory view. The theory has much to say with regard to the firm's motivation for seeking out a highly qualified individual who is able to provide the firm with unique knowledge assets in his or her capacity as a NED, but is silent with regard to the NED's motivation. In fact, it could be said that here we encounter a paradox, which is at the heart of NED service on behalf of a firm. Why would a NED who possesses a specific asset, his or her expertise, agree to share this expertise for a relatively insignificant remuneration? What motivates such an individual to serve as a NED rather than as a well-paid consultant?

In line with our observations concerning the fact that agency theory provides little guidance concerning the motivation for an individual to monitor a firm and its managers of which he or she is by definition independent, the RBV likewise provides little insight into the motivation of an individual to provide a firm with the benefits of his or her skills, competencies, and experience as a NED, when this position is often poorly remunerated, and is increasingly exposing him or her to damaging liability claims.

As with agency theory, we recognize that the RBV is also subject to methodological weaknesses. Like motivation, corporate culture, tacit knowledge, and capabilities, intangible firm resources have proven very difficult to measure (Barney, 1986; Hitt, Gimeno, & Hoskisson, 1998; Kogut & Zander, 1992). In fact, the inability to measure the impact of these elements is seen as an overall weakness of the RBV (Robins & Wiersema, 1995).

We believe, however, that it is important for researchers to gain insights into the motivation of these individuals, who are seen as indispensable actors in corporate governance, for the very reasons cited in both the agency theory and RBV literature, moving toward an integrative model of motivation for the NED.

Toward an Integrative Model of Motivation

The agency theory and RBV frameworks, which have been employed comprehensively to explain a firm's motivation for employing a NED, do not directly address the question of the motivation for an individual to become a NED. The literature dealing with NEDs has offered suggestions which seek to explain what may motivate an individual to serve as a NED, including prestige, expansion of personal contacts, and exposure to different business structures and experiences (Hambrick & Jackson, 2000), but the foundations of these viewpoints are not empirical. There is a corporate governance literature which seeks, empirically, to explain how individuals could be motivated to serve as NEDs, and the conclusion usually takes the form of a suggestion to align the interest of the NEDs with the interests of the owners by increasing the ownership stake of the NEDs themselves (Hambrick & Jackson, 2000; Pass, 2004). This emphasis on the alignment of interests is firmly embedded in the agency theory framework, yet it is usually framed in terms of motivating NEDs after they have agreed to serve, and thus does not directly address the question of what might motivate a NED to serve in the first place.

Thus while agency theory sees the NED's value primarily in the role as a monitor of the firm's management, it does not explain the paradox of why a person with few, if any, significant ties to the firm would agree to monitor the management of that firm. While the resource perspective of board research, in conjunction with the wider RBV of the firm, sees the NED as a valuable source of skills and experience which could contribute to the competitive advantage of the firm, it does not venture to explain why a highly qualified individual would be willing to share his or her valuable skills and experience with a firm that he or she, admittedly, does not have close ties with, and for which the remuneration is often quite low.

We believe that it is important to integrate the question of motivation into board research in light of the perceived crisis in the recruitment of NEDs as a result of the increased responsibilities associated with the job, as well as the potential for increased liabilities following corporate scandals which have affected NEDs' personal assets. We believe that an integrative model of non-executive director motivation must build upon both agency theory and the RBV of the firm, yet expand the boundaries of research to include other perspectives. Here we provide a number of promising theoretical perspectives and hypotheses which may be useful in constructing a model of NED motivation.

One of the most interesting theoretical developments, which could have an impact on the exploration of NED motivation, is stewardship theory. *Stewardship theory* has emerged as an addition to agency theory in the literature, which seeks to explain management behavior (Davis, Schoorman, & Donaldson, 1997). We believe that it could also shed light on director motivations. Stewardship theory takes exception to agency theory's depiction of individuals as individualistic, opportunistic, and self-serving, requiring a proactive alignment of interests at best, and monitoring, at worst. As NEDs can be considered agents of the owners much like managers can, stewardship theory's observations concerning managers might be able to be applied to directors as well. Stewardship theory suggests that, contrary to agency theory's viewpoint, people may be motivated less by individual goals than is commonly believed. According to this framework, individuals serving as directors would be more inclined to embrace and seek to attain the goals of the organization, rather than their own personal goals. Stewardship theory is operationalized by combining the psychological attributes of the director with firm context (Davis et al., 1997). It is important to note, however, that while stewardship theory is seen as a promising avenue of research into manager and director motivations, it is a relatively new theory and needs to be validated by further research (Davis et al., 1997).

Based on the insights of stewardship theory, we propose the following hypothesis concerning motivation for service as a NED:

> **H1**: An individual serving as a NED will be at least as motivated to serve the organization as to serve his or her own interests.

Theories concerning motivation have moved beyond a biological focus to a focus on social cognition (Pincus, 2004) and recent research into human motivation has focused on social cognitive theories. Social cognitions are cognitive processes and structures through which individuals regulate their motivation (Cervone, 1991). While most of the literature dealing with social cognitions has dealt with subordinates (Phillips, 1995), a growing body of research is addressing the social cognitions of leaders (Chemers, 2002). The social cognitions theory framework endeavors to explain a wide range of human behaviors, including motivation (Bandura, 1997). This theoretical framework depicts the motivation of leaders as being the result of a dynamic process through which the leader's social cognition, the firm context, and his or her behavior interact (McCormick & Martinko, 2004).

The basis of social cognitive theories of motivation is that all humans have needs for effective interactions with the environment (White, 1959). Built upon this fundamental need are other needs, including the need for achievement (McClelland, 1961), the need for cognition (Cohen, Stotland, Wolfe, 1955), the need to fit in, and the need for power (Atkinson, 1958). Each of these needs in the SCT framework could shed light on the motivations of individuals to serve as NEDs. Indeed, they have been hinted at in the indications of researchers of boards of directors that NEDs are motivated by the prestige associated with their positions. Such motivations on the part of NEDs could help to explain the paradoxes that, as we have pointed out, are associated with service as a NED.

The SCT of human motivation leads us to propose the following hypotheses with regard to NEDs:

H2a: Individuals serving as NEDs will be motivated by a need for achievement.

H2b: Individuals serving as NEDs will be motivated by a need for cognition (i.e., a need to exercise their faculties of thought and knowledge).

H2c: Individuals serving as NEDs will be motivated by a need to fit in.

H2d: Individuals serving as NEDs will be motivated by a need for power.

One further area of study which could lead to insights regarding NED motivation concerns corporate social responsibility. Corporate social responsibility is an increasingly important area of research in its own right, and some studies in the area of corporate social responsibility have indicated that this field could provide insight into the motivations of NEDs. One study looked specifically at the level of corporate social responsibility of executive versus NEDS, and found that the NEDs had a significantly higher level of CSR than their executive counterparts (O'Neill, Saunders, & McCarthy, 1989). Some research has concluded that NEDs are often motivated by what they perceive to be their responsibility toward the firms, which they serve, as well as society at large (Frederick, 1983; Ibrahim & Angelidis, 1995). In light of these results, we may conclude that attitudes toward social responsibility may be an influential factor in the motivation of an individual to serve as a NED.

Thus, the corporate social responsibility perspective of human motivation leads us to propose the following hypotheses:

H3: Individuals serving as NEDs will be motivated by a sense of responsibility toward the firm and toward society as a whole.

CONCLUSION

The chapter has attempted to shed light on one of the dilemmas facing boards of directors today—how to ensure that well qualified and experienced individuals will be motivated to serve as NEDs on corporate boards. The academic community and business practitioners have grown increasingly concerned that the responsibilities and potential liabilities of

NED service will diminish the pool of those willing to be NEDs, and that this will have a negative impact on corporate performance.

In our view, these concerns have highlighted the fact that theories dealing with corporate governance research, namely agency theory and the RBV of the firm, are incomplete when studying NEDs. Corporate governance research has emphasized the rationale for and the impact of NEDs on corporate boards, as well as the competences required of NEDs. What these theories have not adequately considered is the motivation of individuals to be NEDs. Therefore, knowledge concerning NED motivation is a weak link in the corporate governance research, which needs to be remedied.

A better understanding of motivation will enable firms to identify and encourage those individuals who are most likely to contribute their skills and experience to firms through corporate boards. In order to expand existing knowledge concerning the motivations of NEDs, three areas of research could enrich understanding about the motivation of NEDs:

- *Stewardship Theory*, which takes exception to the agency theory perspective and suggests that individuals are more motivated by collective goals for the good of the organization than has commonly been assumed;
- *Social Cognitive Theory*, which considers motivation as a function of common human needs, which can be identified, such as the need for achievement, the need to fit in, and the need for power; and
- *Corporate social responsibility*, which suggests that NEDs may be motivated by their feelings of social responsibility.

The fact that the motivations of NEDs go beyond a purely functional role of control, opens new perspectives for consultants. Indeed, the increasing complexity of the control of management requires that those who seek to become NEDs possess a large set of competencies which are difficult to find in one person. With regard to consultants, it is possible that they assume the role of advisors to NEDs, and in doing so, they can allow the NEDs to assume responsibility even if do not have all the required competencies. Nevertheless, it is important for consultants to understand those factors that motivate directors to serve, and to adapt their own service and perspective to this reality. If the three areas—stewardship theory, social cognitive theory, corporate social responsibility are embraced, a number of ramifications ensue:

- from a stewardship theory perspective, consultants will need to be aware and attentive to the moral and ethical principles of the directors, and to how they define and interpret their unique function;

- from an social cognitive theory perspective, they will need to be more attentive to the directors' desire for a sense of personal achievement; and
- from the corporate social responsibility perspective they will work together with the NED to identify what they consider to be the social responsibility of the firm. In essence, the function of the consultant of an NED would not only be to provide advice and competence, but also to help the NED to define and clarify precisely what it means to be a director. This "human touch," or the personalization of the relationship between a consultant and the NED, is one of the most important dimensions of the emerging market for board consulting.

REFERENCES

Atkinson, J. W. (1958). *Motives in fantasy, action and society.* Princeton, NJ: Van Nostrand.

Bandura, A. (1997). *Self-efficacy: The exercise of control.* New York: Freeman.

Barney, J. B. (1986). Organizational culture: Can it be a source of sustained competitive advantage? *Academy of Management Review, 11*(3), 656–665.

Barney, J. B. (1991) Firm resources and sustained competitive advantage. *Journal of Management, 17*(1), 99–120.

Baysinger, B. D., & Butler, H. (1985). Corporate governance and the board of directors: Performance effects of changes in board composition. *Journal of Law, Economics, and Organization, 28*(1), 101–134.

Baysinger, B. D., & Hoskisson, R. E. (1989) Diversification strategy and R&D intensity in multiproduct firms. *Academy of Management Journal, 32*(2), 310–332.

Berle, A. A., & Means, G. (1932). *The modern corporation and private property.* New York: MacMillan.

Bhagat, S., & Black, B. (1999). *The uncertain relationship between board composition and firm performance. The Business Lawyer, 54*(3), 921–963.

Boussouara, M., & Deakins, D. (2000). Trust and acquisition of knowledge from non-executive directors by high technology entrepreneurs. *International Journal of Entrepreneurial Behaviour and Research, 6*(4), 204–226.

Brickley, J. A., Coles, J. L., & Terry, R.L. (1994). Outside directors and the adoption of poison pills. *Journal of Financial Economics, 35*(3), 371–390.

Cervone, D. (1991). The two disciplines of personality psychology. *Psychological Science, 2*, 371–377.

Chemers, M. M. (2002). Efficacy and effectiveness: Interpreting models of leadership and intelligence. In R. Riggio, S. Murphy, & F. J. Pirozzolo (Eds.), *Multiple intelligences and leadership* (pp. 139–160). Mahwah, NJ: Erlbaum.

Cohen, A., E. Stotland, E., & Wolfe, D. (1955). An experimental investigation of need for cognition. *Journal of Abnormal and Social Psychology, 51*(2), 291–294.

Daily, C. M., & Dalton, D. R. (1992). The relationship between governance structure and corporate performance in entrepreneurial firms. *Journal of Business Venturing, 7*(5), 375–386.

Daily, C. M., & Dalton, D. R. (1994). Outside directors revisited: Prescriptions for CEOs and directors. *Journal of Small Business Strategy, 5*, 57–68.

Daily, C. M., & Dalton, D. R. (2003). Dollars and sense: The path to board independence. *Journal of Business Strategy, 24*(3), 41–43.

Dalton, D. R., Daily, C. M., Ellstrand, A. I., & Johnson, J. L. (1998). Meta-analytic reviews of board composition, leadership structure, and firm performance. *Strategic Management Journal, 19*(3), 269–290.

Davis, J. H., Schoorman, F. D., & Donaldson, L. (1997). Toward A stewardship theory of management. *Academy of Management Review, 22*(1), 20–48.

Ezzamel, M. A., & Watson, R. (1993). Organizational form, ownership structure, and corporate performance: A contextual analysis of U.K. companies. *British Journal of Management, 4*(3), 161–176.

Fama, E. F. (1980). Agency problems and the theory of the firm. *Journal of Political Economy, 88*(2), 288–307.

Fama, E. F., & Jensen, M. C. (1983). Separation of ownership and control. *Journal of Law and Economics, 26*(2), 301–324.

Finkelstein, S., & Hambrick, D. C. (1990). Top management team tenure and organizational outcomes: The moderating role of managerial discretion. *Administrative Science Quarterly, 35*(3), 484–503.

Fleischer, A., Hazard, G. C., & Klipper, M. Z. (1988). *Board games: The changing shape of corporate power.* Boston: Little, Brown.

Frederick, W. (1983). Corporate social responsibility in the Reagan era and beyond. *California Management Review, 25*(3), 145–156.

Godfrey, P. C., & Hill, C. W. L. (1995). The problem of unobservables in strategic management research. *Strategic Management Journal, 16*(7), 519–533.

Gomez, P. -Y. (2004). Power of top management vs. the role of the board: History of theories. *International Studies of Management and Organizations, 34*(2), 37–62.

Gomez, P. -Y., & Korine, H. (2005) Democracy and the evolution of corporate governance. *Corporate Governance: An International Review, 13*(6), 739–752.

Gomez-Mejia, L. R. (1994). Executive compensation: A reassessment and a future research agenda. *Research in Personnel and Human Resources Management, 12*, 161–222.

Grant, R. M. (1996). Toward a knowledge based theory of the firm. *Strategic Management Journal, 17*, 109–122.

Hambrick, D. C., & D'Aveni, R. A. (1992). Top management team deterioration as part of the downward spiral of large corporate bankruptcies. *Strategic Management Journal, 15*, 241–250.

Hambrick, D. C., & Jackson, E. M. (2000). Outside directors with a stake: The linchpin in corporate governance. *California Management Review, 42*(4), 108–127.

Hitt, M. A., Gimeno, A. J., & Hoskisson, R. E. (1998). Current and future research methods in strategic management. *Organizational Research Methods, 1*(1), 6–44.

Hitt, M. A., & Ireland, R. D. (1986). Relationships among corporate level distinctive competencies, diversification strategy, corporate structure and performance. *Journal of Management Studies*, *23*(4), 401–416.

Hoskisson, R. E., & Hitt, M. A. (1990). Antecedents and performance outcomes of diversification: A review and critique of theoretical perspectives. *Journal of Management*, *16*(2), 461–509.

Hoskisson, R. E., Hitt, M. A., Wan, W. P., & Yiu, D. (1999). Theory and research in strategic management: Swings of a pendulum. *Journal of Management*, *25*(3), 417–466.

Hoskisson, R. E., & Turk, T. A. (1990). Corporate restructuring: Governance and control limits of the internal capital market. *Academy of Management Review*, *15*(3), 459–477.

Huse, M. (2005). Accountability and creating accountability: A framework for exploring behavioral perspectives of corporate governance. *British Journal of Management*, *16*(s1), s65–s79.

Huse, M. (1998). Researching the dynamics of board-stakeholder relations. *Long Range Planning*, *31*(2), 218–226.

Ibrahim, N. A., & Angelidis, J. P. (1995). The corporate social responsiveness of board members: Are there differences between inside and outside directors? *Journal of Business Ethics*, *14*(5), 405–413.

Jensen, M. C., & Meckling, W. H. (1976). Theory of the firm, managerial behavior, agency costs, and ownership structure. *Journal of Financial Economics 3*(4), 305–360.

Kakabadse, A., Ward, K., Korac-Kakabadse, N., & Bowman, C. (2001). Role and contribution of non-executive directors. *Corporate Governance*, *1*(1), 4–7.

Kogut, B., & Zander, U. (1992). Knowledge of the firm, combinative capabilities, and the replication of technology. *Organization Science*, *3*(3), 383–397.

Lewicki, R. J., & Bunker, B. B. (1996). Developing and maintaining trust in work relationships. In R. M. Kramer & T. M. Tyler (Eds.), *Trust in organizations: Frontiers of theory and research* (pp. 114–139). Newbury Park, CA: SAGE.

McClelland, D. C. (1961). *The achieving society*. Princeton, NJ: Van Nostrand.

McCormick, M. J., & Martinko, M. J. (2004). Identifying leader social cognitions: Integrating the causal reasoning perspective into social cognitive theory. *Journal of Leadership and Organizational Studies*, *10*(4), 2–12.

McNulty, T., & Pettigrew, A. (1996). The contribution, power, and influence of part-time board members. *Corporate Governance: An International Review*, *4*(3), 160–179.

Mizruchi, M. S. (1996). What do interlocks do? An analysis, critique and assessment of research on interlocking directorates. *Annual Review of Sociology*, 22, 271–299.

O'Neill, H., Saunders, C., & McCarthy, A. (1989). Board Members, Corporate Social Responsiveness, and Profitability. *Journal of Business Ethics*, *8*(5), 353–358

Pass, C. (2004). Corporate governance and the role of non-executive directors in large UK companies: An empirical study. *Corporate Governance*, *4*(2), 52–63.

Pearce, J. A., & Zahra, S. A. (1992). Board compensation from a strategic contingency perspective. *Journal of Management Studies*, *29*(4), 411–438.

Phillips, J. M. (1995). Leadership since 1975: Advancement or inertia? *The Journal of Leadership Studies, 2*, 58–80.

Pincus, J. (2004). The consequences of unmet needs: The evolving role of motivation in consumer research. *Journal of Consumer Behavior, 3*(4), 375–387.

Rhoades, D. L., Rechner, P. L., & Sundaramurthy, C. (2000). Board composition and financial performance: A meta-analysis of the influence of outside directors. *Journal of Managerial Issues, 12*(1), 76–91.

Robins, J., & Wiersema, M. F. (1995). A resource-based approach to the multibusiness firm: Empirical analysis of portfolio interrelationships and corporate financial performance. *Strategic Management Journal, 16*(4), 277–299.

Rosenstein, S., & J. G. Wyatt (1990). Outside directors, board independence, and shareholder wealth. *Journal of Financial Economics, 26*, 175–191

Short, H., Keasy, K., Wright, M., & Hull, A. (1999). Corporate governance: From accountability to enterprise. *Accounting and Business Research, 29*(4), 337–352.

Spender, J. C. (1989). *Industry recipes: An enquiry into the nature and sources of managerial judgement.* Oxford, England: Blackwell.

Tosi, H. L., & Gomez-Mejia, L. R. (1994). CEO compensation monitoring and firm performance. *Academy of Management Journal, 37*(4), 1002–1016.

Wagner, J. A., Stimpert, J. L., & Fubara, E. I. (1998). Board composition on organizational performance: Two studies of insider/outsider effects. *Journal of Management Studies, 35*(5), 655–677.

Waldo, C. N. (1985). *Boards of directors: Their changing roles, structure, and information needs.* Westport, CT: Quorum Books.

Weir, C., & Laing, D. (2001). Governance structures, director independence and corporate performance in the UK. *European Business Review, 13*(2), 86–95.

Wernerfelt, B. (1984). A resource based view of the firm. *Strategic Management Journal, 5*(2), 171–180.

Westphal, J. D. (2002). Second thoughts on board independence: Why do so many demand board independence when it does so little good? *The Corporate Board, 23*(136), 6–10.

White, R. W. (1959). Motivation reconsidered: The concept of competence. *Psychological Review, 66*(5), 297–333.

Wood, M., & Patrick, T. (2003). Jumping on the bandwagon: Outside representation in corporate governance. *Journal of Business & Economic Studies, 9*(2), 48–53.

Yermack, D. (1986). Higher market valuation with a small board of directors. *Journal of Financial Economics, 40*(2), 186–211.

Zahra, S. A., & Pearce, J. A. (1989). Boards of directors and corporate financial performance: A review and integrative model. *Journal of Management, 15*(2), 291–334.

Zahra, S. A., & Stanton, W. W. (1988). The implications of board of directors composition for corporate strategy and performance. *International Journal of Management, 5*(2), 229–236.

CHAPTER 9

CROWDING OUT OF TRUST AND ITS IMPACT ON MANAGEMENT CONSULTING

Michael Nippa and Jens Grigoleit

Corporate governance (CG) has been a major subject of both scientific research and practical discussion on corporate management (Daily, Dalton, & Canella, 2003). Although alternative approaches exist, research on CG is predominantly based on the rationale proposed by agency theorists (Daily et al., 2003; Davis, Schoorman, & Donaldson, 1997). Based on the assumption that managers are inherently opportunistic and selfish, agency theory argues that they will constantly try to betray owners in order to maximize personal benefits (Jensen & Meckling, 1976; Shleifer & Vishny, 1997; Williamson, 1985). Such a pessimistic view of human nature (Davis et al., 1997; Moran & Ghoshal, 1996) leads to systematic and mutual distrust. Consequently, agency theory based CG mainly builds on explicit behavioral control, the use of explicit performance-related incentives, punishment in case of misconduct, and extensive monitoring (Sundaramurthy & Lewis, 2003). With regard to monitoring, the role and performance of existing corporate boards, whether one-tiered (as, for example, in the United States) or two-tiered (as in Germany), are currently questioned. Critics complain that board members are in cahoots

Board Members and Management Consultants: Redefining the Boundaries of Consulting and Corporate Governance, pp. 171–190
Copyright © 2008 by Information Age Publishing

with top managers and do not fulfill their primary purpose (i.e., monitoring management as representatives of corporate shareholders; see Jensen, 1993; Shleifer & Vishney, 1997).

Apparently, agency theory ignores the economic benefits of alternative forms of CG, for example based on stewardship theory (Davis et al., 1997; Donaldson & Davis, 1994). If managers show—other than assumed—loyal and collaborative behavior and behave like stewards serving in the full interest of their shareholders, explicit monitoring and control becomes less important. In this case trust-based relationships between managers and owners are more efficient (Malhotra & Murnighan, 2002). Instead being monitored and controlled, managers should be empowered. However, empowerment increases the risk that managers would misuse their power. Therefore, empowerment and trust go hand in hand (i.e., trust is a necessary precondition for this type of governance system; see Sundaramurthy & Lewis, 2003). Consequently the role and function of the board of directors and its members are extended. Board members would not act as intelligent agents of shareholders only, but provide important explicit and tacit knowledge, serve as coaches and sparring partners, and/or mobilize social capital and networks (Van der Walt & Ingley, 2003).

While there are no unambiguous decision rules regarding when to rely on trust and when not, recent research finds support for the thesis that the use of explicit control is perceived as a signal of distrust and, therefore, will erode the perpetuation of trust (Falk & Kosfeld, 2004; Fehr & Fischbacher, 2002; Malhotra & Murnighan, 2002). Accordingly, agency based CG may lead to a crowding out of trust between corporate owners and management. Furthermore, amplifying monitoring (i.e., application of explicit control) will enforce opportunistic behavior, thus provoking a self-fulfilling prophecy.

Systematic crowding out of trust in the upper echelons of corporations may have significant economic effects for management consultants. If the role and function of outside board members will be restricted to monitoring, knowledge transfer will be eclipsed. In such instances, top management consultants may fill the gap based on their function as knowledge provider (Nippa & Petzold, 2002). Additionally the need for independent evaluations of strategic management decisions will mount. Particularly outside board managers confronted with imminent liability suits will increasingly seek coverage and assured certification offered by management consultants (Nippa & Petzold, 2002).

They main objective of this chapter is to provide scientific support for the proposition that agency-based CG will systematically crowd out trust between corporate owners and managers and respectively inside and outside directors. Our subordinated objective is to examine possible impacts on management consulting. In order to achieve these objectives, we will begin by briefly describing alternative perspectives on CG. Second, we will define trust and distrust, depict fundamental interdependencies, and emphasize their effect on CG. Third, we will present organizational mechanisms that foster crowding out of trust. Finally, we will discuss the impact on management consulting.

ALTERNATIVE VIEWS ON CG

Since CG is a complex issue that involves many parties with different interests and objectives, it has been discussed quite controversially (Daily et al., 2003). This discussion refers to different fields of science, spanning from economic and organization theory to accounting, law, psychology, and politics. As a result, the term "corporate governance" has become somewhat "fuzzy" (Turnbull, 2000). In a very broad definition, CG includes all activities that are related to managerial decision making and control systems within any organization. However, following the mainstream of literature, we restrict our analysis to direct relations between corporate owners and the board of directors as their agent and corporate managers in the context of separate ownership and control. As proposed by Shleifer and Vishny (1997), CG deals with "the ways in which suppliers of finance to corporations assure themselves of getting a return on their investments" (p. 737)

The need for an explicit CG has been attributed to the separation of corporate ownership and corporate management (Berle & Means, 1932; Fama & Jensen, 1983). It leads to a constellation in which corporate owners are principals, who delegate the function of managing the corporation to professional managers, who act as their agents. Because delegated tasks are complex and because future contingencies cannot be foreseen completely, perfect contracts which specify every detail of the relationship are not feasible (Shleifer & Vishny, 1997). Additionally, the performance of managers cannot be sufficiently evaluated by the owners, because they can neither fully monitor managers' input (i.e., effort) nor precisely valuate the future consequences of managerial decisions (Jensen & Meckling, 1976; Milgrom & Roberts, 1992). This leaves room for discrete action, which cannot be monitored by the owners of corporations, thus allowing for managerial misconduct. In view of this problem, the legislator enforced supervisory boards or boards of directors, who were intended to act on behalf and in the interest of all shareholders. Nonexecutive, in particular outside board members, would prevent managerial self-service and ensure appropriate consideration of shareholder interest and maximization of shareholder value. However, installing an organization of shareholder representatives does not solve the fundamental problem resulting from the separation of corporate ownership and corporate management. Rather, it leads to multiple principal-agent relationships and transfers fundamental issues of mutual collaboration such as trust and distrust from an aggregated level to intergroup and interpersonal relationships.

Relationships—collaborations that are characterized by reciprocal dependence, at least partially conflicting interests, and uncertainty regarding the behavior of others (e.g., trust or distrust)—are the main mediators of the decision how to react (i.e., whether to implement explicit control or to rely on trustworthy behavior of the managers). If owners believe that they cannot trust management, they will implement measures that reduce the possibility of betrayal by self-serving managers. If they believe that managers are trustworthy, in contrast, they can abstain from monitoring because control becomes redundant or even counterproductive.

IMPACTS OF TRUST AND DISTRUST ON CG

Trust and distrust are ubiquitous phenomena and important variables that determine human behavior and human interaction in particular. Because trust and distrust are of relevance in various disciplines and situations, many different definitions of these terms can be distinguished (Bigley & Pearce, 1998; Rousseau, Sitkin, Burt, & Camerer, 1998). Academic debates about trust and distrust and the number of respective publications have increased enormously during the last years. Therefore, we will only give a comprehensive overview of current research in order to provide a basis for further analyses and discussions with regard to CG.

Definitions of Trust and Distrust

According to Cummings and Bromiley (1996), trust can be defined as a belief of an individual that another individual will undertake efforts to uphold his or her commitments, that he or she will act honestly, and that the individual will not try to gain personal advantages on others' account, even when faced with an opportunity for it. Similarly, distrust may be defined as the belief that the other person will act opportunistically (i.e., that he or she does not care about harming others when seeking his or her own interest or that he or she will purposely harm others, if there is a chance of taking personal advantage).

Transferring these general definitions to interpersonal relations in business or economic contexts, it is important to realize that:

- Trust and distrust are aspects of social interaction. They involve two or more persons, groups, or organizations whose actions are interdependent (Becerra & Gupta, 2003; Rousseau et al., 1998).

- Trust is always associated with personal vulnerability (Mayer, Davis, & Schoorman, 1995). Without a latent chance of being misused, exploited, or disappointed, trust literally does not exist. Trust and distrust are based on beliefs and expectations about definite human behavior. Beliefs and expectations refer to the fact that trust and distrust are of relevance only in situations characterized by uncertainty. Relying on trust (as well as relying on distrust) can prove wrong in the future. The perception of such a risk of failure is a constituting part of *conscious trust*; otherwise one would speak of blind trust (Johnson-George & Swap, 1982; Luhmann, 1979; Kee & Knox, 1970). Similarly, if a person or group certainly knows that she or he will be harmed or exploited, distrust loses its meaning and relevance.

- Trust and distrust cannot be comprehensively explained on the basis of calculative behavior alone as both are—to a considerable degree—based on intuition and emotions. Because trust and distrust are characterized as beliefs, they only emerge in situations of limited knowledge. For instance, preferences and intentions of other people are in most cases unpredictable. Therefore, one has to make assumptions without being able to rationally prove them. Trust and distrust fill the gap of missing information, which allows for decision making that otherwise would be impossible because of insufficient data (Luhmann, 1979; Nooteboom, 2002).

If trust and distrust have to be characterized as beliefs, they are distinguished from a situation where there is no belief and no assumption (i.e., a situation of perfect unconsciousness or of perfect predictability). Consequently, the opposite of trust is not distrust, as commonly thought. Instead of a single continuum of trust and distrust one has to assume a dual continuum (Lewicki, McAllister, & Bies, 1998; Luhmann, 1979; Sitkin & Roth, 1993; Swift, 2001).

An important part of the academic literature on trust deals with questions and concepts of processes that facilitate or foster trust among persons or groups. Frequently different sources of trust are distinguished (Lewicki & Buncker, 1996):

- *Calculus-based trust,* which stems from rational considerations of the situation and the consequences of possible actions on the distribution of cost and utility. Calculus-based trust can result from credible information regarding the intentions or competence of another as well as from the fact that in certain situations breach of trust is impossible as the trusted partner would harm himself by it.

* *Knowledge-based trust,* which derives from repeated interaction over time and refers to past experiences that reveal information on the personal characteristics of the interacting individual.

* *Identification-based trust,* which results from personal identification, causing the interacting parties to effectively understand and appreciate each others' wants. Through this interaction, the partners develop common goals, which they try to reach through mutual cooperative behavior. Feelings of identification are also fostered by the common affiliation to certain groups or social categories.

It is noteworthy to add that trust cannot be based on one of these three sources alone (Nooteboom, 2002). Neither a purely calculative trust, which even can be seen as a "contradiction in terms" (Williamson, 1996, p. 274), nor a purely affective or identification-based trust explains interpersonal trust comprehensively.

THE IMPACT OF TRUST AND DISTRUST ON CG SYSTEMS

Fundamental trust and distrust between interacting persons or groups imply completely different forms of governance. If owner respectively nonexecutive board members of a corporation trust "their" executive managers, they will grant them a high degree of freedom and independence in order to reduce unnecessary justification burdens and to motivate them. The decision to trust managers is regularly based on the belief that they will not misuse their freedom and betray the corporation and its shareholders (Bigley & Pearce, 1998). By granting freedom, the mechanism of reciprocity is stimulated as well (Gouldner, 1960). If managers honor the grant as a gift, they normally feel obligated to return an adequate gift (e.g., by acting in favor of corporate owners). Granting trust breeds more trust (i.e., it reinforces itself; see McEvily, Zaheer, & Perrone, 2002; Nooteboom, 2002).

Given an initial distrust in management, owner respectively nonexecutive board members will most likely implement a governance system based on extensive monitoring in order to protect the firm and their interests from exploitation deriving from opportunistic management behaviors. They may even try to make use of this opportunism by applying explicit incentive systems that aim to motivate managers to behave in the interest of the firm through seeking to maximize their own wealth. Consequently, if the relationship between nonexecutive board members and top management is characterized by distrust, they will most likely implement a CG system that refers to agency reasoning. In the case that mutual trust dominates intraboard collaboration, a stewardship-based CG system appears to be more appropriate.

In order to develop a model of CG that simultaneously incorporates both approaches, one has to analyze factors that foster or hamper the emergence and stability of trust and distrust. At first glance, trust and distrust substitute each other. From this perspective, explicit control is unnecessary—*if* people trust each other. Consequently trust becomes obsolete, if collaboration and cooperation is based on complete control (Malhotra & Murnighan, 2002). Yet, because complete control is illusionary, residual trust is always needed (Knight, 1947). Similarly, abstaining from any kind of control and purely relying on unconditional trust is rather irrational and often characterized as "blind" trust (Malhotra & Murnighan, 2002; Sundaramurthy & Lewis, 2003). Therefore, neither absolute trust nor absolute explicit control appears to be an efficient solution. Additionally, due to self-enforcing mechanisms inherent in both concepts, mixing both behaviors also turns out to be problematic. Accordingly, one has to assume that CG systems either are based on a very large degree of mutual trust between owners and managers or on the extensive use of explicit control.

Interestingly, the behavioral assumptions—namely opportunism and self-interest underlying agency theory—increasingly dominate both CG research and CG practice. Consequently distrust, explicit monitoring, and controlling are widespread. Thus a question that arises is why trust-based forms of CG are very rarely discussed and proposed. One possible explanation is that trust is not apparent in business transactions as asserted (see, for example, Williamson, 1993, 1996). However, reflecting the vast amount of academic research on trust in business relations and respective findings that prove its impact, this argument obviously does not hold. Another more realistic explanation presumes that trust is crowded out by extensive use of explicit control. This thesis finds fundamental support from works provided by Douglas McGregor (1960, 1966), who argued that a significantly authoritarian approach of management tends to become a self-fulfilling prophecy.

A Crowding Out of Trust

Current research in the field of behavioral economics shows that measures proposed by agency theory may initiate serious side-effects under certain conditions. A frequently analyzed effect is the crowding out of intrinsic motivation through the use of explicit incentives (Barkema, 1995; Deci & Ryan, 1985; Frey, 1997). This motivational crowding out effect is widely acknowledged and accepted, even by economists (Bénabou & Tirole, 2003; Kreps, 1997). We assume that not only intrinsic motivation, but also trust tends to be crowded out, if agency theory-based CG measures, in particular explicit monitoring and controlling, are implemented.

Basically this thesis is built on two arguments. First, trust is superseded because the concept of trust fundamentally conflicts with the behavioral assumptions used by agency theorists. Second, implementation of extensive monitoring and explicit incentives will lead to an erosion of trust or a decreased probability that trust will emerge in a given situation.

Crowding Out Initiated by Defective Assumptions of Agency Theory

According to the basic assumptions of agency theory, individual decision-making is based on rational calculation limited only by informational restraints and bounded rationality (Milgrom & Roberts, 1992). Quite contrary, trust cannot be built based on pure calculation relying on objective facts, but is grounded on subjective beliefs, expectations and emotions. Thus, the "decision" to trust is more like a conjecture. Since trust cannot be sufficiently explained by calculation, its existence—given the assumptions of agency theory—has to be doubted if not considered to be impossible at all (Nooteboom, 2002; Williamson, 1993).

Decision making based on expectancy values that rely on arithmetic means—as generally implicated by economics—contradicts trust as well. It systematically neglects the fact that there are different types of managers, some of which might behave trustworthy and others opportunistically. It rather assumes that the probability of opportunistic behavior is the same in any time and situation. Similar to the rationale used by Akerlof (1970) in explaining "lemon markets," the economic advantage of economically superior alternatives is systematically underestimated, if mean values are applied. With regard to CG, this means that all managers are treated as being opportunistic, despite the general experience that some managers are opportunistic, while others are trustworthy (Milgrom & Roberts, 1992). However, applying the improper, negative generalization justifies respectively coercively demands that rely on the use of explicit control and extensive monitoring.

The second substantial contradiction between the concept of trust and economic theory is related to the assumption of ubiquitous selfish behavior of all participants involved. Based on this behavioral assumption one has to conclude that individuals will harm others, if they expect to personally profit from it (Williamson, 1996). Since it is impossible to design complete contracts for complex tasks such as managing a corporation, exploitation of one contractual party by the other party can never totally be ruled out. Thus, agency theorists have to assume that opportunism will affect every agency relationship under certain situations (Williamson, 1993). Further, a person consciously ignoring chances to enhance his personal interest contravenes the general principle of self-interest maximization and/or rationality. Since trust is based on the substantiated expectation of nonopportunistic behavior within relationships, its relevance has to be denied by new institutional economics in general and agency theory in particular (Nooteboom, 2002).

Applying the assumptions underlying agency theory clearly leads to a denial of the existence of any trust in business relations, which many agency theorists and practitioners restrain from doing so. The fact that the concept of trust contradicts fundamental assumptions of agency theory is not a sufficient explanation and justification for our crowding out thesis. Consequently, it is necessary to analyze the impact of the exertion of explicit control on interpersonal trust in CG relations.

Crowding Out Initiated by Explicit Control

Many measures that are designed and implemented to achieve coordination in organizations have a strong influence on the development of trust in business relationships. Particularly incentive and monitoring systems are of great importance in this context (e.g., Ferrin & Dirks, 2003).

At first glance, measures implied by agency theory do not contradict trust. Control measures implemented to prevent opportunistic behavior will even encourage trust to a certain degree (Sitkin & Roth, 1993). As mentioned above, trust is founded on expectations. If monitoring reduces uncertainty about the plausible behavior of managers, it bears the potential to enhance the belief that they will not exploit existing discretion and are trustworthy. Furthermore, the higher the perceived protection against potential damage resulting from managerial opportunism and the greater the liability of managers, the easier trust may emerge. Following such arguments, measures of control enable an improved predictability of managerial behavior and therewith decrease the danger of false expectations. Consequently, one can argue that the application of distrust-based CG systems proposed by agency theory paradoxically enhances the possibility that trust will emerge and sustain.

However, this position neglects some substantial effects that determine the relationship between corporate owner respectively nonexecutive board members and executive managers.

Reciprocity

Reciprocity is a fundamental characteristic of human behavior that has been recognized as one of the most substantial mechanisms for efficiently coordinating social interaction (Blau, 1964; Gouldner, 1960). Reciprocity means that if the decision or behavior of a person is perceived as positive (or negative) by another person, it will lead to an accordingly positive (or negative) reaction (Fehr & Falk, 2002; Fehr & Fischbacher, 2002). Remarkably, reciprocity—like trust—cannot be sufficiently explained by applying assumptions of purely rational and self-interested decision making. Rather it has to be regarded as an inherent, internalized norm which is mainly pursued without cognitive analysis. For example, most human beings feel inclined to repay received gifts. Similarly they tend to "repay" behavior that harms them (i.e., they seek revenge). This behavior is of special relevance, because people—contradictory to traditional economic reasoning—thereby do not necessarily consider economic benefits (i.e., they do not show purely self-serving behavior; see Blau, 1964; Fehr & Gäechter, 2000).

Through abandoning explicit control, corporate owners and their board representatives consciously put the corporation in a situation of implicit vulnerability, which can be considered as an expression of trust and commitment (McEvily et al., 2002). Additionally, a conscious renunciation to monitor and to control will reduce justification pressures exerted to managers (Nippa & Petzold, 2005). Furthermore, it should strengthen the motivation for achievement of managers by giving them the freedom to decide rather autonomously. In this respect, trust granted by their principals ought to be perceived as a gift by managers. Under the assumptions of reciprocity, this gift obligates managers to repay. They will, for instance, show loyal behavior and more effort to increase corporate and shareholder value. If one follows this argument, granting trust will stimulate and promote trustworthy behavior.

On the contrary, if managers perceive that the board withdraws trust or opposes them with distrust by introducing measures of explicit control, they may interpret this behavior as a signal of negative attitudes against them (Malhotra & Murnighan, 2002). Assuming that intensified monitoring and increased pressure for justification are perceived as inadequate and/or unfair by managers, the latter will feel little inclination to show cooperative behavior (Barkema, 1995; Fehr & Fischbacher, 2002; Fehr & Gäechter, 2000). Particularly managers who have been actively engaged by the corporation and who have put their personal interests last, will feel betrayed and will change their behavior (Davis et al., 1997). Applying agency theory based CG measures, therefore, may damage a collaborative exchange relation and erode trust. Simultaneously, this will decrease the psychologically-based retentions of managers against opportunistic behaviors and will thereby increase the tendency to concentrate on their personal advantages, showing self-serving behavior and losing any ethical scruples (Luhmann, 1979).

Psychological Reactance

The theory of psychological reactance is based on the observation that individuals will react to a perceived restriction of their freedom by expressing an attitude and/or behavior that is directed against the restricting measure. For instance, people will show a strong preference for decisions or actions that are forbidden or unwelcome. Furthermore, people regularly try to circumvent or sabotage the regulation that imposes respective limitations on them (Brehm, 1989; Lessne & Venkatesan, 1989).

Applied to CG systems, one can expect that managers develop psychological reactance towards the measures that restrict their behavior and freedom of choice (i.e., measures of explicit control). Therefore, extensive CG regulations may lead to psychological reactance of managers. The consequences of such behavior for CG systems are serious. Reactance serves as an incentive for behavior and decisions that directly harm the corporation. Although measures of explicit control decrease the probability of such behavior, using explicit control directly promotes aversive behavior that sometimes has even more serious consequences.

According to the behavioral concepts of reciprocity and psychological reactance mentioned above, applying measures of monitoring and explicit incentives may cause a reinforcing spiral of opportunism and, thus, a crowding out of mutual trust. This provokes the paradoxical consequence that the use of measures to prevent or at least to curb opportunistic behavior inherently reinforces it. Trustworthiness of managers is not increased, but rather decreased.

Crowding Out of Trust as a Reinforcing Cycle

Crowding out trust is intensified by reinforcing effects of distrust initiated by a system of explicit control (Luhmann, 1979). If managers perceive that the owners or nonexecutive board members withdraw their trust, they will most probably be more prone to show opportunistic behavior. They may even think that this behavior is expected anyway so that there is nothing wrong about it. As the first signs of opportunism become obvious, the fears of the initially only slightly suspicious board members are confirmed and they will most probably intensify their control activities in order to avoid further damage (Ghoshal & Moran, 1996). Due to effects of reciprocity and psychological reactance already elaborated, this will lead to even stronger negative reactions. Consequently, even more sophisticated control systems and institutions will be implemented. Simultaneously, manager will react with more refined forms of opportunistic action (Sundaramurthy & Lewis, 2003). A reinforcing cycle of mutual distrust emerges, which will elude manageability due to inherent dynamic forces (see Figure 9.1).

Based on these insights one has to presume a self-fulfilling prophecy effect (i.e., the application of agency theory leads to a self-fulfillment of its basic assumption of human or managerial opportunism). The theory and its assumptions provoke the emergence of opportunistic and trust-unworthy managers. By enhancing social distance and promoting reactance behavior, it further provokes selfish and scrupulous behavior of managers at the expense of corporate owners.

Relevant Factors Mediating the Effect of Crowding Out of Trust

The phenomena depicted above that crowd out trust seem to represent a general principle transferable to different forms of interpersonal relationships. However, applied to CG relationships certain characteristics of publicly-traded firms may intensify the erosion of trust, which also helps to spread distrust.

Enforced "distance" Between Nonexecutive and Executive Board Members

The relationship between managers and owners of publicly-traded corporations is by nature mainly impersonal (Bhide, 1994). This seems not to be the case for the board of directors, thus supporting trustful relationships between nonexecutives and executives. Yet, such personal ties are increasingly criticized by stakeholders explicitly referring to agency theory. They argue that personal relations between nonexecutives and executives, amalgamation of CEO and chairman (i.e., top manager [agent] is simultaneously chief representative of shareholders [United States], proposal of supervisory board members by CEOs [United States/Germany], or common transition of former CEOs into the position "chairman of the supervisory board" [Germany]) are clear signs of collusion that harm shareholder interests. As such, "Directors' ties to management and the CEO are often stronger than their ties to the company" (Patton & Baker, 1987, p. 18). Consequently separating CEO and chairman, waiting periods, the selection of truly independent supervisory board members (e.g., from small shareholder organizations), and the use of pay-for-performance systems are frequently claimed. However, a

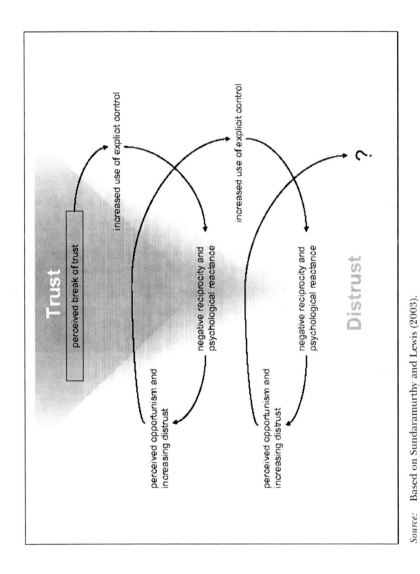

Source: Based on Sundaramurthy and Lewis (2003).

Figure 9.1.   The reinforcing cycle of mutual distrust

relationship that builds on formal, unsuspicious interaction and interpersonal distance generally does not promote the emergence of mutual trust.

Ambiguity of Strategic Decisions

In order to develop and stabilize trust, contents of explicit and implicit contracts as well as the actual behavior of the contractual partners are of great importance. In contrast to simpler assignments, employment contracts for top-managers are characterized by complexity, dynamics, and uncertainty. The corporation's success that may be the primary indicator of executive performance mainly depends on the appropriateness of strategic decisions (Grant, 1998). The task of strategic management exhibits certain characteristics that differentiate it from routine decision making in principle (Harrison & Pelletier, 2000; Nippa, 2001). Unfortunately, it also involves a high degree of ambiguity and uncertainty (Schwenk & Thomas, 1988). Therefore, it is impossible to derive deterministic alternatives and solutions. Accordingly, one can never avert that strategic decisions made in the best interest of the corporation turn out to be wrong, inferior, or inappropriate. Furthermore, one has to take into account that strategic decisions always include subjective evaluations of causes, effects, and alternatives based on heterogeneous, partly conflicting personal interests. For example, minority shareholder may evaluate merger and acquisition or "squeeze-out" decisions differently than the majority holder, the management, and employees. The characteristics of strategic decisions thereby evidently influence trust-building processes and continuity of trustful relationships.

Furthermore, it is quite impossible to retrace and verify the original decision-making process once the decision is made. Nevertheless, depending on the distribution of power, the responsibility for wrong decisions is ascribed to managers. Owner and nonexecutives alike assume and argue that executive managers should have recognized potential difficulties, uncertainties, developments, and resulting failures due to superior information because of attribution errors and biases (e.g., Robbins, 2005, pp. 136–138). The fact that managers also possess only limited information is regularly disregarded (Hendry, 2002). Yet, in retrospect, it is always easier to detect inferior decisions and to identify superior alternatives. Fueled by agency theory, one cannot help suspect managerial incompetence and opportunism as the ultimate cause for inferior decisions and loss of profits. In order to identify responsible managers more easily and in order to prevent further failures and losses, monitoring will, thus, be intensified. However, as mentioned earlier, extensive monitoring, reduced freedom, and increased justification pressure will produce even more distrust, particularly between nonexecutive board members and executives (Malhotra & Murnighan, 2002).

Based on our explanation and discussion, a crowding out of trust and the arising hegemony of distrust-dominated governance relations appear to be a logical consequence. Conditions of the specific situation make it difficult to establish and to stabilize trust. Additionally, the widespread use of agency theory seems to be a factor that complicates trust building even more by systematically crowding out trust and fuelling distrust.

IMPLICATIONS FOR MANAGEMENT CONSULTING

Are there any consequences for top management consultants deriving from this phenomenon? As top management consulting by definition has close relationships with upper echelons of corporations, we assume that the crowding out of trust currently taking place will effect management consulting in at least two ways. First, top management consultants will have to fill the knowledge gap widened by the exclusion of any dependent outside board member or periodic replacement of board members. Second, top management consultants will be increasingly mandated by independent outside board members to review strategic decisions and options proposed by executives and/or the latter in order to justify and certify these decisions.

Additional Demand for Knowledge Provision

Referring to the different economic functions top management consultants fulfill (Nippa & Petzold 2002), one can expect an increasing demand for management resources offered and provided by these individuals and firms. Management consultants support management by making special resources, like time and capacity as well as knowledge and information, temporarily available to them. Under the premise that agency theory-based CG systems will significantly alter board composition and collaboration among nonexecutive and executive board members, the demand for firm-specific, strategic expertise will soar. Following Simons' assumption that managerial work is primarily decision making (Simon, 1965), management consultants support managerial decision making by providing professional, content-related, and methodological information and knowledge. If, for whatever reason, executives are no longer able to pick industry or functional experts from their personal network, they will have to rely even more on specialized management consultants. Additionally, separating the board of directors into insiders and outsiders will further lead to interest-driven demand for independent advice regarding strategic decisions—particularly, if outside board members are primarily selected based on their independence, and not based on their expertise and/or their social network from multiple board memberships.

Additional Demand for Decision Enforcement

Top management consultants possess special reference power based on their independence and reputation. Therefore they become a means to enforce or justify favored strategic alternatives by providing an accepted, sometimes unquestionable reference (Nippa & Petzold, 2002). Especially top management consulting companies are able to certify the superiority of ambiguous strategic decisions that are disputed by different stakeholders.

Confronted with (1) increased skepticism from different shareholders, shareholder organizations, analysts, and business journalists that result in additional investor communication, (2) easier legal challenges of decisions, and (3) higher personal risks and threats resulting from new laws, rigid law enforcement, and less insurance coverage, executive and nonexecutive board members are seeking justification and certification (Nippa & Petzold, 2005). As strategic management decisions are usually ambiguous and heuristic, the quality of these decisions cannot be solely and unequivocally evaluated in monetary or quantitative terms. Management decisions are to be classified as experience and credence goods, which are difficult to evaluate with regard to their quality (Darby & Karni, 1973; Nelson, 1970). Therefore, the reputation of decision makers may serve as a substitute indicator of quality. Especially management consulting companies, which have earned a respective reputation ("brand name"), may be employed for political and power-related purposes by different interest groups. The more the relationship between owner, their board representatives and managers is characterized by distrust instead of trust, and the more decisions and behavior are ambiguous, the more independent arbitrators, expert witnesses, and certifiers are needed. Hence, one can assume that top management consultants will profit from agency theory-based CG systems currently implemented.

CONCLUSIONS

The chapter emphasized trust as a relevant alternative for designing CG systems. Trust-based CG systems differ with regard to their characteristics and their economic consequences from CG systems based on monitoring and sanctioning as implicated by traditional economic approaches like agency theory. We further argued that the latter system and concepts induce systematic crowding out of trust mainly through the effects of intensified explicit control. Restrictive forms of external supervision as well as a generalized assumption of opportunistic behavior tend to initiate a self reinforcing cycle of distrust.

From this perspective, one has to doubt that agency theory is a generally applicable and adequate foundation for designing efficient CG systems. Although it may be adequate for corporations (i.e., publicly-traded companies with disperse and mainly autonomous shareholders), it may lead to economically suboptimal solutions by disregarding important benefits of trust. The dominance of agency theory-based approaches in the discussion on CG (Daily et al., 2003) may already reflect the self-fulfilling prophecy effect of assuming ubiquitous opportunism.

Yet, to encourage a fruitful progress of management research and economic theory, it is necessary to take the inherent limitations of currently applied approaches into account. Following the argument, CG theory would be enhanced by applying a multiparadigmatic perspective that includes economic explanations as well as approaches and insights from behavioral science. A complementary use of different perspectives and approaches—for instance, based on a contingency model—may provide a more realistic and appropriate perspective on CG relations than one that is based on a single approach.

We propose, therefore, that a strand of future research might evaluate the economic consequences of trust and distrust, especially regarding the resulting costs of CG in detail. Costs resulting from the crowding out effect of trust should be included into the calculation of governance costs. We further propose to initiate empirical studies aimed at providing assumptions with regard to CG costs and benefits of various measures (e.g., legal acts) and of the systems in total. Because the development of trust is contingent on the specific situation, there should also be further research regarding the preconditions of trustworthy and opportunistic behavior and their ramifications for consultancy at the highest organizational levels.

REFERENCES

Akerlof, G. A. (1970). The market for "lemons": Quality uncertainty and the market mechanism. *Quarterly Journal of Economics, 84*(3), 488–500.

Barkema, H. G. (1995). Do top managers work harder when they are monitored? *Kyklos, 48*(1), 19–42.

Becerra, M., & Gupta, A. K. (2003). Perceived trustworthiness within the organization: The moderating impact of communication frequency on trustor and trustee effects. *Organization Science, 14*(1), 32–44.

Bénabou, R., & Tirole, J. (2003). Intrinsic and extrinsic motivation. *Review of Economic Studies, 70*(3), 489–520.

Berle, A. A., & Means, G. C. (1932). *The modern corporation and private property.* New York: Macmillan.

Bhide, A. (1994). Efficient markets, deficient governance. *Harvard Business Review, 74*(6), 128–139.

Bigley, G. A., & Pearce, J. L. (1998). Straining for shared meaning in organization science: Problems of trust and distrust. *Academy of Management Review, 23*(3), 405–421.

Blau, P. M. (1964). *Exchange and power in social life.* New York: Wiley.

Brehm, J. (1989). Psychological reactance: Theory and applications. *Advances in Consumer Research, 16*(1), 72–75.

Cummings, L. L., & Bromiley, P. (1996). The organizational trust inventory (OTI): Development and validation. In R. M. Kramer & T. R. Tyler (Eds.), *Trust in organizations: Frontiers of theory and research* (pp. 302–330). Thousand Oaks, CA: SAGE.

Daily, C. M., Dalton, D. R., & Cannella, A. A., Jr. (2003). Corporate governance: Decades of dialogue and data. *Academy of Management Review, 28*(3), 371–382.

Darby, M. R., & Karni, E. (1973). Free competition and the optimal amount of fraud. *Journal of Law and Economics, 16*(1), 67–88.

Davis, J. H., Schoorman, F. D., & Donaldson, L. (1997). Toward a stewardship theory of management. *Academy of Management Review, 22*(1), 20–47.

Deci, E., & Ryan, R. (1985). *Intrinsic motivation and self-determination in human behavior.* New York: Plenum Press.

Donaldson, L., & Davis, J.H. (1994). Boards and company performance: Research challenges the conventional wisdom. *Corporate Governance: An International Review, 2*(3), 151–160.

Falk, A., & Kosfeld, M. (2004). *Distrust: The hidden cost of control* (Working Paper). University of Zurich, Germany.

Fama, E. F., & Jensen, M. C. (1983). Separation of ownership and control. *Journal of Law and Economics, 26*(2), 301–326.

Fehr, E., & Falk, A. (2002). Psychological foundations of incentives. *European Economic Review, 46*(4/5), 687–724.

Fehr, E., & Fischbacher, U. (2002, March). Why social preferences matter: The impact of non-selfish motives on competition, cooperation and incentives. *The Economic Journal, 112,* C1–C33.

Fehr, E., & Gächter, S. (2000). Fairness and retaliation: The economics of reciprocity. *Journal of Economic Perspectives, 14*(3), 159–181.

Ferrin, D. L., & Dirks, K. T. (2003). The use of rewards to increase and decrease trust: Mediating processes and differential effects. *Organization Science, 14*(1), 18–31.

Frey, B. S. (1997). *Not just for the money: An economic theory of personal motivation.* Cheltenham, England: Edward Elgar.

Ghoshal, S., & Moran, P. (1996). Bad for practice: A critique of the transaction cost theory. *Academy of Management Review, 21*(1), 13–47.

Gouldner, A. W. (1960). The norm of reciprocity: A preliminary statement. *American Sociological Review, 25*(2), 161–178.

Grant, R. (1998). *Contemporary strategy analysis: Concepts, techniques, applications* (3rd ed.). Malden, England: Blackwell.

Harrison, F. E., & Pelletier, M. A. (2000). The essence of management decision. *Management Decision, 38*(7), 462–469.

Hendry, J. (2002). The principal's other problems: Honest incompetence and the specification of objectives. *Academy of Management Review, 27*(1), 98–113.

Jensen, M. C. (1993). The modern industrial revolution, exit, and the failure of internal control systems. *The Journal of Finance, 48*(3), 831–880.

Jensen, M. C., & Meckling, W. H. (1976). Theory of the firm: Managerial behavior, agency costs and ownership structure. *Journal of Financial Economics, 3*(4), 305–360.

Johnson-George, C., & Swap, W. C. (1982). Measurement of specific interpersonal trust. *Journal of Personality and Social Psychology, 43*(6), 1306–1317.

Kee, H. W., & Knox, R. E. (1970). Conceptual and methodological considerations in the study of trust and suspicion. *Journal of Conflict Solution, 14*(3), 357–366.

Knight, F. H. (1947). *Freedom and reform.* New York: Harper.

Kreps, D. M. (1997). Intrinsic motivation and extrinsic incentives. *American Economic Review, 87*(2), 359–364.

Lessne, G., & Venkatesan, M. (1989). Reactance theory in consumer research: The past, present and future. *Advances in Consumer Research, 16*(1), 76–78.

Lewicki, R. J., & Bunker, B. B. (1996). Developing and maintaining trust in work relationships. In R. M. Kramer & T. R. Tyler (Eds.), *Trust in organizations: Frontiers of theory and research* (pp. 114–139). Thousand Oaks, CA: SAGE.

Lewicki, R. J., McAllister, D. J., & Bies, R. J. (1998). Trust and distrust: New relationships and realities. *Academy of Management Review, 23*(3), 438–458.

Luhmann, N. (1979). *Trust and power.* Chichester, England: Wiley.

Malhotra, D., & Murnighan, J. K. (2002). The effects of contracts on interpersonal trust. *Administrative Science Quarterly, 47*(3), 534–559.

Mayer, R. C., Davis, J. H., & Schoorman, F. D. (1995). An integrative model of organizational trust. *Academy of Management Review, 20*(3), 709–734.

McEvily, W.J., Zaheer, A., & Perrone, V. (2002). *Vulnerability and the asymmetric nature of trust in interorganizational exchange* (Working Paper). Carnegie Mellon University, Pittsburgh, Pennsylvania. Retrieved January 9, 2005, from http://www.wiwiss.fu-berlin.de/w3/w3sydow/EURAM/pdf_2003/McEvilyZaheerPerrone_EURAM03.pdf

McGregor, D. (1960). *The human side of enterprise.* New York: McGraw-Hill.

McGregor, D. (1966). *Leadership and motivation.* Cambridge, MA: MIT Press.

Milgrom, P., & Roberts, J. (1992). *Economics, organization and management.* Englewood Cliffs, NJ: Prentice-Hall.

Moran, P., & Ghoshal, S. (1996). Theories of economic organization: The case for realism and balance. *Academy of Management Review, 21*(1), 58–72.

Nelson, P. (1970). Information and consumer behavior. *Journal of Political Economy, 78*(2), 311–329.

Nippa, M. (2001). *Strategic decision making: Nothing else than mere decision making?* Freiberger University Working Papers 01/ 2001.

Nippa, M., & Petzold, K. (2002). Functions and roles of management consulting firms: An integrative theoretical framework. In A. F. Buono (Ed.), *Developing knowledge and value in management consulting: Research in management consulting* (pp. 209–230). Greenwich, CT: Information Age.

Nippa, M., & Petzold, K. (2005). Impacts of justification behavior—The forgotten costs of corporate governance. In K. Cool, J. Henderson, & R. Abate (Eds.), *Restructuring strategy,* Strategic Management Society Book Series (pp. 251–268). Oxford, England: Blackwell.

Nooteboom, B. (2002). *Trust: Forms, foundations, functions, failures and figures.* Cheltenham, England: Edward Elgar.

Patton, A., & Baker, J. C. (1987). Why won't directors rock the boat? *Harvard Business Review, 65*(6), 10–14.

Robbins, S.P. (2005). *Organizational behavior* (11th ed). Upper Saddle River, NJ: Pearson Education.

Rousseau, D. M., Sitkin, S. B., Burt, R. S., & Camerer, C. (1998). Not so different after all: A cross-discipline view of trust. *Academy of Management Review, 23*(3), 393–404.

Schwenk, C. R., & Thomas, H. (1988). Effects of strategic decision aids on problem solving: A laboratory experiment. In J. H. Grant (Ed.), *Strategic management frontiers* (pp. 400–413). Greenwich, CT: JAI Press.

Shleifer, A., & Vishny, R. W. (1997). A survey of corporate governance. *The Journal of Finance, 52*(2), 737–778.

Simon, H. A. (1965). *Administrative behavior.* New York: Free Press.

Sitkin, S. B., & Roth, N. L. (1993). Explaining the limited effectiveness of legalistic "remedies" for trust/distrust., *Organization Science, 4*(3), 367–392.

Sundaramurthy, C., & Lewis, M. (2003). Control and collaboration: Paradoxes of governance. *Academy of Management Review, 28*(3), 397–415.

Swift, T. (2001). Trust, reputation and corporate accountability to stakeholders. *Business Ethics, 10*(1): 16-26.

Turnbull, S. (2000). Corporate charters with competitive advantages. *St. John's Law Review, 74*(1), 89–173.

Van der Walt, N., & Ingley, C. (2003). Board Dynamics and the Influence of Professional Background, Gender and Ethnic Diversity of Directors. *Corporate Governance: An International Review, 11*(3), 218–234.

Williamson, O. E. (1993). Calculativeness, trust, and economic organization. *Journal of Law & Economics, 36*(1), 453–486.

Williamson, O. E. (1985). *The economic institutions of capitalism.* New York: Free Press.

Williamson, O. E. (1996). *The mechanisms of governance.* New York: Oxford University Press.

PART IV

A NEW PROFESSION: THE CONTRACT, THE RESPONSIBILITIES, AND THE FUTURE

CHAPTER 10

ENABLING OR FACILITATING DISCRIMINATORY BOARD PRACTICES IN BOARD APPOINTMENTS

Where Are the Women?

Susan M. Adams

Women comprise a disproportionate percent of corporate boards in most countries while accounting for a growing amount of the worldwide consumer and labor force (Hausemann, Tyson, & Zahidi, 2006; "Women and the World," 2006). Among the *Fortune* Global 200 companies, the United States has the highest percent of women directors where 17.6% of board seats are filled by women in the 75 *Fortune* Global 200 companies (Corporate Women Directors International, 2007). At the other end of the spectrum, Asian countries have the lowest female representation with 1.3% of the board seats of Japan's 27 companies in the *Fortune* Global 200 filled by women. These numbers show a slow improvement over studies conducted during the last 10 years but only measure the largest firms where female representation is the highest. This is a nontrivial point since smaller

Board Members and Management Consultants: Redefining the Boundaries of Consulting and Corporate Governance, pp. 193–201

companies have consistently yielded smaller percentages of women on their boards (cf. Burke, 2000).

Norway is an exception to these trends. There, a wide range of boards are seeing a dramatic jump in female board representation due to recent legislation requiring all listed firms to have 33% to 50% women directors, depending on the size of the board, by 2008 or face delisting and dissolution. In 2006, 28.8% of the board seats in Norway were filled by women, up from 22% 2 years earlier (Thomas, 2006) demonstrating that quicker change to the status of women on boards is possible.

While there is a growing case for corporate board diversity, the management consultant's responsibility and opportunity for promoting diversity on boards is less clear. Obvious characters such as the CEO (chief executive officer), board chair, board nominating committee, and search firms are clearly responsible for considering all candidates that can provide benefits for the firm. More broadly, employees, activist shareholders, and agents of the organization such as management consultants can be influential in acting on behalf of the welfare of the organization and thus, should bear responsibility for promoting diversity when it can be beneficial to the company.

The focus of this chapter is to identify when and how management consultants should be involved in advancing the cause of corporate board diversity. First, the business and social cases for board diversity are reviewed followed by identification of where consultants are directly and indirectly involved in influencing board diversity. Finally, a more consultant-centric rationale is offered for using the influence of management consultants to facilitate the process of female board appointments to benefit their clients, and ultimately, their own success.

THE BUSINESS CASE FOR BOARD DIVERSITY

A growing body of research (e.g. Bilimoria, 2000; Carter, Simkins, & Simpson, 2003; Daily & Dalton, 2003; Erhardt, Werbel, & Shrader, 2003; "2006 Census," 2004) leads to the conclusion that firm performance is positively related to gender diverse boards. Erhardt and colleagues included ethnic minorities in their investigation of the relationship between diversity and firm performance. They found that both return on investment and return on assets were positively related to board diversity. Similarly, Carter and colleagues found that boards with women or minorities were positively related to firm value (as measured by Tobin Q). Direct research has yet to dissect the causal mechanisms responsible for this link between women on boards and firm performance but authors conducting related research offer insights into potential causal factors. With the ultimate goal of firm performance, the business case for promoting gender diversity on boards is based on at least three issues. First is the representation of the female view to better understand the purchasing processes and product preferences of women as consumers and shareholders. Second is the issue of board dynamics and third is talent development. Individually, or taken together, these factors support the recommendations of Conger, Finegold, and Lawler (1998) in promoting board effectiveness by promoting understanding of products and processes to minimize risks and make sure that top talent is being employed for the company's benefit.

The Female View

Research indicates that gender diversity on corporate boards can help boards understand the increasingly influential female consumer view. Women can provide more resources for a board through their unique perspectives on the organization's products and organizational processes (Bilimoria, 2000; Daily & Dalton, 2003). This is not a trivial issue given the expanding role of female consumerism where women make over 80% of the buying decisions. The consumer influence of women also goes beyond personal and family spending since the majority of purchasing managers for companies are women (Popcorn & Marigold, 2000). A better understanding of the female view can help business organizations serve their customers better which, in turn, can lead to better firm performance.

Board Dynamics

Studies about workgroups suggest the need for diversity to enhance the prospect of having issues fully debated (Cascio, 2004; Sonnenfeld, 2004). This social systems perspective may help explain findings relating board diversity and positive firm performance. Different dynamics in the boardroom are likely to occur when diverse perspectives are represented. Diversity of thought can promote a wider array of discussions and provide a more complete picture of issues so that boards can make better decisions.

There is a caveat to the promotion of this type of diversity on boards. Diversity has been given a bad name in many circumstances because it has not been properly executed. All too often, a woman or minority is elected to a board supposedly, to get a different view. However, the individual chosen thinks very similarly as the rest of the board, most likely due to similar backgrounds, lifestyles, and education. Similarity is probably what was attractive about the individual as a candidate in the first place since similarity is related to favorable performance evaluations (Pulakos & Wexley, 1983). For example, there is a small pool of women serving on boards and as high level executives in large firms (Daum, Neff, & Norris, 2006; "2006 Census," 2006). They tend to be exceptional women who blazed the trail for others. Their experiences competing effectively in the corporate world more closely mirror, or exaggerate, those of men rather than the vast majority of women they supposedly represent. Most of the high powered women have similar career paths and similar or higher levels of education from the same universities as their male counterparts ("Leading CEOs," 2007). While the observable demographic characteristic of gender may lead some to think that a different view is represented, the individuals may in fact have little diversity of thought. As is discussed later, there are times when observable diversity is valuable to a board. Other times, nonobservable diversity based on values, experiences, and thought processes (Erhardt et al., 2003) is what is needed. Consultants can help their clients by providing ways to identify the type and level of diversity needed and how to find appropriate candidates.

Some researchers say that there is strong evidence for making a social and moral case for including women on boards, but a less convincing business case can be "argued on the basis of hard evidence" (van der Walt & Ingley, 2003, p. 232). Instead of paying attention to diversity, they suggest focusing on the merits of candidates and the potential social capital candidates can offer as strategic resources for the firm. Fondas (2000), however, proposes that diverse boards that include women are more apt to achieve the increase in social capital that van der Walt and Ingley highlight. She suggests that the objective, outsider view that women offer can enhance the three functions of board work: providing governance oversight, linking the firm to its environment, and providing strategic direction. Thus, the presence of women on boards alters the board dynamics. Westphal and Milton (2000) provide further support for Fondas' conclusions on a conditional basis. They found that directors with previous experience as a minority director, such as being the only women or only person of color, are not reluctant to voice their views and the presence of minority directors enlarges the social networks available to the firm. But, according to Westphal and Milton, the extent to which minorities can contribute effectively depends on whether they are accepted into the "in group" (the more favored group that is granted greater responsibility) as opposed to the "out group" of the board. Women who rise to the level of director status are usually external directors, coming from varied backgrounds with diverse perspectives. They must cross such high hurdles that they often develop the capability to share their different ideas in a compatible manner (Fondas, 2000). Moreover, a critical mass of women and minorities increases the likelihood of their influence on board behavior (Kramer, Konrad, & Erkut, 2006).

The Development of Potential Talent

The third factor that can lead to firm performance is executive mentoring for the development of all potential talent. Women on boards can aid in the advancement of women within organizations. Their mere presence signals that attainment to high profile positions is possible and women directors can provide valuable mentoring to women executives. This is where observable diversity rather than unobservable diversity matters. There is a glass ceiling attributed to women's careers in business as the data shared at the outset of this chapter show. There are women who feel stuck in the politics of organizations who have the desire and qualifications to rise in their organizations ("Study of 353 Fortune 500 Companies," 2004). Recent legislation, particularly in the United States and the United Kingdom, has made the work of corporate boards very time consuming necessitating a larger pool of board candidates to fill seats. Women stuck at lower levels of their organizations can provide an expanded pool of diverse talent for board appointments. However, the potential talent needs mentoring to access the upper ranks of businesses to prepare them better for board service. Therefore, having more board-ready women serve on boards can have this side effect of unleashing an untapped pool of talent that benefits businesses.

THE SOCIAL CAUSE CASE FOR BOARD DIVERSITY

The statistics presented in the opening show a disproportionate representation of women on boards in relation to their roles in society as consumers and employees. Beyond the business case that suggests tapping diversity of thought to understand the influence of women as consumers and a positive influence on board and organizational processes, there is the issue of fairness. Is it fair to exclude the stakeholder voice of women? Exclusionary practices for board searches compound the glass ceiling barrier for career advancement that women face. The "good old boy network" is still used by many boards to identify potential board candidates despite espoused practices of a more open process. "Getting on the radar" for consideration as a viable candidate is a tough endeavor for women that do not belong to the same social networks as their male counterparts. Creating change to this process requires working through local politics with multiple approaches (Adams & Flynn, 2005a, 2005b). The InterOrganization Network (ION—www.IONWomen.org) is a group of women's organizations dedicated the advancement of women on boards that is combating the social network problem in this manner. ION offers assistance to boards and search firms by providing a list of women candidates that meet the board's specified criteria. ION shows that there are ways to access the pool of qualified women and little excuse to say there are no qualified women available. Boards and their search firms are simply not looking in the right places.

The social and business cases presented here suggest that boards are neglecting their fiduciary and moral responsibilities to act in their shareholder's best interest by not appropriately implementing board diversity that could benefit their stakeholders.

LEGAL INDUCEMENTS FOR BOARD DIVERSITY

As with most changes, resistance is expected. Changing board appointment practices is particularly complex given the power plays and competing demands that dominate organizational life. Such a change requires techniques that push and pull to force and seduce change (Adams & Flynn, 2005b). Several countries are using the legal avenue to gain compliance. Norway and Spain, for example, have legally mandated quotas. Sweden is threatening. Other countries such as New Zealand and Israel require government owned organizations to fill quotas.

While an outcomes approach is used in the countries just mentioned, a process approach is used in the United States. A provision in the 2002 Sarbanes-Oxley Act requires disclosure of the search process in publicly available regulatory documents. Boards are open to regulatory sanctions and potential discrimination lawsuits if candidates find a discrepancy between practice and what is said in the documents. To limit such risks, boards are using search firms to provide lists of candidates to supplement their personal input. Even this practice can lead to lawsuits by not overseeing and encouraging search firms to be inclusionary. Outsourcing the work does not outsource one's fiduciary responsibility.

CONSULTANT TOUCH POINTS

Consultants can influence the board appointment process in a number of direct and indirect ways.

- *Advising*—Consultants can provide direct advice to boards, search firms and executives about the risks involved and ways to avoid exclusionary practices in candidate searches.
- *Succession planning*—Consultants can encourage comprehensive human resources programs to grow the pipeline of qualified women for board service.
- *Awareness programs*—Consultants can provide training seminars, white papers, and journal articles targeted to executive women, CEOs, and boards about preparing for women for board service and how to find qualified women for boards.
- *Training* – Consultants can work with universities and organizations that train board members, or create their own programs.
- *Sponsorships*—Consultants can sponsor activities that educate and aide various constituencies involved in promoting women on boards. For example, Deloitte assists The Chicago Network (www.thechicagonetwork.org) in conducting its annual census of women on boards. KPMG provides funding for ION in its work to raise awareness of the issue and to provide lists of qualified candidates to boards with open seats.

CONSULTANTS AS FACILITATORS OR ENABLERS

Many consultants have the opportunities to help clients through the touch points outlined above. Beyond the moral case of promoting gender equality and fairness, there are valid, albeit selfish, reasons consultants should facilitate the consideration of women candidates for corporate boards. As the business case suggests, there is a benefit for the client in acquiring the additional female view, in board dynamics that promote deeper discussion, and in the development of organizational talent. These factors can lead to better firm performance which means that the consultant is working the best interest of the client by encouraging serious consideration of qualified female candidates.

Enabling neglect of the pool of qualified women for boards can make the consultant culpable in discriminatory behavior. This is not an issue that is going away. In fact, large well-organized groups are working internationally to change the status of women on boards. Catalyst, Corporate Women Directors International, ION, and search firms around the globe are conducting census reports on a regular basis to track progress. At this writing, the demand for a quota in the United Kingdom is being considered. And, investment fund managers are taking notice. TIAA-CREF (Teachers Insurance and Annuity Association–College Retirement Equities Fund), for example, funded the critical mass study of women on boards (Kramer et al., 2006) and is a vocal advocate for transparency. Socially responsible funds, such as the Calvert Fund, are also exercising pressure with their investments.

Knowledgeable consultants can educate clients in the business and social cases for board diversity. Thus, they are guiding their clients toward achieving the benefits of diversity and away from the legal and social risks of neglect. The bottom line for consultants is an enhanced reputation that can lead to retained and new clients; and the associated income.

REFERENCES

Adams, S. M., & Flynn, P. M. (2005a) Local knowledge advances women's access to corporate boards, *Corporate Governance: An International Review, 13*(6), 836–846.

Adams, S. M., & Flynn, P. M. (2005b) Actionable knowledge: Consulting to promote women on boards, *Journal of Organizational Change Management, 18*(5), 435–450.

Bilimoria, D. (2000). Building the business case for women corporate directors. In R. J. Burke & M. C. Mattis (Eds.), *Women on corporate boards of directors: International challenges and opportunities* (pp. 25–40). Boston: Kluwer Academic.

Burke, R. J. (2000) Company size, board size and numbers of women corporate directors. In R. J. Burke & M. C. Mattis (Eds.), *Women on Corporate Boards of Directors: International Challenges and Opportunities* (pp. 157–167). Boston: Kluwer Academic.

Carter, D. A., Simkins, B. J., & Simpson, W. G. (2003). Corporate governance, board diversity, and firm value. *The Financial Review, 38*, 33–53.

Cascio, W. F. (2004) Board governance: A social systems perspective. *Academy of Management Executive, 18*(1), 97–100.

Conger, J. A., Finegold, D., & Lawler, E. E. (1998). Appraising board room performance. *Harvard Business Review, 76*(1), 136–148.

Corporate Women Directors International. (2007). *Corporate Women Directors International 2007 Report: Women Board Directors of the 2006 Fortune Global 200.* Retrieved August 13, 2007, from http://www.globewomen.com/summit/2007/2007_global_200_cwdi_report.htm

Daily, C. M., & Dalton, D. R. (2003) Women in the boardroom: A business imperative. *Journal of Business Strategy, 24*(5), 8–10.

Daum, J. H., Neff, J., & Norris, J. C (2006). *Spencer Stuart 2006 board diversity report.* Retrieved July 20, 2007, http://www.spencerstuart.com/research/boards/955/

Erhardt, N. L., Werbel, J. D., & Shrader, C. B. (2003). Board of director diversity and firm financial performance. *Corporate Governance: An International Review, 11*(2), 102–111.

Fondas, N. (2000) Women on boards of directors: Gender bias or power threat? In R. J. Burke & M. C. Mattis (Eds.), *Women on corporate boards of directors: international challenges and opportunities* (pp. 171–177). Boston: Kluwer Academic.

Hausemann, R., Tyson, L. D., & Zahidi, S. (2006). *The Global Gender Gap* Leading CEOs: a statistical snapshot of S&P 500 leaders. (2007). *Spencer Stuart.* Retrieved July 20, 2007, from www.spencerstuart.com/research/articles/975/ *Report 2006.* Geneva, Switzerland: World Economic Forum.

Kramer, V. W., Konrad, A. M., & Erkut, S. (2006). *Critical mass on corporate boards: Why three or more women enhance governance* (Report No. WCW 11). Wellesley, MA: Wellesley Centers for Women.

Leading CEOs: a statistical snapshot of S&P 500 leaders. (2007). *Spencer Stuart.* Retrieved July 20, 2007, from www.spencerstuart.com/research/articles/975/

Popcorn, F., & Marigold, L. (2000). *EVEolution: The eight truths of marketing to women.* New York: Hyperion.

Pulakos, E. D., & Wexley, K. N. (1983). The relationship among perceptual similarity, sex, and performance ratings in management-subordinate dyads. *Academy of Management Journal, 26*, 129–139.

Sonnenfeld, J. A. (2004). Good governance and the misleading myths of bad metrics. *Academy of Management Executive, 18*(1), 108–113.

Study of 353 Fortune 500 Companies Connects Corporate Performance and Gender Diversity. *Catalyst News Release, January 26, 2004.* Retrieved January 27, 2004, http://www.catalystwomen.org/

Thomas, C. W. (2006). Women on European boards: Scandinavia extends its lead. *Egon Zehnder International.* Retrieved July 20, 2007, from http://www.egonzehnderknowledge.com/knowledge/content/articles/index.php?article=2426

2006 Census: Women Board Directors. (2006). *Catalyst.* Retrieved July 21, 2007, http://www.catalyst.org/knowledge/wbd.shtml

van der Walt, N., & Ingley, C. (2003). Board dynamics and the influence of professional background, gender and ethnic diversity of directors. *Corporate Governance: An International Review, 11*(3), 218–234.

Westphal, J. D., & Milton, L. P. (2000). How experience and network ties affect the influence of demographic minorities on corporate boards. *Administrative Science Quarterly, 45*(2), 366–398.

Wolfman, T. G. (2007). The face of corporate leadership. *New England Journal of Public Policy, 22*, 37–72.

Women and the world economy: A guide to womenomics. (2006, April 12). The *Economist*, pp. 60-61.

CHAPTER 11

HOW SARBANES-OXLEY IS TRANSFORMING CORPORATE BOARDS AND IMPACTING CONSULTING

Intended Effects and Unintended Consequences

Rickie Moore

Launched in the wake of the corporate scandals that rocked the world at the turn of the twentieth century, the Sarbanes-Oxley (SOX) law has become a principal vehicle of the radical reform of the governance of firms (Clark, 2005). As corporate boards scramble to comply, SOX and its requirements are creating new opportunities and dilemmas for firms and consultants across the globe. From the new restrictions about the composition of the Board of Directors (BoD), the profile of independent directors (IDs) and service providers to the new moral and legal

Board Members and Management Consultants: Redefining the Boundaries of Consulting and Corporate Governance, pp. 203–214
Copyright © 2009 by Information Age Publishing
203

hazards and dilemmas for consultants, the unfurling consequences of SOX are profoundly transforming both the corporate consulting environment and the way business is conducted. According to Linck, Netter & Yang (2005), findings from their survey of 7000 public companies have revealed that SOX had dramatically increased the cost of corporate boards; the cost was more important for smaller firms, and audit committees meet more than twice as often post-SOX as they did pre-SOX; boards were also larger and more independent post-SOX, more firms were separating the posts of CEO and Chairman of the BoD, and some were establishing nominating and governance committees as part of their new organization.

With the already short supply of suitably qualified IDs according to the new regulations, firms are increasingly turning to consultants to fill these newly enforced SOX ID positions. In accepting this new evolution in their roles and responsibilities as SOX IDs (Daily & Dalton, 2003), consultants will quickly find themselves caught up in new tensions and quandaries as they challenge and pit their knowledge and advice against each other within the board and within firm. For some companies, not only are their board rooms increasingly becoming major handicaps and constraints as they comply with the new legal definitions and requirements—IDs, mandates, separation, and so forth, but so too are their external relationships. Despite its well intended effects, SOX is resulting in a number of unintended consequences that challenge, and will eventually undermine, its ambition and its promise.

NEW ROLES, NEW RULES AND NEW KIDS ON THE BLOCK

In keeping with SOX, one of the most important missions of the "new" SOX-ID is to oversee the executives that are responsible for the daily operations of the firms. In principle, the purpose of the SOX-ID is to introduce more objectivity in the supervision of firm executives through the use of a "new set of untainted, unrelated and neutral yet powerful eyes" (D'Aquila, 2004). If, in the past, the BoD was often considered as a group of "agreeing buddies and friends," SOX now legally requires firms to have boards comprising a majority of IDs, who are experts and who are unrelated to and have had no prior connections to either the firm or the board.[1] Legislators felt that by eliminating all potential and possible con flicts and by making IDs legally responsible and accountable for the firm's operations, directors that were totally independent and unconnected with the firm, would be less likely to turn a blind eye and better able to disclose all wrong doings. Firms are therefore being forced to identify and recruit the new 'type' of directors in order to comply with SOX requirements.

For almost 6 decades, the consulting industry has established its reputation of having largely contributed to the growth and the success of its clients especially in the private sector. The renowned management consultant has championed the consulting industry and played a pivotal role in the development of the discipline and the practice of management and management theory. Having extensive industry experience and knowledge, consultants train, advise and coach CEOs, Senior and Middle Management – their typical clients on the conduct of their business. Fulfilling a diversity of roles, missions and profiles, and serving in a number of capacities, consultants have long been regarded as thought leaders, fountains of knowledge, conceptors, initiators and vectors of change in organizations.

Given the sheer volume of its membership and the sudden explosion in demand for talented IDs fuelled by SOX, the consulting industry ideally constitutes a natural and well-furnished source of potential candidates that are appropriately qualified and SOX-compliant. As such, consultants from all disciplines—legal, strategy and financial, and so forth, are becoming prime targets for firms and organizations to fill the positions of IDs on the boards in the new SOX defined and controlled business environment. Consequently, the solicitation of consulting firms and consultants has simply skyrocketed. However, in essence, SOX created a "double edged hoola hoop" for consultants. On the one hand, the sudden spiking demand constitutes a new opportunity for them to be invited and enticed into new high profile positions on corporate boards. As this new SOX-induced (r)evolution unfolds,[2] several consultants may choose to warmly welcome the opportunity to be an ID. On the other hand, the new constraints and implications that come with the function of the new SOX-defined ID are not only numerous, but are now legally and penally binding. In addition, there is one major caveat—that is, as mentioned previously, they cannot become IDs of the firms with which they have been connected. If they do, there will be a problem of conflict of interest, and both the firm and the consultant will be legally liable for noncompliance and violation of the law. Audit and consulting firms would find this opportunity particularly problematic because if one of their employees accepts to become an ID that would automatically disqualify the audit or consulting firm from working for the company (the new firm of the former employee). Further dilemma and conflict could ensue if a competitor of the audit or consulting firm is also working for the company as the new ID would be able to become familiar with the prices and practices of the competitor of his or her former employer.

Resource Dilemmas for IDs and Auditors

Given the profile of the ideal ID as defined by SOX, firms are being pushed to "engage" IDs that are most knowledgeable in the sectors or areas of the firm's operations, and who are totally new to the firm. For Peng (2004), the obligation to find IDs that are skilled and competent in the functions they will be required to perform becomes a critical matter for firms and has induced new effervescence and efflorescence in the consulting industry. With their combined and new massive need for several SOX-IDs, companies are facing problems of supply and demand, quality and liability. In addition, they are confronted with a new legalized resource problem that is costing much more than was anticipated (D'Aquila 2004); they will be forced to swap IDs that are very knowledgeable of the firm and its operations for ones that are not. This trade-off can prove to be a very pricey and difficult transaction. With the "no strings attached in any way, shape or form" between the firms and the IDs prior to their appointment, firms have no choice but to comply or risk facing very severe sanctions and stiff penalties including hefty fines and delisting from the stock exchanges. Firms, therefore, must pay the price of compliance. For some CEOs and boards, complying with this obligation requires a shift in mindset as it could result in letting the "Trojan horse" into the boardroom. The psychological and organizational impact of such a move is not without its repercussions as board behavior and relations will also be forced to change.

Frank Brown of PwC Global Assurance Services, considers that SOX-defined "Independent Directors (IDs) are a scarce commodity." He recommended to all his clients that they should be in the market for truly independent qualified directors whether (they are looking or not) because there aren't that many to go round." Brown (2002) further suggested that one way of increasing the pool was to look at potential directors coming out of the legal community, and consulting professions with a broad background in the business.

One of the direct outcomes of this (r)evolution is that executive search firms, like consultants, have experienced an increase in solicitation of their services. Client-firms, cognizant of the pains of recruiting, are increasingly turning to these firms to help them not only fill management positions, but board positions as well. Executive search firms are now, more and more, being asked to identify and recruit suitable candidates that match the new SOX profile. For these search firms, the implementation of SOX has brought new life and opportunity to the staffing and human resources industry, and they are ideally positioned to benefit. As they streamline their operations and occupy the new niche, some have launched new innovative products and services, and are advertising their

expertise in ID search, and their specialization in ID placement. Ultimately, SOX has unintendedly generated new revenue streams for the
executive search firms. By extension, SOX may also create new conflict
and dilemma if an executive search firm is providing both IDs and other
executives to a client-firm. Such a situation could lead to a direct or indirect connection between the client-firm and its new IDs and other executives via the search firm—which raises the issue as to how many degrees of
separation are necessary in order not to be considered as having an
implicit connection. To avoid the problem, firms might choose to have
different search firms for each category of profiles. The concern then
becomes after how many appointees would an executive search firm no
longer be considered "independent and unconnected" and able to provide a client-firm with its services.

Alien Experts and Professional Risk

In effect, the requirement that corporate boards had to be comprised
of a majority of IDs who are very familiar with their roles and responsibilities, and thus the operations of the executives who they are legally
required to oversee and supervise, and at the same time, be unconnected
and unrelated to the firm, translates into firms engaging "knowledgeable
yet expert aliens and outsiders." However, this obligation poses a number
of problems as many IDs also have full-time jobs. They cannot be part-
time IDs with a double work-load and double pay, and unable to devote
an unlimited amount of time to the company in order to legally and satis-
factorily fulfill their SOX ID responsibilities. As a SOX ID, they will have
to give up all other employment in order to serve on the board. SOX[3]
specifically states:

> (3) FULL-TIME INDEPENDENT SERVICE.—Each member of the
> Board shall serve on a full-time basis, and may not, concurrent with
> service on the Board, be employed by any other person or engage in
> any other professional or business activity.

With the new legal and penal responsibilities and shackles that come with
the position of the ID, some consultants would be reluctant to drink from
the "poisoned chalice" by serving as an ID on a board. The question can
thus be asked as to which consultants would be willing to risk everything
for something that they cannot fully and totally oversee, control or supervise (Epstein, 2003).

Firms would be taking a major risk if they were unable to find IDs that
have the appropriate skills and who are willing to give up everything to
serve on the board and fully perform their legal duty, and proceed to
appoint IDs that are less skilful or knowledgeable than the persons they

will oversee, or are insufficiently available to do their job thoroughly. The dilemma that results from this situation is the possible public doubt and lack of confidence (Castellani, 2003), about the guarantee and certainty obtained from an ID that is neither sufficiently familiar nor competent in the role that he or she is expected to play, or who is not thoroughly knowledgeable about the firm's operations, or who has not spent enough time exercising his or her function. Paradoxically, such a situation of the 'green long-distance alien expert' would have the inverse effect and increase the likelihood of fraud and misreporting, rather than decrease or eliminate them.

From Judge and Jury to Judge or Jury

One of the major principles of the SOX reforms was the separation of the functions of accounting, auditing and consulting in order to reduce the likelihood of malpractice, and to increase the level and quality of independence within and among client firms and their service providers. The target of this separation is the professional and personal relationships between corporate Board members and service provider firms. Whereas in the past, one service provider could cumulate several functions and be both the judge and jury of their client, that is, an auditing firm hired by a company could also provide consulting or other services to the company, the new SOX restrictions, by delimiting the types and number of roles and services that could be provided by subcontracting or service-supplier firms, are forcing both parties to make choices. Within the new SOX guidelines, an auditing firm hired by a company is legally prohibited from also providing consulting or other services to the company. As a result, new market opportunities have been created for service providers as previously 'locked-in markets' have been opened up.

Change, Change, Then Change Again: The New Life Cycle of Auditing Service Providers

With its emphasis on independence, one of SOX's new legal requirements is the changing of auditors every five years. According to SOX:[4]

> it shall be unlawful for a registered public accounting firm to provide audit services to an issuer if the lead (or coordinating) audit partner (having primary responsibility for the audit), or the audit partner responsible for reviewing the audit, has performed audit services for that issuer in each of the 5 previous fiscal years of that issuer.

Apart from the resources required for this renewal process, auditing firms will find themselves changing clients shortly after becoming fully knowledgeable and familiar with their operations. In order to avoid being out of work because of the imposed timed renewal, auditors will be forced to diversify into new sectors and to grow their existing client base. Auditors will therefore surf and ride the waves of the firms in order to maintain and develop their client portfolios and activity. Potential conflict and dilemma could also occur should two consulting or audit firms, providing identical services to competing clients, merge. SOX then becomes an impediment to the development to merger and acquisitions among consulting firms and among audit firms as it could eventually result in the loss of valuable clients. Consciously deciding to get rid of a profitable client in order to comply with SOX will be very tough choice and lead to much turmoil and internal conflict.

Agency Issues, Confidentiality and Disclosure: Moral Hazard for the ID

As firms scramble to redo their boards, the new law also introduced new agency issues (Daily et al., 2003) and a real dilemma for IDs. In the pre-SOX period, total confidentiality and nondisclosure were considered as standard operating procedures (SOPs) for consultants and Board members as both were required to sign nondisclosure agreements (NDAs) with the firms. A typical NDA would read: I agree that I shall not during, or at any time after the termination of my employment with the Company, use for myself or others, or disclose or divulge to others including future employees, any trade secrets, confidential information, or any other proprietary data of the Company in violation of this agreement.

This legally enforceable document has not only served as a deterrent, but also as a foundation for building strong relationships between Board members and the firm, and between consultants and their clients. The implementation of SOX however, has led to a modification of these procedures. If in the pre-SOX era, IDs and consultants were expressly forbidden from communicating or disclosing confidential and proprietary information obtained in the firm, today IDs are legally required to disclose all necessary information and denounce all malfeasance (see Table 11.1).

The use of information obtained in the course of an ID's engagement is increasingly becoming a new source of controversy, and will affect his or her relationship with the firm. With the new internal control mechanisms required by the law, and new regulations being placed on IDs to inform the board and the legal authorities of any malpractices discovered (Ivancevich et al., 2003), *whistle blowing* is becoming a skill that IDs have to learn. This is a real dilemma for IDs as the need for transparency and information disclosure introduced by SOX, brought its own set of perils (Edmunds, 2004; Hecht, 2002). For IDs, failure to report the "appropriate" information would be equated to

**Table 11.1   Pre- and Post-Sarbanes-Oxley:
Disclosure and Confidentiality**

Pre-Sarbanes-Oxley	Directors and Consultants	
Disclosure	• Oath of secrecy • Not legally required (Facultative, Personal Ethic)	
Confidentiality	• Required (Contract of nondisclosure—Agreement)	
Post-Sarbanes-Oxley		
	Directors	*Consultants*
Disclosure	• Legally required (Law)	• Not legally required (Facultative, personal ethic)
Confidentiality	• Only those aspects or areas where there is no malpractice or wrongdoing	• Required (Contract of nondisclosure–agreement) • Sworn to secrecy

encouraging malpractice, being an accomplice to the problem, and would make them legally accountable and penally liable for the consequences. As a result of SOX, IDs will be legally required to "*snitch*" on their colleagues and firms, and can therefore find themselves in a "damned if I do and damned if I don't situation." If the firm in which the ID is employed becomes embroiled in legal controversy, the reputation of both the firm and the ID concerned will be at stake. In addition, should an ID be identified as not having provided the appropriate oversight and control, he or she could be held legally liable and accountable for the problem. Theoretically, if any wrongdoing goes unnoticed, or there is fraud, either with or without the ID's knowledge, he or she could be held liable. The unfolding debate is one of competing loyalties, and moral and ethical responsibilities.

An interesting twist to this situation would be the case of a consultant that has obtained wide industry experience, and is fully knowledgeable of and conversant with the tricks of the trade or standard industry practices (SIP) used by a number of CEOS and firms, and who accepts the job of an ID in a nonclient firm within the same industry. Very often CEOs can engage in practices that are unknown to the BoD and that can have very negative impacts on the firms, and through his or her experience, a consultant is thus better prepared and armed to identify and detect such situations or malpractice. A typical example would be a decision to invest in a new technology, or to withdraw from certain markets, or underinvest in certain products without the explicit approval and validation of the board. CEOs, for a number of reasons, may misrepresent the information that they communicate to their boards or present it in a way that favors their chosen position. Hence, while the CEOs may not necessarily lie to their boards, they can knowingly and wilfully manipulate the information they provide and the way they provide it. Within the current legal framework, a consultant who discovers any wrongdoing is not legally required to inform the Board and appropriate authorities. The decision to denounce their clients is thus based on the consultant's personal and professional deontologies. Will consultants be putting themselves out of a job as potential IDs if they are known to have mastered the "tricks of the trade" of their clients, and could, from the outset, be in a position to "spill the beans?"

As mentioned previously, former consultants that accept the new job as IDs, would be legally prohibited from "covering" for the CEOs, and be required to announce their malpractices should they discover them. Will consultants-turned-IDs accept the risk of defamation and criminal liability for not reporting and disclosing illegal and unethical practices by their CEOs? How can consultants-turned-IDs ethically and effectively resolve the tensions of their new relationships with their CEOs?

If the corporate world is still in shock and in the recovery mode from the first blast of SOX, more dilemmas are yet to come.

Experienced but Unknowledgeable, Trans-sectoral and Geographic Mobility

With the restrictive requirements that define the profile of the ID, consultants that have significant experience in a function within a sector could also find themselves targets for ID positions by firms in sectors of which they are relatively un-knowledgeable. Given the lead-time and learning required by the new ID to fully comprehend the practices of the firm, those CEOs that are ill-intentioned would hope that by the time the ID can discover, investigate and report the malfeasance, the CEO would be long gone. Closing such a 'loophole' is not going to be easy, as requiring specific sector experience raises the bar and narrows the field of candidates. Consequently, this situation would force consultants-wanting-to-become-IDs to specialize in a sector or a field, and stimulate and increase their geographic mobility.

Local Law and Global Effect

Not only did the introduction of SOX transform corporate governance and consulting as they were practiced in the United States, it is also having a number of unintended impacts on foreign firms and around the world (Higgs, 2003). With the globalized nature of business and the financial industry, SOX also applies to foreign-owned firms listed on, or operating in U.S. markets. These firms, like their American counterparts or subsidiaries, are also required to comply with the new regulations and to adopt corporate governance practices that are not necessarily required in their home countries (Weiland, 2005). For some cultures and countries, the auditor-client, consultant-client relationships are sacrosanct and regulated by laws that demand total confidentially. Hence, auditors and consultants can therefore not be held liable in the home country, but can be forced to turn over their notes in the United States in the case of a malpractice investigation. This situation creates a legal quagmire, as foreign firms operating in the United States will have to either implement duplicate procedures, or adopt the American norms that can be perceived as being unpatriotic.

The Phoenix Effect: From Director to Auditor and From Auditor to Consultant

To prevent the evolution from independence to dependence, SOX has imposed a 5 year term limit on both the auditors and board members; auditors are allowed to serve for one term while board members may be considered for a second term (maximum). Every five years a firm will be forced to either replace its auditors or its IDs or both, and this forced rotation guarantees new business for Executive search firms and modulates the emergence of new IDs, and is also creating a number of other unintended consequences on consultants and the consulting industry. Without many options available to them, former IDs and auditors that can no longer legally serve in the firms or on boards will launch into new careers as consultants because they can formalize and commercialize their industrial experience to a wide range of clients, especially their former peers and counterparts—CEOs, boards, and even other consultants. Brown (2002) also noticed "the change in trend in the last 24 months as a number of IDs that were recently retired, were becoming senior partners of accounting firms, and performing very prominent functions as chairmen or, members of audit committees in a number of firms." As consultants remain "untouched" for now by SOX and its reforms, the consulting industry will increasingly become the destination and industry of choice for the former IDs and auditors who are not yet ready to quit the business environment.

CONCLUSION

If SOX has started or is starting to achieve its intended impacts on curbing corporate malfeasance and corruption, its unintended consequences are progressively emerging. While the evaluation of the effectiveness of SOX is underway (Carbasho, 2003), and the jury is still out, its obligations are transforming Boardrooms and creating new opportunities (Levinson,

2003), and dilemmas for consultants and the consulting industry around the world. Naturally, firms are turning to consultants to assist them in the implementation of corporate governance measures (Parker, 2005), and the requirements of SOX—that is, reporting procedures, new management practices, and so forth, that would allow them to comply with the law. Further, academics engaged in research on firms and specific dimensions of business will no doubt soon find themselves as prime candidates for jobs as IDs.

As the changes permeate the firms, IDs will increasingly defend their independence, control and responsibility. Disclosure, information sharing, transparency and confidentiality will become serious issues of contention between the consultants of the different stakeholder groups (middle management, unions, employees, etc.) in the firm and the BoD. Consequently, the outcome of any crossfire among the various consultants would most likely result in a field day for lawyers and judges in the courts as it would be the lawyers, not the consultants, that battle each other for vindication, and the judges, not the CEOs, that arbitrate the pertinence and relevance of the advice and counsel provided by the consultants.

NOTES

1. Sarbanes-Oxley Act of 2002, H.R. 3763, Section 108 (a) (b) (1) (A) (ii).
2. See Accountability—http://www.independensector.org/issues /sarbanesoxley.html
3. See Sarbanes-Oxley Act of 2002, H.R. 3763, Section 101 (e) (3).
4. Sarbanes-Oxley Act of 2002, H.R. 3763, Section 203 Audit Partner Rotation (j)

REFERENCES

Brown, F. (2002). *Implications of Sarbanes Oxley.* PricewaterhouseCoopers. http:// Retrieved December 10, 2005, from www.pwcglobal.com/extweb /manissue.nsf/DocID/C01A0777ED2010D4CA256C93002B277C.htm

Carbasho, T. (2003). Accounting firms say implications of Sarbanes-Oxley still unfolding. *Pittsburgh Business Times* Retrieved December 20, 2008, from http:/ /pittsburgh.bizjournals.com/pittsburgh/stories/2003/03/31/focus5.html

Clark, R. C. (2005). Corporate governance changes in the wake of the Sarbanes-Oxley Act: A morality tale for policy makers too. Harvard Law School Discussion Paper No. 525. Retrieved July 14, 2008, http://www.law.harvard.edu /programs/olin_center

Castellani, J. J. (2003). Implementation of the Sarbanes-Oxley Act and restoring investor confidence. The Business Round Table. Testimony before Senate Committee on Banking, Housing and Urban Affairs, October 2, 2003.

D'Aquila, J. M. (2004). Tallying the cost of the Sarbanes-Oxley Act. *The CPA Journal*. Retrieved October 10, 2005, from http://www.nysscpa.org/cpajournal/ 2004/1104/perspectives/p6.htm

Daily, C. M., & Dalton, D. R. (2003). Dollars and sense: The path to board independence. *Journal of Business Strategy, 24* (3), 41–43.

Daily, C. M., Dalton, D. R., & Cannella, A. A., Jr. (2003). Corporate governance: Decades of dialogue and data. *Academy of Management Review, 28*, 371–382.

Epstein, R. A. (2003). Sarbanes overdose. *National Law Journal, 25*(23), A17.

Edmunds, A. (2004). Leveraging the Whistle-Blower Protection Provision for SOX compliance. *The Sarbanes-Oxley Compliance Journal* Retrieved October 12, 2005, from http://www.s-ox.com/feature/article.cfm?articleID=257

Hecht, C. (2002). Audit Committee and Management Disclosure Requirements of the Sarbanes-Oxley Act, Retrieved October 12, 2005, from http:// www.accounting.smartpros.com/X35188.xml

Higgs, D. (2003). *Review of the role and effectiveness of non-executive directors.* London: January.

Ivancevich, J. M., Duening, T. N., Gilbert, J. A., & Konopaske, R. (2003). Deterring white-collar crime. *Academy of Management Executive, 17*(2), 114–127.

Linck, J. S., Netter, J. M., & Yang, T. (2005). Effects and unintended Consequences of the Sarbanes-Oxley Act on Corporate Boards. Working Paper, AFA, Social Science Research Network.

Levinson, M. (2003, January 15). Get on Board. *CIO Magazine.* December 13, 2005, from http://www.cio.com/article/011503/board.html?printversio=yes

Parker, A. (2005, Feb. 9). New Rules help "big four" firms double fees. *Financial Times*, p. A1.

Peng, M. W. (2004). Outside directors and firm performance during institutional transitions. *Strategic Management Journal, 25*(5), 453–471.

Sarbanes-Oxley Act of 2002, H.R. 3763.

Wieland, J. (2005). Corporate governance, values management, and standards: A European perspective. *Business and Society, 44*(1), 74–93.

ABOUT THE AUTHORS

Susan M. Adams is an associate professor of management at Bentley University. Her current research and consulting interests focus on the interplay of individual and organizational growth and most recently on the advancement of women in leadership positions. She holds a PhD in management from Georgia Institute of Technology.

Jose Luis Alvarez is director of the Center for Corporate Governance at Instituto de Empresa in Madrid, Spain. He holds a PhD in organizational behavior from the Harvard Business School, where he has also served as visiting professor. He is also visiting professor at INSEAD, France, since 2001. His main research focus is on the role and careers of top executives, doing extensive consulting on the design, processes and evaluation of boards of directors and top management teams.

Anthony F. Buono, series editor, has a joint appointment as professor of management and sociology at Bentley University, and is founding coordinator of the Bentley Alliance for Ethics and Social Responsibility. His current research and consulting interests focus on the management-consulting industry, organizational change, and interorganizational alliances, with an emphasis on mergers, acquisitions, strategic partnerships, and firm-stakeholder relationships. He holds a PhD with a concentration in industrial and organizational sociology from Boston College.

Xavier de Sarrau is an attorney at law, member of the Geneva and Paris bars. He acts as an advisor to families and private groups on their key activities and concerns in the tax, legal, and governance areas. He is also a founding partner of Sarrau Thomas Couderc, a law firm based in Paris, specializing in private equity transactions. He works extensively with clients and contacts who are based in various jurisdictions, in particular France, the United Kingdom, the United States and Switzerland. He started his professional life as a tax attorney and, subsequently, held various management positions in the former Andersen Professional Services network as country managing partner for France, then area managing partner for EMEIA (Europe, Middle-East, India, and Africa) and, ultimately, managing partner—Global Management Services.

David Finegold is the dean of the School of Management and Labor Relations at Rutgers, the State University of New Jersey. Prior to joining Rutgers, Dr. Finegold was a professor at the Keck Graduate Institute in Claremont, Californa and at USC's Marshall School of Business. He is the author of more than 70 journal articles and book chapters and has written or edited six books. He consults and provides executive education and coaching to public and private sector organizations on issues about talent management and employee development, corporate governance, integrating ethics into strategic decision making, and designing effective organizations.

Jonas Gabrielsson is assistant professor at CIRCLE, Lund University, and the Norwegian School of Management—BI, in Oslo. His current research interest is about the governance of research-based ventures, with a focus on how board characteristics and board activities in the early phases of a venture's development affect organizational life chances. He is also interested in the interactions and relationships among key actors in the process of decision making and control over firm resources in these ventures.

Pierre-Yves Gomez is a full professor of strategic management at EM Lyon (France) and director of the French Corporate Governance Institute. His research focuses on corporate governance and political foundations of management science. He is currently working on the links between corporate governance and strategy. He has published numerous articles on political economy and strategy and several award-wining books in French including *Qualité et Théorie des Conventions* and *La République des Actionnaires*, and in English including *Trust, Firm and Society* and *Entrepreneurs and Democracy*, both with Harry Korine from the London Business School.

Jens Grigoleit is a PhD candidate in the Faculty of Business Administration at the Technische Universität Bergakademie Freiberg and visiting scholar at the University of Technology, Sydney. His research focuses on competing concepts of corporate governance, especially on the impact of trust, social capital, and tacit knowledge.

Kevin P. Hendry is a consultant in strategy and corporate governance and a facilitator with the Australian Institute of Company Directors. He was formerly vice president and managing director of Asia Pacific for Monsanto and was also a member of the global management team for Monsanto's nutrition and consumer products business. He has also been an adjunct lecturer in strategic management at the University of Queensland and is currently undertaking his PhD on the role of the board in firm strategy.

Morten Huse is professor of innovation and economic organization at the Norwegian School of Management—BI, in Oslo, and visiting research professor at Bocconi University in Milan. His current research interests are entrepreneurship and boards of directors with focus on stakeholder and behavioral perspectives, and on governance in SMEs and family firms. He was formerly the chairperson of the National Association of Corporate Directors (StyreAkademiet) in Norway.

Geoffrey C. Kiel is deputy vice chancellor and dean of business at The University of Notre Dame Australia. He has had an extensive career as a management consultant, senior manager, management educator and academic researcher. He has been published in journals such as the *Journal of Marketing Research*, *Business Horizons* and the *European Journal of Marketing*. His current research focuses on corporate governance and he is the coauthor of the major Australian practical guide to governance, *Boards that Work* and *Board, Director and CEO Evaluation*.

Harry Korine (PhD INSEAD) is a teaching fellow at the London Business School and senior research fellow at the French Corporate Governance Institute, Lyon. He also serves as chairman of Forma Futura Invest, Inc., an asset management company based in Zurich, Switzerland. His new book is titled, *Entrepreneurs and Democracy: A Political Theory of Corporate Governance* (Cambridge University Press, forthcoming, with Pierre-Yves Gomez).

Edward Lawler, III is distinguished professor of business and director of the Center for Effective Organizations in the Marshall School of Business at the University of Southern California. He has consulted with over one hundred organizations on employee involvement, organizational change, and compensation and has been honored as a top contributor to the fields of organizational development, organizational behavior, corporate governance, and human resource management. The author of over 300 articles and 38 books, his articles have appeared in leading academic journals as well as *Fortune*, *Harvard Business Review* and leading newspapers including *USA Today* and the *Financial Times*.

Alessandro Minichilli is junior assistant professor at Bocconi University in Milan, where he received is PhD in business administration and management. His teaching activities and research interests are in the area of corporate governance, with a focus on boards of directors from a behavioral perspective. He is also interested in family businesses, and the board characteristics in those kinds of firms.

Rickie A. Moore is an associate professor at EM Lyon Business School and is also an associate researcher in the Institute for Socio-Economics of Organizations. He works in the domains of strategic management, organizational performance and effectiveness, performance measurement and management, management consulting intervention methodologies, and new venture creation. He holds visiting teaching and research appointments in several universities worldwide, conducts intervention research in several firms and institutions, and serves on the boards of several firms and international organizations. He is currently chair of the Management Consulting Division of the Academy of Management. He holds a PhD in management sciences from the University Jean Moulin Lyon 3.

Gavin J. Nicholson is a senior lecturer at the Queensland University of Technology and has spent the past 8 years consulting on corporate governance and strategy to large Australian public companies, government-owned corporations, not-for-profit organizations, statutory authorities and research organizations. Coauthor of numerous international journal articles, he is also coauthor *of Boards that Work* and *Board, Director and CEO Evaluation*. His PhD investigates the strategic impact of boards of directors and he regularly presents his research findings to various groups throughout Australasia, Europe, and North America.

Michael Nippa is a professor of management, leadership, and human resources at the Technische Universität Bergakademie Freiberg and Visiting Scholar at the Marshall School of Business (USC) and the Australian Graduate School of Management (UNSW). His research integrates international management, strategic leadership, organization, innovation, management consulting, and corporate governance.

Joan E. Ricart is the Carl Schrøder professor of strategic management and chairman of the General Management Department at IESE Business School, University of Navarra. He is president elect of the Strategic Management Society, director of the scientific committee of EIASM, and was President of the European Academy of Management from 2001 to 2006.). He has published several books and articles in international and national journals on subjects as strategy, economics, organization, and corporate governance. He holds a doctoral degree in industrial engineering, UPC, a PhD in managerial economics from Northwestern University, and a doctor in economics from UAB.

David Risser is a corporate governance analyst for Nestor Advisors Ltd, a London-based consultancy company providing a wide range of corporate governance related services. He is also an associate researcher at the French Institute of Corporate Governance (IFGE). French and Czech, David holds a postgraduate diploma (DEA) in banking, finance, and international economics from the University Lyon Lumière.

David G. Russell is a researcher at the French Corporate Governance Institute, and teaches strategy and corporate governance at EM LYON, in Lyon, France. He is a visiting professor at the Catholic University of Lyon, the Paris Graduate School of Management, the University of Birmingham, and Hong Kong Polytechnic University. His current research interests focus on board human capital, nonexecutive directors, and cross-national studies of boards of directors. He is currently working toward a PhD with a concentration in corporate governance at the University of Birmingham.

Thierry Tomasi was admitted to practice at the Paris Bar in January 2004 and has worked in the litigation and arbitration practice of Denton Wilde Sapte in London and Paris, before joining the Litigation and Arbitration Department of Sarrau Thomas Couderc in Paris, in May 2005. He holds two postgraduate degrees in international law (University of Paris-Panthéon Assas) and an LLM in International Business Law (University of London-King's College).

Printed in the United States
215380BV00003B/8/P